EVALUATING CHILDREN'S INTERACTIVE PRODUCTS

The Morgan Kaufmann Series in Interactive Technologies

Series Editors: Stuart Card, PARC; Jonathan Grudin, Microsoft; Jakob Nielsen, Nielsen Norman Group

EVALUATING CHILDREN'S INTERACTIVE PRODUCTS

Principles and Practices for Interaction Designers

Panos Markopoulos

Janet C. Read

Stuart MacFarlane

Johanna Höysniemi

The Morgan Kaufmann Series in Interactive Technologies
AMSTERDAM • BOSTON • HEIDELBERG • LONDON
NEW YORK • OXFORD • PARIS • SAN DIEGO
SAN FRANCISCO • SINGAPORE • SYDNEY • TOKYO
Morgan Kaufmann is an imprint of Elsevier

ELSEVIER

MORGAN KAUFMANN PUBLISHERS

Publisher:	Denise E. M. Penrose
Publishing Services Manager:	George Morrison
Project Manager:	Marilyn E. Rash
Assistant Editor:	Mary E. James
Copyeditor:	Debbie Prato
Proofreader:	Dianne Wood
Indexer:	Kevin Broccoli
Cover Design:	Joanne Blank
Cover Image:	© Young-Min Yoon
Typesetting/Illustration Formatting:	Charon Tec
Interior/Cover Printer:	1010 Printing International Ltd.

Morgan Kaufmann Publishers is an imprint of Elsevier.
30 Corporate Drive, Suite 400, Burlington, MA 01803

This book is printed on acid-free paper.

Library of Congress Cataloging-in-Publication Data

Evaluating children's interactive products : principles and practices for interaction designers / Panos Markopoulos . . . [et al.].
  p. cm. — (The Morgan Kaufmann series in interactive technologies)
Includes bibliographical references and index.
ISBN 978-0-12-374111-0 (alk. paper)
1. New products—Design and construction. 2. Interactive multimedia—Evaluation.
3. Children's paraphernalia—Evaluation. 4. Child consumers. I. Markopoulos,
P. (Panos)
TS171.4.E93 2008
006.7—dc22   2008008693

For information on all Morgan Kaufmann publications, visit our Web site at
www.mkp.com or *www.books.elsevier.com*.

Printed in China
08 09 10 11 12   10 9 8 7 6 5 4 3 2 1

Working together to grow
libraries in developing countries

www.elsevier.com | www.bookaid.org | www.sabre.org

ELSEVIER   BOOK AID International   Sabre Foundation

CONTENTS

6   BEFORE THE EVALUATION 90

PREFACE

This book is for students, researchers, and practitioners who design or evaluate interactive products for children. It does not require background knowledge in computer science, human factors, psychology, or design, although concepts from these areas of knowledge are used in the book. This is a handbook rather than an introductory textbook or an academic treatment of this topic, and it aims to provide practical and sound advice for how best to evaluate interactive products. This advice is based on accumulated experience with such evaluations and on research results in the new and fast-growing subdiscipline of human–computer interaction (HCI) that focuses on products for children.

This book's title could have been *Evaluating Interactive Products for and with Children*. Indeed, it was developed from a tutorial with that cumbersome, albeit accurate, title that we have given at several specialist conferences. It covers evaluation methodology for supporting interaction design for products, systems, software applications, toys, games, and specialized appliances intended to be used by children.

Most, but not all, of the time, the evaluation methods discussed in this book require the participation of children. This participation reflects a changing perspective in our field and in society in favor of an increasingly active and responsible role for children. Our focus on *interaction design* means that several aspects of products that might need to be evaluated are outside this book's scope—for example, whether the product or system is safe to use or whether it functions according to its technical specifications.

The design of interactive technology has been studied for many years. Initially, this study concentrated on the ergonomics of use, but later included the cognitive and even social aspects of interaction. Today, this field contains a substantial body of knowledge with regard to interaction design and the more narrowly scoped field of usability engineering (UE). Within these areas of practice, and the related research field of HCI, a host of methods are available for evaluating interactive products. Given the initial focus of these fields (interaction design and UE) on supporting work-related adult activities, much of the associated methodology works well when the intended users of the products are adults at their workplaces.

Paradoxically, if a central tenet of HCI is to base design on understanding users, the methods and techniques proposed in mainstream HCI are often defined, described, and practiced as if they were user independent. Our book stems from a growing conviction that we must break loose from this frame of mind. We argue that there is an increasing need to revisit methodologies developed for office workers or adult consumers, to adapt them, and to develop new ones that fit the diversity of contexts, products, people, and uses that interaction design is faced with today.

One area where routine HCI methods need serious revision, or are even considered inappropriate, is in the study of children and children's products. Notions of usability, tasks, and performance must be revisited or put into the context of broader concerns for children, such as their development, their learning, and whether they have fun while using a product. Assumptions about how users will behave and what can be expected of them in the context of an evaluation often fall apart when working with children rather than adults. The need for new methods, adaptations of existing methods, and (eventually) a book arose out of the realization that people who evaluate products with children need specific, up-to-date advice on methodology that is not readily available.

How to Use This Book

You are probably reading this book because you need to evaluate a product with children. If this is the first time you have worked with them, or even the first time you have done an evaluation in any context, you will find here a gentle introduction to what is different when working with children that provides step-by-step guidance for setting up an evaluation study, running it, and interpreting its results.

If evaluating children's products is already part of your job, this book gives you advice on how to perform evaluations more systematically, and it brings your practice and knowledge up to date with related research. The chapters offer you a wider range of methods and helps you weigh the pros and cons of each.

We hope that researchers will also find this book interesting. It provides an overview of a new and vibrant research field and exposes gaps in current methodologies that future research must address. We also hope it conveys our enthusiasm for this research area, where so much interesting work is taking place and so much still needs to be done.

Instructors can use this book to support a specialized course on its topic. It can also be used as supplementary reading for courses on interaction design or human–computer interaction. Compared to textbooks on these more general topics, you will find what we hope is a complete and self-contained handbook on how to proceed with setting up an evaluation with children.

If this is the first handbook you have read on the topic of evaluating products, we believe it can provide a solid foundation and a good introduction to how evaluations should be done. You will learn about the place of evaluation in the design process and be introduced to a wide variety of methods. Although this book focuses on children, it takes a broader view than many related sources on what methods are useful for evaluating products and how to combine or adapt them. This book provides a different and valuable perspective even if your interests are not primarily in working with children. It provides in-depth coverage of many of the issues skimmed over by other books—issues that are very important in actual evaluation practice—such as how to design a survey, how to do observations, and how to use diaries.

Whereas earlier texts placed a lot of emphasis on how to insert usability in a company and the practical procedures that should be followed, this book focuses more on the soundness of the methodology and on helping you to appreciate the quality of the data you collect and the conclusions you can draw from it. Our focus stems from working with children, but we believe that this perspective is one that needs to be emphasized more in evaluation methodology in general, and we hope our book is a relevant contribution in that direction.

This Book's Organization

Evaluating Children's Interactive Products: Principles and Practices for Interaction Designers is organized in four parts.

Part 1, Children and Technology, provides a brief introduction to working with children, children's technology, and interaction design for those who are new to the field. It discusses how ethical issues should be dealt with when working with children, and provides an overview of evaluation methodology, introducing concepts and terminology that are important to consider when shaping and defining an evaluation.

Part 2, Evaluating with and for Children, provides a step-by-step practical guide for an evaluation, including what you need to do before, during, and after an evaluation session. The chapters pay special attention to how the involvement of children affects a study.

Part 3, Methods of Evaluation, goes deeper into different methods, discussing how methods that were originally developed for evaluating adults' products must be adapted. It introduces a number of new methods and techniques that can be used for evaluating products with children. This part also discusses how to record interaction, the intricacies of doing Wizard of Oz studies, and how to do inspections— that is, appraisals of interaction design without the involvement of children.

Part 4, Case Studies, presents three case studies that illustrate some challenging issues of working with children.

Acknowledgments

Many people have contributed to the production of this book.

We thank the various members of the Interaction Design and Children community for their research in advancing this field and their helpful discussions with us at conferences or during our tutorials. Special thanks go to Libby Hanna, Alissa Antle, Tilde Bekker, and Wolmet Barendregt for sharing some of their experiences in the invited-guest boxes in the book.

Thanks to Marthin Boschman for his work in the KidsLab; to Janneke Verhaegh, Iris Soute, and Angelique Kessels for their contribution to the case study in Chapter 17; and to Boris de Ruyter for supporting the groupware we used while writing the book. Thanks also to Matthew Horton, Diana Xu, Akiyo Kano, Emanuela Mazzone, and William Carter for their assistance in the evaluation studies reported in Part 2 and for their overall contributions to the text.

We are grateful to colleagues and friends who responded enthusiastically and quickly to our last-minute requests to use their illustrations. Thanks go to Lucas Noldus, Albert Willemsen, and Martijn Willems of Noldus Information Technology;

Anne Jansen and Johan Spiik of Tobii Technology; and Sarah Price of the London Knowledge Lab.

We thank Juan Pablo Hourcade, Tom McEwan, Kirstin Alexander, Pamela Qualter, Judy Robertson, and Gilbert Cockton for reviewing the chapters, encouraging us, pointing out information we might have missed, and offering constructive critiques. You helped make this book better than we could have made it if left to our own devices.

Finally, we thank all the children, students, and colleagues who took part in our research during the last few years and especially those who helped assemble some of the materials for this book.

Panos, Janet, Stuart, and Johanna

ABOUT THE AUTHORS

Panos Markopoulos initially studied electrical engineering and computer science at the National Technical University of Athens and then moved into the field of human–computer interaction at Queen Mary University of London, where his focus was on model-based design and the intersection between software engineering methods and human–computer interaction. In 1998, he moved to The Netherlands, where he worked briefly at Philips Research on television-based user interfaces. He is now an associate professor in the Department of Industrial Design at the Eindhoven University of Technology. Panos chaired the inaugural Interaction Design and Children (IDC) Conference in Eindhoven in 2002. His current research and teaching concerns ambient intelligence and interaction design for children, focusing on design methods and novel application concepts.

Janet Read has a first degree in mathematics from the University of Manchester, United Kingdom. After teaching mathematics for several years, she moved into human–computer interaction where she specifically studied the usability of handwriting recognition interfaces for children. Currently a senior lecturer at the University of Central Lancashire, she teaches general and advanced human–computer interaction, interaction design, and child–computer interaction, and she leads the lively Child–Computer Interaction (ChiCI) research group. Janet's current research is concerned with text input technologies, children's use of tangible technologies, and the investigation of methods for the design and evaluation of children's technology.

Stuart MacFarlane graduated with a degree in mathematics from the University of London and began his career as a teacher. He moved on to a PhD in human–computer interface evaluation at Heriot-Watt University and became a senior lecturer in human–computer interaction at the University of Central Lancashire, where he was involved in a number of projects on the design and evaluation of interactive products for children. Stuart cofounded the ChiCI Group at the university in 2002. He was the chair of the IDC Conference in 2003 and, with the other three authors, developed tutorials about evaluation and children that were presented at a number of conferences in 2003 and 2004, which eventually led to this book. He now works at Edge Hill University.

Johanna Höysniemi's interests include design, technology, usability, and social media. After obtaining her MSc in software engineering at Tampere University in Helsinki, she continued studying in the Medialab at the University of Art and Design Helsinki. She then received a PhD in interactive technology at the University of Tampere. During her PhD research, she designed and evaluated physically interactive computer games for children. Johanna was cochair of the IDC conference in 2006. More than 200 children have taken part in various evaluation studies as part of her research. Since 2006, she has been working in industry as a senior interaction designer with several international technical companies. In the future, she plans to continue designing products with and for children.

To Annick, Josephine, Emiel, John, Helen, Janno, Elodie, Jonathan, Toshi, Aki, and Kenneth, who have supported us in this endeavor by their patience and their understanding.

To researchers and practitioners past and present who, knowingly or otherwise, gave us reason to think this book could be written.

To lost moments, and lost nights that, whilst gone forever, can, having seen the fruit of their demise, be remembered without regret.

– Panos, Janet, Stuart, and Johanna

PART 1

CHILDREN AND TECHNOLOGY

CHAPTER 1

WHAT IS A CHILD?

Doug Larson once said, "A child is a person who can't understand why someone would give away a perfectly good kitten." In a book written for evaluators of interactive products for children, a child who would not give away a kitten is interesting but not especially illuminating! This chapter gives the reader a sense of children and childhood. It outlines some basic child psychology, introduces some of the developmental theories that might assist in understanding the world of children, and puts children's worlds into context.

In this somewhat brief chapter, it is impossible to do justice to the enormous wealth of knowledge about children and their development, so the reader is particularly encouraged to consult other texts.

There are many definitions of *childhood* and *being a child*. The most frequently used definition comes from the United Nations Convention on the Rights of the Child (UNCRC), which was ratified by 191 countries in 1989. In the definition, a child is "every human being below the age of 18 years unless under the law applicable to the child, majority is attained earlier." Other definitions assume that childhood ends at the age of 16.

Age and Children

It is tempting, and often necessary, to use age as a limiting factor when discussing children, but age is a very blunt metric because it assumes that at one specific point in time, a person leaves childhood and enters adulthood. Age-related definitions take little account of the gentle shifts and fluctuations between the states of adulthood and childhood (and do not even consider babyhood!). Postmodernists, such as Le Dasberg (1989) and Philip Veerman (1992), led a movement against age-related definitions with their "cultural relativist" view that acknowledges the significant differences between peoples and societies and the need to respect and maintain these differences. They argued that childhood is a relative concept that changes "according to historical time, geographical environment, local culture, and socioeconomic conditions" (Kuper, 1997, p. 13).

The authors of this book respect this postmodernist view and believe that although childhood is generally defined by biological age, the differences across cultures and societies that impact on children and childhood cannot be ignored. Most of the content of this book is concerned with children between the ages of 4 and 13. Within these rough boundaries, biological age is for the most part deliberately kept out of the text, but where we speak of "young" children, we are generally referring to those children under the age of 6 or 7, with "older" children being those aged 8 or above. Given the significant differences across cultures and countries, these distinctions should be used with care, especially when thinking about children who are 7, 8, and 9.

Learning about Children

However children are defined, by far the best way to learn about them is to spend time with them. This is easy for those with their own children, but for the reader without the appropriately aged children, there are still many opportunities to interact with this very special audience. Some possibilities include helping out in schools, coaching a sports team, and working in after-school care centers. More informal possibilities can include spending time with the children of friends and family and going to places where children congregate. Having a cup of coffee at McDonald's can provide an illuminating glimpse into the lives of children. Children's spaces can also be partially investigated from a distance: Watching children's TV programs, reading children's books, and observing what kinds of things they like to buy can all be revealing. It is not always possible to learn about children in such an interactive way. The remainder of this chapter provides a brief overview for readers who want to know more.

Theories of Child Development

In broad terms, children have similarities and differences. As a population they change over time in similar ways: They grow bigger, get stronger, and learn more. However, across a similar population, individual children can also have many differences. Child development is the study of these differences and similarities.

An understanding of child development is necessary for individuals who want to carry out evaluation studies with and for children. This understanding will help prevent errors in judgment, minimize poor design of evaluation studies, and provide more believable results.

Studies in child development began in the seventeenth and eighteenth centuries with a lively debate as to whether children developed as a result of nurture (a view held by John Locke, 1632–1704) or nature (Jean Jacques Rousseau, 1712–1778). In the years that followed, many (often conflicting) broad theories of child development were proposed, with the intention that these theories could explain and make predictions about children.

The earlier development theories tended to involve large age groups and offered explanations for many different general phenomena, but more recent theories have focused on small age groups or precisely defined groups of children, often studying a limited field of interest. Several development theories are outlined in the next section, and then we examine some of the specific findings about child development as they relate to the involvement of children in the evaluation of interactive products.

Perspectives on Child Development

Kail (2002) identifies five major theoretical perspectives in child development: biological, psychodynamic, learning, cognitive-developmental, and contextual. In this chapter, we briefly touch on each of these views. The reader is encouraged to reflect on how acceptable these theories are in the modern world and how the ideas proposed might affect evaluation studies.

Biological

Theories that take a biological perspective uphold the nature side of the debate: that external factors, people, and events have little or no effect on the child's development. One such theory—the maturational theory (Arnold Gesell, 1880–1961)—argues that children should be left to develop in their own ways. Another theory—the ethological theory—assumes that experience has an impact but only if it occurs at the "right" time. Konrad Lorenz (1903–1989) supported this view by claiming that certain learning can only take place if it happens at the right moment.

Psychodynamic

This perspective on child development includes the works of Sigmund Freud (1856–1939) and his student Erik Erikson (1902–1994). Freud's work essentially offers a theory of personality defined with these three components:

- Id (primitive instincts)
- Ego (practical, rational behavior)
- Superego (the moral component)

These are supported by a theory of psychosexual development that argues that development best occurs when the child's needs (which vary at different stages) are met. Erikson's work was more focused on the social aspects of development, and he produced a psychosocial theory that a person's lifetime is divided into eight stages, each with its own challenges. Erikson's work was not only about children; it considered a person's entire life. The stages that are of most interest to evaluators of children's products are shown in Table 1.1.

Erikson made the following assertions:

- Around the ages of 4 or 5, children become competitive and begin to prefer sex-appropriate activities. They also begin to feel both responsibility and guilt.
- Children are not able to use their own initiative until around age 7, at which time they also learn to follow rules.
- By age 13 (adolescence), children are aware of who they are but may experience minor delinquency, self-doubt, and rebellion.

Our own work with children supports these assumptions. The novice evaluator can take some important lessons from this theory: Almost all children are competitive (see Figure 1.1); the older they are, the more they are able to follow rules; and

Table 1.1

Erikson's Theory

Psychosocial Stage	Age	Challenge
Initiative versus guilt	3–6	To develop a willingness to try new things and to handle failure
Industry versus inferiority	6–adolescence	To learn basic skills and to work with others
Identity versus identity confusion	Adolescence	To develop a lasting integrated sense of self

Figure 1.1
*Children playing
competitively at a
computer.*

as they approach adolescence, they sometimes become difficult to manage. This clearly makes the last group a difficult one for evaluation studies!

Learning

Early theorists who were concerned with learning upheld the view of John Locke that children were born as blank slates and that they became who they were chiefly by instruction. B. F. Skinner (1904–1990) proposed the idea of "operant conditioning"—that is, the provision of punishment to change errant behavior and the provision of reinforcement to reward good behavior. Thus, children could be taught to be good by giving rewards and punishments because they would associate the reward or punishment with the action that earned it. Skinner's work has greatly influenced much of the current practices in schools and homes.

Tip

You may find that children of the same age from two different schools will behave quite differently in your evaluation studies.

Figure 1.2

Often, the reward for children in an evaluation study is a trip out or an interesting activity.

More recently, Albert Bandura (1925–) expanded on the work of Skinner with his sociocognitive theory of learning. He proposed that when rewarded or punished, children try to figure out what is going on and the reason for the reward or punishment, and, as a consequence, they begin to understand their abilities and talents (self-efficacy).

For evaluators, understanding the influence of rewards is critical. If children are engaged in an evaluation activity for which there is a reward, they will expect certain things to have taken place. The child may believe that the reward was given because he gave the correct answer to a question. This, however, may make the child less critical than the evaluator would like him to be. If no reward is given, the child might assume that she has done something bad or answered a question incorrectly. In our view, rewards are seldom needed; taking part is reward enough (see Figure 1.2).

Cognitive–Developmental

The focus in the cognitive-developmental perspective is on the child's mind and what is going on inside it. Essentially the domain of Jean Piaget (1896–1980), cognitive-developmental theories are based on the belief that children act as scientists and in so doing actively construct meaning as they discover how the world works.

Stage	Ages	Key Points for Interactive Product Design
Sensorimotor	Birth–2	
Preconceptual Thought	2–4	
Intuitive Thought	4–7	Children can use symbols and words and can distinguish reality from fantasy. In the latter part, they can take into account the viewpoint of others.
Concrete Operations	7–11	Children can classify things and understand the notion of reversibility and conservation. They can think logically but not abstractly.
Formal Operations	11+	Thinking is about ideas. They can consider various solutions without having to act them out and can deal with hypothetical situations.

Table 1.2

Piagetian Stages of Development

Piaget's theory of development (1970) is still much used, and evaluators who work in the research domain will often encounter references to it in academic texts. The Piagetian stages of cognitive development are very helpful in describing the key stages of intellectual and language development. By referring to a Piagetian stage, writers can address a "small" age group of children without getting too concerned with biological age. The Piagetian stages are shown in Table 1.2.

Evaluators of interactive technology would do well to examine Piaget's work closely. He made several interesting observations of the way children behave at the different stages, and his observations on children's egocentric behavior before the age of around 7 are especially informative. In addition, his ideas on learning indicate that in most instances an evaluation of an interactive product should consider how learning has an impact or how it takes place.

From around the age of 7, children clearly attempt to work out what is going on around them, and their ability to do so is central to many evaluation studies. When you ask a child, "Did you like this software?" a complex process happens as the child contemplates the statement, establishes what was *really* being asked, and constructs an answer.

Sociocultural

The work of Urie Bronfenbrenner (1917–2005) is the most frequently used contextual view of development. His view is of a child developing within a complex system

Figure 1.3

Bronfenbrenner's model.

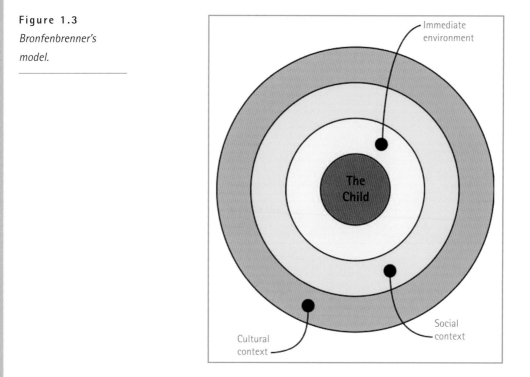

with many interactions. Bronfenbrenner's work was no doubt influenced by the work of Lev Vygotsky (1896–1934), in which the communication from adult to child of cultural systems and belief systems was investigated. In Bronfenbrenner's model (see Figure 1.3), the child interacts with each of the three contexts as part of a system. This means that as the child acts on the context, the context also acts on the child.

Context is essential in evaluation studies with children. A common problem is where children take part in an evaluation in school and are asked to be critical of a product that is placed in front of them. Depending on the school ethos and culture, criticism may or may not be encouraged, so children in one school who are faced with a different context will not necessarily answer the same as children from another school. Evaluators must both consider context and find ways to break through the potential problems associated with it.

Summary

The preceding theories are important because they explain the differences in children across both a single age group and a lifespan. For evaluation studies, however, it is often necessary to be able to make some assumptions about a cohort of children with respect to their abilities and skills at a given point in time. The next section of this chapter presents some more general statements about child development milestones.

Typical Stages of Development

Theories of child development are intended to explain the differences and similarities in the three features of children that change with age: physical development, socioemotional development, and cognitive development.

Physical

Physical development is generally associated with the size of the child, the child's movement skills, and the related gross- and fine-motor skills. Children grow rapidly in the first two years of their lives, and then they follow standard growth curves, meaning that their physical size at later ages can be estimated quite easily from their size at age 2. As shown in Figure 1.4, the diversity in size, both within a cohort and

Figure 1.4

The One Laptop per Child (OLPC) Project has been producing small laptops that use no electricity. Note that the design is well suited to small children. Source: From www.olpc.com.

Figure 1.5

An example of writing at age 4. Note the poor spelling and the uneven formation of letters, all indications of poor motor skills and language immaturity.

across a time span, is important. It is estimated that children are growing taller at a rate of about 1 cm (0.40 inch) per decade, and yet within a single cohort children of a single sex may normally differ in size by up to 15 cm (6 inches) at age 6 and up to 22 cm (8.5 inches) at age 12. Thus, the design of seating and the position of dry-wipe boards and the like in a usability lab that will be used by children should take these variations into account.

Between the ages of 2 and 6, fine-motor and gross-motor control improves a great deal. Children move from barely being able to draw a circle to being able to construct clear images and to write legibly. Figure 1.5 shows a child's uneven and badly spaced writing. During the same time period, they learn to jump, throw, and balance. Interestingly, by around age 10 girls have better fine-motor control than boys, while boys perform better than girls at strength-related gross-motor activities. With the upsurge in technology that incorporates physical play, like the Nintendo Wii, it is also worth noting that as children become adolescents the strength of boys is significantly increased as their muscles grow with the onset of puberty.

Socioemotional

The most important aspect of socioemotional development is an appreciation of how relationships affect development, with the caregiver–child attachment setting

Figure 1.6
Friends playing together.

the stage for future relationships, emotional and self-development are both important themes. The self-esteem of children is associated with emotional development.
Although it is known that preschool children have very high levels of self-esteem,
with time, and possibly directly as a result of entry into the educational system, this
self-esteem declines, with around 15 percent of those 9 to 10 years old having very
low self-esteem; the self-esteem of girls being, in all cases, lower than that of equiv-
alently aged boys.

Other social habits change in different ways. Prejudice, for instance, is known to
decline as children mature, and friendships become stronger. As children get older,
they demonstrate what are known as prosocial behaviors (see Figure 1.6)—that is,
they act altruistically (for the benefit of others). This is important when children are
working in pairs or groups as it may result in interference even when children have
been told not to help one another.

Cognitive

Cognitive development includes intellect and language. It is concerned with the way
individuals learn to think, their memory, their problem-solving abilities, and their

reasoning. In this area, children start to learn language around the age of 1 and, surprisingly, learn an average of ten words a day for the next 16 years. This learning is not level—during the early years children learn more slowly, with the greatest learning occurring in the middle years. Between the ages of 3 and 5, children think in an egocentric way and solve problems illogically; as they get older, they become rational and learn to understand other people's points of view.

Cognitive development and, more specifically, language is crucial in evaluation studies. It is worth noting that the variation across children is fairly wide. Although most children will be able to read simple language by around the age of 7, some will have great difficulties with expressing themselves using written language.

Child Development and the Evaluation of Interactive Products

Table 1.3 suggests some questions that evaluators might consider when planning an evaluation.

Table 1.3

Questions about Child Development

Developmental Features	Issues to Be Noted
Physical Development	• Is it physically and ergonomically possible for a test participant to operate the input devices or use any other test-related equipment? • Are input devices suitable for a specific age group? • Is the interior design of the test space appropriate for both small and big test participants?
Socioemotional Development	• Is the test situation socially understandable and safe for a test participant? • Can a child adapt to a new situation alone and without a peer or a familiar adult? • Is the number of adults versus children balanced? • How dependent are test participants on adults' help and attention? • Do children aim at pleasing or annoying adults? • What behavior of the test administrator might decrease or increase the openness of the test situation? • Can a child cooperate in a way that is required when performing a test together with another child? • Can the test situation cause distress or feelings of failure for a child, and does this affect the situation and results obtained? • Can a test situation make children feel afraid? How can you prevent that? • Can you encourage a child during a test? Does it affect a child's subjective assessment of a product's qualities? • Does a child understand that the product is being evaluated and not the child? How does the child feel about being part of testing and how well he or she is doing in it? • Does a child have a positive feeling about testing once it is over?

Developmental Features	Issues to Be Noted
Cognitive Development	• Does a child understand what he or she is expected to do? • Does a child understand what "carrying out a task" means? • Are test tasks understandable and memorable? • Can a child use the product independently? • Does a child understand cause-and-effect relationships that are necessary for using the product? • Are a child's problem-solving skills mature enough in terms of test tasks? • Are there any features in the test situation that distract a child's thinking and attention? • Is the cognitive load too big for a child? Do the methods used for testing add to this load? • Can a child recollect previous activities and thinking? Can retrospective methods that rely on this recollection be used? • Can a child read? If not, how are test tasks to be presented to the child and how should an adult remind a child who forgets what he or she is supposed to be doing? • Can one use written forms or language as a part of testing? • Can a child understand the language and concepts used by a test supervisor? • Can a child write? Can the child respond in writing? • How well can a child verbalize thoughts? • Can a child respond to questions during an interview? Do the child's answers contain enough for the purposes of the evaluation?

Table 1.3

Cont'd

The Temperament of Children

Irrespective of stage of development, each child has a unique temperament. Temperament is especially interesting in evaluation studies because it can have a significant effect on both the evaluation methods to be used and the results gathered. Differences in temperament can have a considerable effect on the usefulness and validity of a user study. Unlike many other aspects of children, temperament is unlikely to change over time, with most children having the same temperament throughout their lives.

Temperamental Dimensions

Chess and Thomas (1996) have identified nine different temperamental dimensions:

Activity level. Different children work at different paces. Some are quite slow to do tasks whereas others race along.

Distractability. The degree of concentration the child has. Hanna et al. (1999) consider that in a usability study preschool children can concentrate for about 30 minutes, but some children will be distracted as many as 15 or 20 times.

Sensory threshold. How sensitive the child is to noise and other sensory interruptions. Some children have a very low threshold to noise, and this affects their performance.

Approach withdrawal. The response of a child to a new situation—whether eager to take part or more hesitant. A reluctance to take part does not always imply a problem with an activity.

Adaptability. The ease with which a child can switch to new things. Some children, especially those with some autistic-spectrum disorders, can be very upset by different situations and will not perform as well as they might had the situation been more familiar.

Persistence. The length of time a child will spend on a difficult task. Some children give up more easily than others.

Intensity. The energy level of a response. One child may be extremely enthusiastic about a product whereas another may seem less engaged. Although this might be all about intensity, it can also be attributed to other aspects of temperament.

Mood. Whether a child is pessimistic or optimistic.

It is clear from this list that special care must be taken to accommodate the different temperaments of children.

Figure 1.7

Younger children are happy working in mixed pairs, but as they get older they are more likely to want to work in same-sex groups at the computer.

Tip

Allow for variable sensory experiences. If the child has to react to a noise, don't assume that because *you* heard the noise the child should respond as well.

Reducing the Effects of Temperament

The following actions will help reduce the effects of temperament on evaluation studies:

Activity level. If children work in pairs (see Figure 1.7), be sure to allow the slower one ample time to finish. Make sure that children who finish tasks early don't distract others.

Distractability. Use an area as free from external distractions as possible. Remove clutter from the evaluation space, turn off mobile phones, do all you can to reduce passing traffic (mainly people, not cars!).

Sensory threshold. Take control of lighting and sound. Where possible, ask the children if they are comfortable with the surroundings. If feasible, allow children to control the noise level of any sound output and the contrast and brightness of the screen.

Approach withdrawal. Use familiar locations for the children and familiar language. Find out the words generally used by the children—for example, *evaluate* is not a "child" word, and using such words only increases the strangeness of the situation.

Adaptability. Make sure all instructions are very clear, and where possible give children a chance to practice with any technology. If planning two or three different activities, make the transitions easy by using similar instructions.

Persistence. Prepare for children stopping before the end by putting the most important tasks first. Encourage persistence by telling the children how long the evaluation will take and providing information to show them their progress.

Intensity. Mix different methods so all children find a comfortable way to give their opinions. For instance, don't just rely only on facial expressions to judge a response.

Summary

This chapter provided a brief overview of child development theories and highlighted the diverse nature of children, their lack of homogeneity, and their widely differing talents and motivations. Of great importance in evaluation studies is recognizing this variance in children and taking account of their differences, abilities, and needs.

Further Reading

You can find an easy-to-read overview of child development and child psychology in Kail (2002) and Smith, Cowie, and Blades (2003). Hundreds of books on child development are available; some are based at high-level audiences, so care should be taken!

It is also worth reading the educational curricula from the county (or state in the United States) in which you are working. These documents specify what children will learn in their school years and can give you a good indication of children's abilities at different stages.

Exercises

1. A local usability company has been asked to evaluate a website that is primarily aimed at English-speaking children aged between 5 and 8. Based on what you learned in this chapter, write a short e-mail (fewer than 200 words) that outlines the most important things you think the evaluator should know about children.

2. Several published guidelines for designing interactive products for children are available—for example, "Children like bright colors." Identify a specific guideline, and discuss how it matches the developmental and temperamental needs of children.

CHAPTER 2

CHILDREN AND INTERACTIVE TECHNOLOGY

The last 20 years have seen an explosion in the availability and range of technology for children, with the result that in most of the Western world children are significant users of interactive technology. By the beginning of the twenty-first century, 98 percent of American households had a TV, 70 percent had computers, 68 percent had video games, and 52 percent had Internet access (Woodward and Gridina, 2000). The computer and video game industry is now worth about $1.7 billion, and the market for educational software and related technologies is comparable.

Children's adoption of technology has evolved rapidly. In schools, one in four lessons in the United Kingdom uses information and communication technology (ICT), and a survey of those 2 to 17 years old found that on average they engaged with interactive technology for over one hour a day. Some children spend a large proportion of their out-of-school time using interactive technology (Department for Education and Skills, 2005). Within the children's sector, the most prolific interactive technology user group is teenagers, with those who are 12 to 15 years old being very active (Wartela et al., 2002).

These statistics show that interactive technology plays a huge part in children's lives. This chapter presents an overview of the different technologies used by children, explores interactivity, and considers several of the primary issues that relate to how children use technology.

Interactive Products

This book is about the evaluation of interactive products, so in this section we take a closer look at the concept of interactivity. We examine definitions of interactivity and consider how interactivity varies across products. In addition, we clarify what is meant by *interactive technology* in the context of this book.

What Is Interactivity?

Interactivity is a term that is used in several different contexts. In the context of human communication, two individuals are said to be interacting if they are communicating (orally or otherwise) with enough connectivity that each individual's changes in behavior can be observed by the other. The interaction in this instance would be manifested as spoken language, body movements, or facial expressions.

Another form of interaction is mediated by products or artifacts. Sometimes referred to as human-to-artifact interaction, man–machine interaction, or human–computer interaction (HCI), this form of interaction relies on the ability of the "nonhuman" actor (the product or the artifact) to demonstrate behavior that is (or appears) interactive.

Interactivity is therefore more than the look or feel or the functionality of a product. The interactivity of a product can really only be discovered by observing it in use or predicting its use. The term *interactive technology* suggests that something extra is added to an interaction by the technology. Thus, the technology must operate in such a way that particular inputs result in specific (different) outputs.

Therefore, a stuffed animal is not an interactive product (even though a child will interact with it). One that purrs when you stroke it has perhaps a very low (and uninteresting) level of interactivity, but a stuffed animal that "listens" to a child and responds in different ways according to the spoken input is much more interactive. Products that interact with children need to be able to respond to their "conversations"; one example of such a product is the Clicker Word Processor that is designed in such a way that the software provides specific help to children while they are using it (see Figure 2.1).

Measuring Interaction

There are many ways to determine the degree of interactivity a product provides. Luckin (2001) developed three profiles to describe interaction:

Profile 1: busy–quiet. Measured by the number of actions taken, thus interaction is considered *busy* when many actions occur and *quiet* when only a few actions take place.

Profile 2: exploration–consolidation. This is the extent to which the child's action leads to an experience or to information. The interaction might result in a small increase in understanding or a significant confirmation.

Profile 3: hopper–persistent. The child might constantly switch tasks during the interaction or may stay with one task.

These profiles of interaction are useful to describe what happens when a child interacts with technology. They do not, however, explain *why* children choose

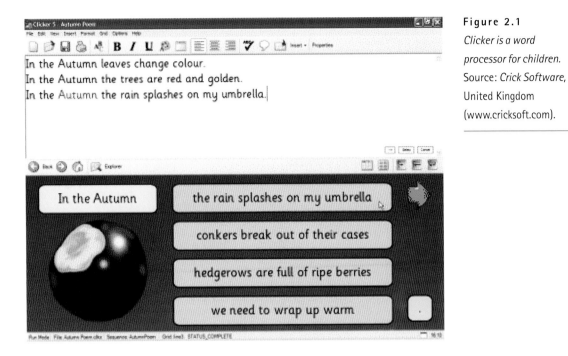

Figure 2.1

Clicker is a word processor for children. Source: *Crick Software,* United Kingdom (www.cricksoft.com).

particular technologies. Children choose interactive technologies for many reasons: boredom, social activity, comfort, and learning, among others.

Interactive Products for Children

Interactive technology for children can be characterized in many ways: their level of interactivity (possibly demonstrated by profiles of children who use it or by a count of their interactive features), their portability (handheld, desktop), their location (school, home), or their connectivity (stand-alone, networked). A good way to categorize children's interactive products is by their purpose.

In many books and reports, children's products are divided into the two broad categories of education and entertainment, with the term *edutainment* meaning those products that mix the two genres (Bruckman and Bandlow, 2003). This "division into two" came from the early days of computing when products for children were either games (remember Pac-Man?) or educational applications. Classifications tend to vary according to context. Ingram (1984) classified interactive products for education according to four genres: didactic (drill and practice), content-free (word processors and so on), recreational, and diagnostic and screening.

In this book we mix these classifications and come up with three genres. We use the term *enabling technology* to include those "content-free" products Ingram spoke of, but we also include in this definition the fourth Ingram classification: products for diagnosis and screening (Read, 2005). Thus, for the purposes of discussing interactive products, this book uses the classifications of entertainment, educational, and enabling.

Entertainment Products

The largest sector of interactive technology for children is entertainment software and related games technology. The two primary product areas for entertainment are interactive toys and computer (video) games. Interactive TV also comes into this category because it is primarily an entertainment product, although it also claims to educate.

Several highly successful interactive toys are available today, and many of them feature smart robotic technology. Some—mainly aimed at the under-11 market—have a simple, recognizable shape that associates itself with noninteractive products or products that are not technically complicated, which children are already familiar with (e.g., RoboDog, Nintendogs, Barney—see Figure 2.2). Other interactive toys allow more freedom and creativity and generally appeal to older age groups—for instance, Lego Mindstorms.

Computer video games have evolved rapidly since the first table-based and TV-based products like Space Invaders. Computer video games are now created for

Figure 2.2

ActiMates Interactive Barney by Microsoft Corporation.

several competing and complementary platforms, including PCs (Windows and Apple); Sony PlayStation PSP, PS2, and PS3; Nintendo GameBoy, GameCube, Wii and DS; and Microsoft Xbox. These games are marketed for specific age groups, with many products designed for children as young as 3. Many computer video games are spin-offs from, or accompaniments to, movies and TV programs, but sports products and simulation products that have no associated marketing are also extremely popular. To determine the suitability of games for different age groups, games classification systems are available that give adults (and children) some idea of the content of the games being purchased (see *http://www.esrb.org*). In many countries, games are classified by age in much the same way that movies are rated and some games cannot be purchased without proof of age. Given that many adult games have high levels of violence, this is a sensible idea.

Education Products

We define education products as those that help the child learn. Some products that are associated with the education process include testing and evaluative products (like those used to determine a child's IQ or academic potential), but these are not really educative and are more accurately described as "enabling."

Interactive technology that is geared toward learning (education products) is separately targeted and marketed for both home and school use. In general, these are quite different products, but both tend to be available on two major platforms, the Internet and CD-ROM. Recently, some more novel products, like LeapFrog's LeapPad series (see Figure 2.3), have taken educational learning technology away from the PC, and more use is also being made of game consoles, thus bringing learning closer to the child's natural environment.

Many companies manufacture software for learning. These include established educational publishers (e.g., Prentice Hall), media companies (e.g., *NBC News 4 Kids* and the *BBC*), and toy manufacturers (e.g., Mattel). Depending on the emphasis of the manufacturing company, the interactive technology is likely to be particularly strong in those areas in which the manufacturer excels.

Enabling Products

Children spend considerable time in front of general computer applications that are neither educational nor entertaining. These products include search engines, word

Figure 2.3

LeapPad by LeapFrog Corporation.

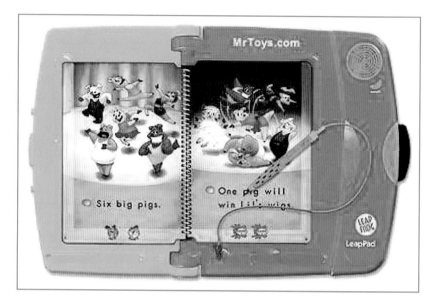

Figure 2.4

This news site from the BBC is specially designed for children, and is similar to NBC News 4 Kids and Channel 1 in U.S. schools.

processors, and graphics packages, as well as more recent technologies like social tools. Although older children will often use adult versions of these products, there are several products that are designed especially for children, including children's news sites with child-friendly language (see Figure 2.4); children's word processors, such as Clicker and TextEase, which have simplified menu structures; and interactive spaces for children to build social networks, such as Bebo (see Figure 2.5).

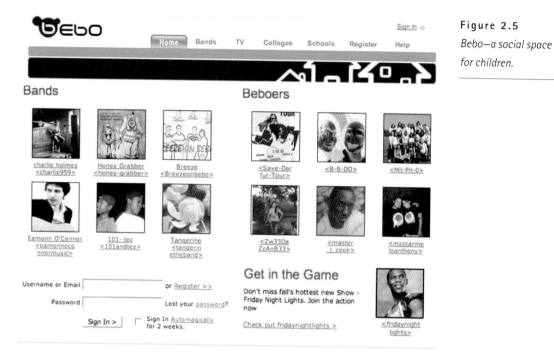

Figure 2.5

Bebo—a social space for children.

As we saw earlier in this chapter, certain products made for the education sector are much better described as enabling products. With the recent rise in e-learning, children of all ages are expected to have access to the Internet and to use it to gather specific content from content management systems that are controlled by their schools. There is potential for huge growth in the provision of online educational services for children. In the United Kingdom, a recent national strategy proposed that all children receive classroom content online and be required to create e-portfolios of their work, browse digital libraries, and take part in e-assessment in their classroom studies (Department for Education and Skills, 2005).

How Children Use Interactive Products

There is a wide variety of interactive technologies, and some of these are multipurpose. In trying to classify technologies into three genres, it is easy to lose sight of the sometimes dual purpose of products and, more interestingly, of the fact that children, being innovative, creative users of interactive technology, will often use products in a way for which they were not intended. The ill-coined term *edutainment computing* comes from this very dilemma. It is certainly possible that a product could be designed to both entertain *and* instruct, but in almost all cases the product has a main purpose. Critics of *edutainment* as a descriptor point out that some such products are sugar-coated education and that they may lead children to expect features from educative products that cannot be delivered and may distract them from more traditional products like books.

The PLU Model

The PLU model outlines and defines how children interact with technology. It emphasizes three different relationships children have with interactive products that align with the three genres of interactive technology. In the PLU model, which was first discussed in Read (2004), children are described as players, learners, or users, and the technologies are described as entertainment, education, or enabling. The relationship of the child to the technology helps when determining how the interactive product might be evaluated later.

Children as players. In this relationship, the child sees the interactive product as a plaything; to satisfy its purpose, the product must amuse or entertain the child.

Children as learners. The interactive product is seen as a substitute school or teacher; it is expected to instruct, challenge, and reward.

Children as users. Here, the child sees the interactive product as a tool; for the product to be useful, it must enable the child and make things easier to do.

A well-designed product will map the purposes of the child to the features of the technology.

In the PLU model in Figure 2.6, both a product and a child's purpose can be mapped in a three-dimensional space, and the distance between them can predict to some extent any mismatch between the technology and the purpose. The model can also be used to assist in the choices of evaluation constructs. Thus, products intended for learning might need to be evaluated for learning, and those intended for fun should be evaluated for fun.

In Figure 2.6, A represents a child's purpose—to learn something while having fun at the same time—and B is the product—which is designed to help the child perform some function. If the distance between these two points is too large, it can be expected that the product will not satisfy the child's goal. This mismatch between

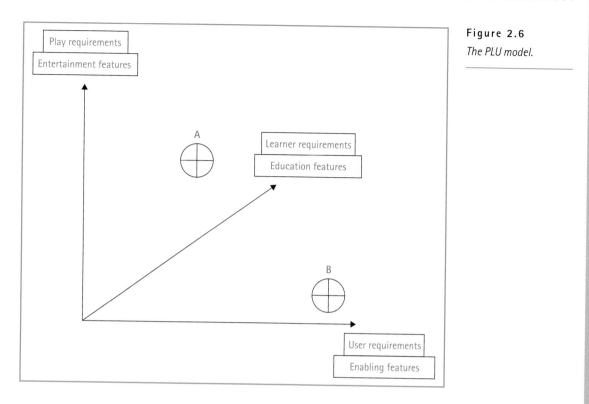

Figure 2.6
The PLU model.

purpose and product can lead to interesting results in evaluations. It is always better to have the children expect roughly what they get! The next section expands on this problem.

Interactive Technology and Evaluation Studies

When carrying out evaluations of technology with children, you should first have some understanding of how children differ from adults in the ways they use technology. It is certainly true that adults, as well as children, also use technology for play, learning, and general use, and adult technology is similarly designed for these same three purposes. However, children interact with the technology differently.

In addition to being a different size, shape, and age from the adults in their world and having different learning skills and emotional maturity, children come to interactive technology already comfortable with it. Marc Prensky (2001) coined the term *digital natives* to describe how children have been born into an interactive world that adults have generally had to discover and understand, as one would a new culture or a new continent. The following are some of the differences between adults and children and their use of technology.

Children as Players

- Children find play very natural, whereas adults may feel "silly." In evaluation studies, it is sometimes difficult to see if children are playing.
- Play is essential for children because it contributes to their development (they do not play just to relax). Children learn by playing, but they may not report that they learned something if the learning was a result of play.
- Children have high levels of imagination, so much of their play can be difficult to see. If asked, the children might say that they have been playing, but the evaluator might not be able to see it.

Children as Learners

- Children have more to learn than adults do, so they have to learn more quickly and efficiently. The effort they report when learning might seem lower than would be expected given the difficulty they may demonstrate on their faces!
- Children learn more easily, and much of what they learn is informal. When asked, children might not even know what they learned.
- Children are into learning; they find it very natural and have a lot of curiosity. It is highly likely that children will learn things that had not been planned into an activity.
- Children's mental models are incomplete, so they may not be able to explain why things are the way they are. They might not be able to give reasons for the things they do.

Children as Users

- Children age more quickly, so their needs for technology keep changing. It is essential to ensure that technology is age appropriate.
- Children have different motivations than adults. They generally only use technology if they want to; they also have much more discretion than adults. If they don't like what is put in front of them, they may walk away.
- Children expect more from ordinary products. They may believe that technology is magic. This can lead to high expectations that may not be realized and may discourage the child.

These differences are worth remembering during evaluations of interactive products. The child is not simply a small adult, and the relationship between product and child must be well understood.

How Good Is Interactive Technology for Children?

Most of the interactive technology children use is at the least beneficial and at best excellent. However, the increased use of interactive technologies and the features embedded in some products have raised fears about the perils of exposing children to them. The focus of this concern is on video games, the Internet, desktop computing, and mobile technology—cell phones, PDAs, iPhones. Some of the concerns are the health implications associated with the sedentary nature of interacting with screen-based applications, the risks associated with possible exposure to pornography or pedophiles, the influence of violent games on the child, and the health and social concerns about overuse of mobile technology.

In the general debate about the harmful effects of interactive technologies on children, both in society at large and in the research community, opinions are divided: Some are very concerned and see all technology as bad; others take a more liberal view. Enthusiasts of interactive technologies are driven by the belief that exposure to technology during early childhood will contribute much to children's academic and professional development. Similarly, many feel that the Internet provides extra educational opportunities. For these reasons, both society and governments encourage the introduction of ICT to children at ever-earlier stages (Plowman, 2003).

There is very little dispute that interactive technologies have a great potential for educational use. Visionaries like Seymour Papert (1980) have long advocated the use of computing technology as an enabling tool to support children's self-directed learning. Much research has been conducted on this concept, and many commercial products have been designed to support it.

With evidence that supports arguments both for and against interactive technology for children, it is clear that technology developers have a responsibility to design their products to meet the needs of children. Products should be designed to accommodate children's size, strength, and dexterity. One example of an appropriate technology for young children is the BigKeys keyboard (Figure 2.7).

Gender and Technology

When it comes to technology, it is important to consider the difference between girls and boys. Whether innate or acquired, girls and boys use interactive technologies

Figure 2.7

BigKeys keyboard.

Source: *From*
Greystone Digital Inc.,
Huntersville, NC (www.
BigKeys.com).

differently. These differences tend to surface round the age of 3 and continue until adolescence. The differences in use are fairly significant until ages 13 to 15, when boys and girls begin to have common interests and participate in activities together.

Most of the studies in this area were conducted by the games industry. Acuff and Reiher (1997) reported the following characteristics:

- Boys are seldom attracted to female game characters; the opposite is not necessarily true.
- Nonaggressive games such as PacMan or Sims may appeal to both boys and girls, but even in these game types aggressive characters and plots are less likely to appeal to girls.
- Sport themes in interactive games and artifacts appeal to both sexes.
- Girls have a stronger interest than boys in communication, such as chat applications.
- Boys may have more interest in content such as sports, financial and business matters, and science and technology.
- Boys identify more with heroic male characters; girls identify with both male and female role models and heroes.

It may be helpful for designers to consult related analyses of children's preferences at different ages to see how these are affected by gender (Acuff and Reiher, 1997). However, a word of caution: Creating and abiding by preferences and characteristics by gender may magnify existing cultural stereotypes. Cassell (2002) reports how some technology manufacturers conformed to an overstereotyped view of girls as users of technology and thus failed to address them as a market and support them as users of these technologies. Designing without a gender bias is a much better way to reach out to both girls and boys, especially if they can adapt the product or game to fit their preferences and tastes.

Summary

This chapter has outlined how technologies for children have developed and has introduced a method by which they can be classified. In particular, it has described the need for evaluators of interactive products for children to take the goals of the children into account when evaluating technologies for different purposes.

The next chapter takes this observation further and looks at the early considerations in planning an evaluation study.

Further Reading

Druin's 1999 book, *The Design of Children's Technology*, is a good introduction to technologies for children. This book looks at several projects where novel technologies were created for and with children. Of particular interest in the book is the discussion of how the products were created and what features the children wanted in them.

A good source for new technologies and news on the latest technologies is the magazine *Technology Review*, published by the Massachusetts Institute of Technology.

Exercises

1. Visit a local store and look at the products that are available for children. If you can, purchase some of them and determine their purpose, predicting what children will do with them, and decide whether they would appeal to either girls or boys or to both.
2. Another useful activity is to guess at what age a child might lose interest in a particular product. Discuss your evaluation of the technology with a colleague, a parent, and a teacher.

CHAPTER 3

THE INTERACTIVE
PRODUCT LIFECYCLE

This chapter will be particularly useful to readers who have a limited knowledge of the overall design process, but it should also serve as a reference point for readers who have more experience. We examine a range of concepts that are relevant to the design of interactive products and define some evaluation terms.

We also look at the product lifecycle, using the Usability Engineering Lifecycle as an example and to show the different places where evaluation is used in the lifecycle. We then discuss different approaches to prototyping and the kinds of prototypes that can be used in evaluations at particular stages. Finally, the roles children play in the evaluation process are examined.

Interaction Design and Evaluation

The term *interactive product* refers to products with some embedded computing and communication capabilities, including interactive software applications that run on generic platforms such as personal computers, cell phones, and game consoles. Interaction design for these products is a relatively new field that has adopted ideas and methods from product design, computer systems design, and industrial manufacturing. Of these three disciplines, industrial manufacturing is the oldest and emphasizes functionality. For example, when you make a hammer the primary consideration is on its fitness for purpose, but safety and durability (both critical factors for hammers!) are also considered important.

Product design, however, is a more recent field that arose as products with similar functionality began to compete in the marketplace. Decisions made in product design are often based on viability, feasibility, and desirability. Indeed, the design of desirable products has become a huge international business. In recent years, the field of product design has extended its scope beyond physical products to address the design of experiences that can be enjoyed through using software products and services.

Computation brings about the potential for almost limitless interactive behaviors. In the early days of computer systems development, designers of such systems emphasized the production of robust, efficient code. With information and communication technology now available to a wider public and significantly affecting everyday life, the design of such systems must address the needs of nontechnical experts and nonprofessional users. Here, the aim is to improve *usability*—in other words, to create products that support people in carrying out their activities and enjoying satisfying experiences mediated by their products or services. This shift of focus has led to the establishment of *human–computer interaction* as a discipline, and it has encouraged new connections between design, media, and computing that have resulted in entirely new fields such as *user experience design* (Forlizzi and Battarbee, 2004; Norman, 2002). *Interaction design* is an umbrella term that describes the processes and techniques that are employed in designing interactive products. Interaction design borrows from all of the preceding areas.

In this book, the term *evaluation* is used to refer to activities that aim to provide feedback and guidance to interaction design, where *interaction* is defined in a broad sense that encompasses fitness for purpose, usability, desirability, performance, and user experience.

The Product Lifecycle

Designing interactive products is usually a complex process that involves a number of smaller-scale activities, such as conceptualizing, development, evaluation, and deployment. To facilitate planning, but also to ensure good practice, a variety of models of the process have been proposed. Such models are called lifecycle models, in an analogy to the biological lifecycle in which life forms mature, reproduce, and create a new generation. In the same way, the development of an interactive product is often followed by evaluations that provide the seeds of concepts for new versions or new products. Lifecycle models typically describe the activities carried out, their deliverables, the roles of the people involved, and how the process moves from one activity to the next.

The Waterfall Model

An early conceptualization of a lifecycle model for software systems was the "waterfall" model, in which the process is seen as a sequence of distinct steps, each of which must be completed before the next one starts (see Figure 3.1). It is widely accepted that such a sequential and inflexible design process is particularly

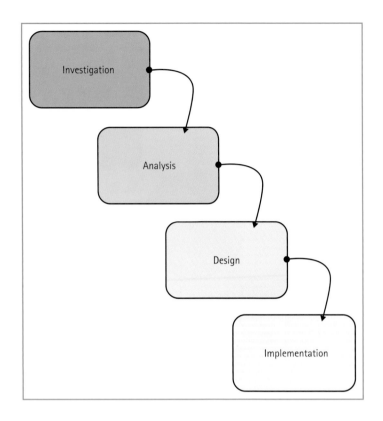

Figure 3.1
A waterfall model for the design of interactive products. This doesn't represent what actually happens; building an interactive product is an iterative process.

inappropriate for designing interactive systems, and here it serves only as a reference framework for describing design activities.

In practice, during the design and implementation stages of the development of an interactive product, there is much negotiation and discussion among the product developers, potential users, and other stakeholders in the system. This is necessary because it is generally difficult to get a clear idea of what is needed for a product without first trying out some ideas and obtaining feedback from various stakeholders.

A *user-centered design* approach assumes that the emphasis during the lifecycle is on engaging with the potential users of the product. This engagement can take place at the early requirements and analysis stages and at the point where the final product is user-tested, but, it is more crucial during the design and build stages. This constant dialogue with the potential users during the design process results in a design being proposed, evaluated, redesigned, reevaluated, and so on, until a design is reached that satisfies the team's criteria well enough to be implemented.

Figure 3.2

A model of human-centered design activities as specified in ISO standard 13407.

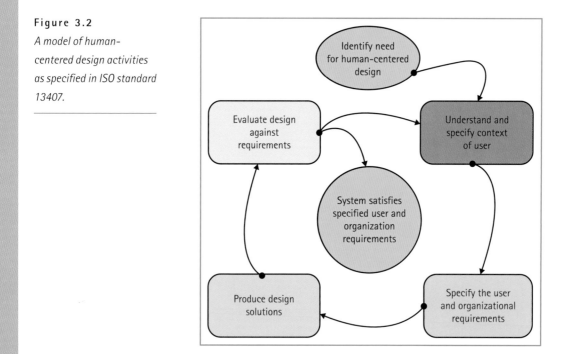

This process is called *iterative design*. This iterative approach is now almost universally accepted and even included in international standards (see Figure 3.2).

The Usability Engineering Lifecycle Model

The model of human-centered design shown in Figure 3.2 explains the tight relationship between evaluation and design activities. From the perspective of project planning, especially when larger design teams need to be coordinated, a more elaborate lifecycle model is needed. This model must detail different concerns to be addressed by the design team, corresponding activities, deliverables, and dependencies between them. The field of *usability engineering* has resulted in some of the most elaborate, yet flexible, processes for involving humans in the design process, in which the role of evaluation becomes an integral part of planning a project.

One very influential and practical model is the Usability Engineering Lifecycle (UEL) model (see Figure 3.3). This model originates from trying to fit usability work with software engineering processes in the domain of information systems for the workplace. Although the terminology, the focus on usability (rather than, say, user

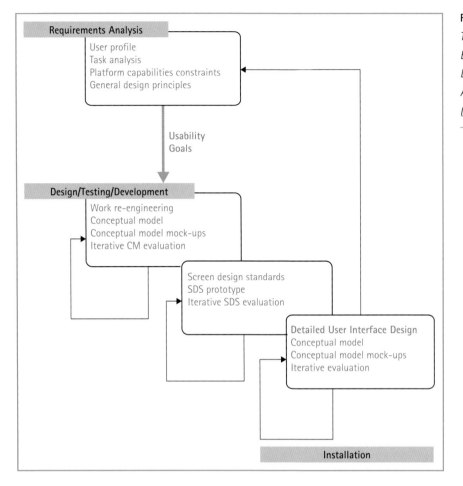

Figure 3.3

The Usability Engineering Lifecycle. Source: *Adapted from Mayhew (1999).*

experience), and the assumptions regarding users and technology very much reflect the origins of this model, it can still provide a practical place to start—for example, designing an interactive product for children.

This section provides a brief explanation of the model. Readers are referred to Mayhew's (1999) book for an extensive description of the method, with practical examples and step-by-step guides for practitioners.

The Usability Engineering Lifecycle model distinguishes three main phases—described on the next page—in the usability engineering of a product: requirements analysis, design/testing/development, and installation. You can see a clear parallel to the activities of Figure 3.1, but note that the arrows feed back from the later activities to the earlier ones, showing that the process is iterative.

Phase 1: Requirements Analysis. Phase 1 includes studying characteristics of targeted users and their tasks to identify usability-related requirements (usability goals); it also includes analysis of generic design principles or technological constraints. The outcomes of these activities are encapsulated in a *style guide* that will guide the design activities that follow. Compared to standard software engineering models, this phase corresponds to requirements gathering.

Phase 2: Design/Testing/Development. Phase 2 is itself structured along levels of abstraction, in which the design progresses from general organization of the interaction to detailed screen content. The corresponding design activities each include an element of the design, creating a mock-up, or *prototype,* to represent the design and evaluating it with users.

Phase 3: Installation. Phase 3 involves installation, evaluation, and obtaining user feedback.

The model advocates returning and iterating the process until the requirements of users are met.

Strengths and Limitations of the UEL

The Usability Engineering Lifecycle describes a relatively linear and structured process. Its strength is that it can provide detailed guidance to a team and a good overview to project management. Its structure might work well with some products and in some organizational contexts, but it may be unnecessarily or excessively structured for other situations. When designing products that are not for the workplace (like most products for children), or when the design team includes only a very small number of people, it may be more appropriate to relax the succession of design activities in Figure 3.3 into a less sequential and more opportunistic transition between stages and to greatly reduce the documentation of design decisions in style guides. Also, for products like cell, or mobile, phones or entertainment applications, installation may need to be more tightly iterated and become an essential part of the design/testing/development cycle. Despite these shortcomings, this lifecycle model remains useful because of its comprehensiveness and because it shows one way to operationalize the general principle of user-centered design.

Using Lifecycle Models

Models of the design process arising from usability engineering and human–computer interaction seem to be the most mature and the most useful in the interaction design process. The lifecycle model in Figure 3.3 (or other, competing ones from these fields) can provide a sound basis for embedding evaluation in the design activity.

It may be necessary to adapt the level of iteration for a specific design process, taking into account the following concerns:

- A software-based application is easier to modify than a hardware one, which means the design process can be more iterative for software.
- Typically, software products have more complex behaviors, making prototyping and evaluation essential.
- Higher levels of interactivity in the product call for a more iterative design process.
- The limited availability of potential users (in this case children) to support the evaluation may limit the number of evaluations that can be done. The involvement of children must be planned carefully.

The Place of Evaluation in the Lifecycle

Evaluation is not simply a stage at the end of the lifecycle when the design is complete. Evaluation can take place at many different stages of the interactive product lifecycle. An early evaluation can be done when only an initial concept is available. Throughout the design process, evaluation can elicit suggested improvements for a wide range of issues—for example, the set of functions provided by the product, the physical appearance or behavior of the product (sometimes called its look and feel), and the situation and labeling of controls and menu choices. When a product is about to be deployed, final *summative evaluations* can be useful to ascertain what, if anything, needs improvement for the next version, as well as to compare the new product with earlier versions (especially useful for marketing). Prior to the release of a finished product, evaluation may take the form of *acceptance testing*.

Using Prototypes in Evaluation

To evaluate particular aspects of the design, the relevant design decisions are captured in intermediate artifacts. In the field of interaction design, these are called prototypes, although in traditional engineering the term carries a slightly different meaning (a first model of a product that will then be reproduced). Often the term *mock-up* is used to contrast to a "real" system, or the term *simulation* is used to indicate that the prototype behaves like a full system only in certain ways. In general, a prototype can be understood as a partial implementation of the intended system and a selective representation of design decisions that the designers need to express and evaluate.

Once a prototype of a product has been created, users can be engaged in simple interactions to see how closely the design fits their preferences or way of working. As the lifecycle progresses, the prototypes tend to develop in detail. To allow for fast iteration and to minimize the costs of revising design decisions, prototypes should be constructed to represent only as much as is relevant for the stage in the lifecycle.

There are many approaches to prototyping, several kinds of prototypes, and several ways prototypes can be classified. The following sections define many of the concepts and terms used to describe prototypes.

Medium Used

Early in the lifecycle, prototypes may be nonfunctional physical mock-ups. If screen-based interactions are involved, they may be *paper prototypes* that are animated by the designer to give an impression of the interaction and the appearance of the product. Paper prototypes, sketches, and other simple techniques such as storyboards are prototyping techniques that typically require very little investment. They allow people who are not trained in the technology to participate in the creation of the designs. This can be especially interesting where young children are concerned.

Where parts of the system functionality are simulated by a human, the prototype is often referred to as a *Wizard of Oz* prototype (discussed more extensively in Chapter 12). Prototyping tools can be used to make interactive software prototypes, and often presentation software can help to portray some aspects of the interaction as a slide show that offers basic interaction. Where the technology is quite challenging to create, video scenarios of simulated use, called *video prototypes*, can provide the basis of an evaluation with users.

Scope

Software prototypes vary considerably. At one extreme there are *wireframe prototypes* (with no real content); other low-content prototypes can include graphically enhanced front ends; and more complete prototypes provide full access to content. *Horizontal prototypes* have limited interactivity, but the entire surface is presented, and *vertical prototypes* have all the functionality and interactivity built into one part of the proto-type. This distinction is easier to understand in the context of graphical interfaces, where a horizontal interface might portray the organization of screens and the navigation between them, illustrating many of the elements of the interface but not supporting their respective functionalities. A vertical prototype might illustrate how the system supports one specific task through a narrow selection of screens and parts of the graphical user interface, all of which are functional.

Fit in the Lifecycle

During the product lifecycle, prototypes can be used in different ways. *Throwaway prototypes* are abandoned after the evaluation once they have served their evaluative purpose; *evolutionary prototypes* are iteratively improved until the final product is reached. During the product lifecycle, many throwaway and evolutionary prototypes may be developed and evaluated.

A similar set of concerns and distinctions for prototypes characterizes product design. During the design of physical products, a range of prototypes might be created. *Form prototypes* are low-fidelity explorations of alternative form designs. *Working prototypes* or *engineering prototypes* refer to technical artifacts that allow simulation of some part of the functionality of the hardware while compromising the appearance of the prototype. Form and engineering prototypes are contrasted in Figure 3.4. *Integrated prototypes* attempt to represent both the form and the function of the final product.

Figure 3.4

Engineering (in child's right hand) and form (left hand) prototypes. The Magic Wand enhances shared reading with sounds supporting the story. Source: Chris Heger, graduation project for the Technical University of Eindhoven.

Purpose

Depending on what information the designers wish to get from the evaluation, it might be appropriate to make different kinds of prototypes. Careful use of resources should mean that only relevant aspects of the product are prototyped and evaluated. In the context of graphical user interfaces, Houde and Hill (1997) distinguish between prototypes that represent the "look and feel" of a product (its presentation and interactive behavior), its functionality, and its role. This classification is reframed here, taking a broader perspective to match the scope of this book. We distinguish between prototypes that help evaluate aspects of interaction relating to the following:

Product role. The *product role prototype* enables its users to understand and evaluate what the designed artifact is supposed to do, what patterns of use are expected to arise, and how this product would be used in a realistic context.

User performance. The *user performance prototype* supports some tasks in sufficient detail and realism to allow the evaluation to gauge how well and how efficiently users can perform their tasks.

User experience (sensory, emotional, or social) of using the product. The *user experience prototype* helps users to experience these experiential aspects of using a product but may be silent regarding functionality and may pay less attention to contextual issues. For example, where a virtual-reality environment is evaluated, a nonfunctional presentation that allows an individual to experience the immersion and interactivity at a sensory level may be sufficient for evaluating the intended experience.

These distinctions are not always as clear-cut in practice; some functionality may need to be supported to make a meaningful experience prototype or to let users experience usage of a prototype in context. In Figure 3.5, these types of prototypes occupy the areas between the angles representing the different types of prototypes.

Traditional usability evaluation focuses on how the design supports users in performing their tasks, with prototypes focusing on interaction and the functionality of the product. Experience prototypes pay more attention to the sensory level, including graphics and sounds. The role prototype requires the essence of product use to be experienced in context.

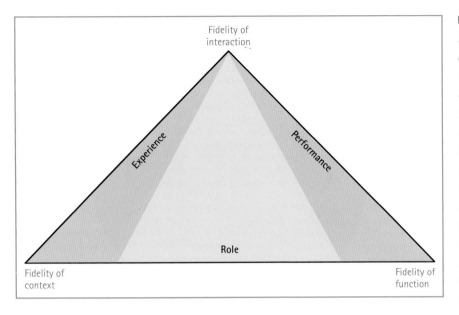

Figure 3.5

*Prototypes can serve
different purposes:
to evaluate the role
a product can play,
to evaluate how a
design supports users
in performing tasks,
and to evaluate the
experiential aspects of
use. Depending on the
prototype's purpose,
different priorities
need to be given to
implementing function,
sensorial interaction, or
contextual realism.*

Involving Children in Design and Evaluation

User-centered design assumes that users will be at least considered but ideally consulted during the development process. This section considers why children's involvement, particularly in an evaluative activity, is preferred and when this user involvement typically takes place.

Figure 3.6 shows a model introduced by Druin (2002) to visualize the relationships among the roles children can play during the design process. The inner circle represents the traditional role of children as end users of technology with no involvement in its design. A user-centered perspective would exclude this practice, although this may very well be one adopted by many developers of products for children. As we move to the outer circles, the role of children changes in two ways: First, it becomes more active and responsible; second, children get involved in more stages of the design activity. A minimal requirement for user-centered design is to involve children as testers of products and as participants in evaluations.

It may seem surprising, but asking children to assist in the evaluation of products for children is not in itself an established practice. A report on the evaluation of educational software for children explains how this evaluation is typically done by teachers or "experts" (Buckleitner, 1999). Sometimes, practical constraints (like

Figure 3.6

*Druin's "onion" model,
which represents different
ways of involving children
in the design of interactive
products.*

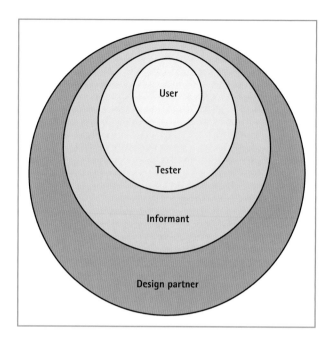

limited time or difficulty in recruiting children) mean that designers conduct an evaluation without using children. In these situations it is common for designers to refer to experts. These may be experts in children, like educators, experts in usability, or expert product designers. In such situations, evaluations typically focus on inspection methods (see Chapter 15).

The opinion of an expert is an educated guess. It is prudent to involve real children in an evaluation in at least one stage in the design process. Participating in an evaluation as a tester is, however, only one of the ways in which children can be involved in the design of a product. Allison Druin (2002) has long advocated that children be involved throughout a project as design partners, and she has introduced a participatory design methodology for doing this called *cooperative inquiry*. Children as design partners contribute their own ideas during the creative design process and maintain a long-term involvement with the adult designers.

This partnership is commendable from the perspective of giving a responsible and participative role to children, but it also presents several challenges that are far from trivial. Child partners cannot be recruited on request, cannot be paid a salary, and cannot miss large parts of school or have their home routines disrupted. Hence, the design activities either need to serve an educational function or must occur during the children's leisure time. Where cooperative inquiry is practiced,

Figure 3.7

Participatory design workshop with children.

designers must be prepared to adjust to children's preferred working and learning styles. Despite these challenges, cooperative inquiry has been applied successfully in industrial settings.

Although this book is not about participatory design and cooperative inquiry, it is compatible with such an approach. Clearly, even in a participatory design project (see Figure 3.7), the assumptions of the design team may need to be tested with other children or evaluated by experts along different design dimensions such as usability, fun, and educational value.

An alternative model proposed by Scaife and Rogers (1999) is the *informant-based* approach, where children are involved as sources of information regularly through-out the design process. Child informants are consulted prior to the design of a product but also regularly requested to test concepts, provide feedback, and sup-port the evaluation of prototypes that are improved iteratively. It is not only the increased involvement and input by children that can help the design process. Children who are consulted repeatedly become gradually attuned to the needs of the design team and thus provide more insightful and critical comments than if they had not had the opportunity to contribute at the first contact (for an example, see the case study in Chapter 18).

Summary

This chapter has outlined the interactive product design lifecycle and, in so doing, has outlined where and when evaluation might take place. Methods by which children can be involved in the design of their own products have been described and the case has been made that in most instances children should be involved in evaluations.

The next chapter looks at some of the barriers and challenges for child involvement by focusing on the ethical involvement of children. After that, their specific involvement as evaluators is explored in greater depth.

Further Reading

The chapter is intentionally brief and introductory. Readers who would like a more thorough overview are strongly advised to consult other published works on this topic. For a foundation in interaction design, we suggest Shneiderman and Plaisant (2004) and Preece, Rogers, and Sharp (2002).

Human–Computer Interaction by Dix et al. (2004) is a solid overview of HCI, with many chapters that outline the general interaction design process, including evaluation methods. Carroll (2002) focuses more on usability engineering for software applications. The specialist book on evaluation by Stone et al. (2005) also provides a good overview.

Some of the pioneering work in the field of interaction design for children can be found in Druin (1999). Reports on applications of the evaluation methods described in this book can be found in the growing literature on interaction design and children. See, for example, the proceedings of the annual Interaction Design and Children conference, which began in 2002.

PART 2

EVALUATING WITH AND FOR CHILDREN

CHAPTER 4

ETHICAL PRACTICE IN EVALUATIONS

Ethics can be defined as "the study of proper action." Ethical behavior is behavior that is "right" in the cultural context in which it occurs. Unfortunately, it is often unclear what course of action is right in a particular situation. This chapter alerts readers to the ethical issues that relate to evaluating products with children.

Compared to working with adults, working with children usually raises numerous ethical and legal issues. It is the responsibility of the evaluator to protect the interests of the children who are participating in an evaluation, as well as those of any adults involved. This protection comes from proper consideration of the ethical issues in a proposed evaluation in advance of the work.

After we introduce some relevant ethical principles and codes of practice, this chapter considers safety and risk assessment and issues of consent, including obtaining consent from both the child and a responsible adult, special issues that may arise if deception occurs, and getting consent for taking and using photographs and video recordings. Other topics include the ethical selection of participants, offering inducements to participants, and protecting participants' privacy. Actual cases illustrating some of these issues can be found in the three case studies (Chapters 16 through 18).

Ethical Principles, Approaches, and Codes

Farrell (2005b) compiled the following ethical principles for evaluation:

- *Respect for other people*—treating all people, including very young children, as autonomous individuals
- *Beneficence and nonmaleficence*—maximizing possible benefits and minimizing harm
- *Justice*—distributing the benefits and any unavoidable harm as fairly as possible

Considering these general principles can make decisions easier, but obviously they are only a starting point.

The *client*, the *administrator* (the person who carries out the evaluation and works directly with any children who are involved), and the *facilitator* (whose role is to meet and greet and see that the event runs smoothly) all have a duty to behave ethically. However, it is the *evaluator* (the person who designs and is in charge of the evaluation) who is responsible—morally and, in many situations, legally—for ensuring that the work is carried out in an ethical way. In a small study, the evaluator, facilitator, and administrator, and even the client, may be the same person, but it is useful to consciously separate the roles.

In the context of an evaluation, ethical problems mainly concern the involvement of people in the study (in the case of this book, usually children), but ethical decisions (particularly about beneficence and justice) are also necessary, even in evaluations that use methods where people are not directly involved as users or respondents—for example, in a heuristic evaluation.

Ethical decisions are subjective, and even experienced evaluators are likely to disagree in some circumstances about whether a proposed action is ethical. One reason for some of the disagreement is that individuals will have different approaches to ethical issues involving children based on their own background, education, and views about children and childhood. Farrell (2005b) describes three different approaches:

- *The utilitarian view,* which emphasizes the outcomes over the processes and seeks the "greatest good for the greatest number."
- *The virtue-based approach,* which "pursues sound moral traits, such as generosity, goodness, kindness, and sympathy" (p. 5). Here, the investigator emphasizes being an overall good person rather than singling out a particular action.
- *The rights-based (deontological) approach,* which focuses on the child participants' moral rights, such as privacy.

Another issue that will affect opinions about what is ethical is the investigator's view of the children involved in the study (directly or indirectly). Are they mainly passive objects of study or active participants who contribute to the study by revealing the important issues? (See Woodhead and Faulkner, 2000.)

Exercises
1. In making judgments about what is ethical and what isn't, it is useful to be aware of your own views and preconceptions. Which of the three ethical approaches (utilitarian, virtue-based, rights-based) is closest to your own view?
2. Consider an evaluation in which you have been involved, have read about, or that you are planning. In that evaluation, are children objects of the study or participants?

Cultural Issues

What is and is not considered ethical is culturally dependent—that is, what is acceptable in one culture may not be in another. For example, attitudes about personal information and authority figures differ among cultures.

Children are in many ways a different cultural group from the adults in their lives in that their attitudes about personal information and privacy may be different from the prevailing adult attitudes (see Figure 4.1). Children's attitudes toward adults in authority (for example, the test administrator or interviewer) vary considerably from one culture to another. Also, cultural views on what "children's rights" are, or whether they have rights at all, will differ widely.

The UN Convention on the Rights of the Child (1989) sets out some basic principles, including the right of children to be consulted over matters that affect them. But these principles aren't necessarily reflected in local custom and practice. Such cultural issues can be a problem when working with groups whose culture is different from one's own or where the evaluation involves people from a number of cultures—for example, an international remote study of a website (Burmeister, 2000).

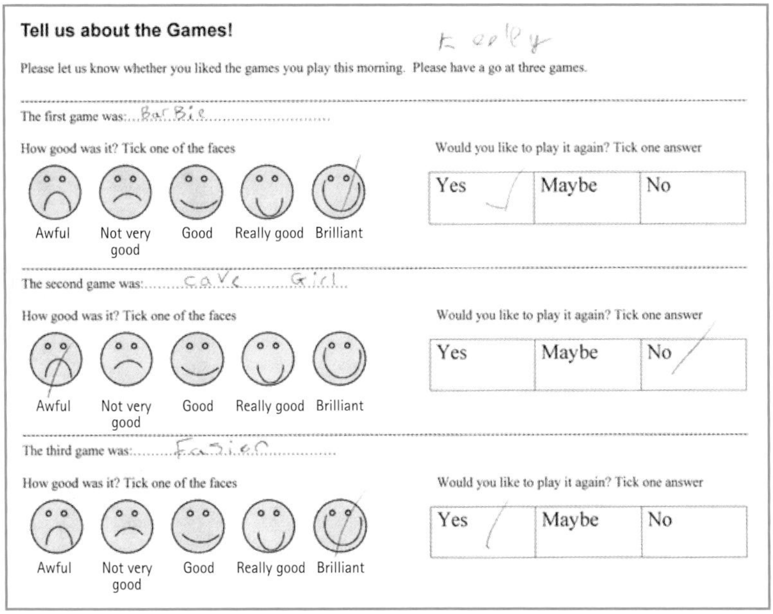

Figure 4.1

A child has written her first name on this evaluation sheet, which was supposed to be anonymous. This isn't uncommon; children often write both their first and last names. Young children don't share adult views about privacy.

Ethical Codes

Organizations, including the Association for Computing Machinery (ACM) and the American Psychological Association (APA), have ethical codes (ACM, 1992; APA, 2002). These codes are not specifically about working with children, but they are nevertheless a useful starting point for evaluators. Alderson (2004) compiled a list of relevant ethical codes, but there are few examples of how these codes can be applied in evaluation practice (Molich et al., 2001), especially where children are involved. It should be noted that *ethical* does not simply mean "obeys a code of ethics"! Following the provisions of a code, such as one of those mentioned in this section, is a useful start, but it does not guarantee that the study is ethical.

The final responsibility for ensuring that a study is done ethically lies with the evaluator, but, as noted earlier, the administrators carrying out the evaluation also have a duty to consider their actions and to behave ethically. It is not sufficient for an administrator to assume that everything is fine simply because it appears to comply with an ethical code and has been approved by the investigator, or even that it has been approved by an ethics committee.

Ethical considerations come into play in any evaluation, not only those that involve people (or children in particular). It is a mistake to assume that ethics need not be considered when a non-user-based method such as heuristic evaluation is being used. The rights of the evaluator, the administrators, and the client may still be at risk. Principles of data protection, confidentiality, and health and safety remain relevant, but more pressing ethical issues arise in situations where children are directly involved.

Ethics and the Law

Most countries have laws that regulate some of the relevant decisions, such as health and safety, child protection, human rights, and data protection legislation. Of course, these laws vary from country to country, so it is difficult to be specific about them here. The general trend in all of these areas is that laws change frequently and are becoming more protective of children. The relatively new concept of "children's rights" is gaining ground in accordance with the UN Convention on the Rights of the Child. In general, an evaluation that is ethical is also likely to be legal, but the reverse isn't necessarily true. Ensuring that the law is being obeyed is a necessary but not sufficient step. It is important that evaluators are aware of the legal position in the jurisdiction they are working in—for example, the minimum age at which a person can give his or her own consent.

Safety and Risk Assessment

When carrying out an evaluation, children should not be placed at any greater risk of any kind (either genuine risk or risk perceived by the child) compared to their normal activities. This might mean physical risk (e.g., using equipment, traveling to an evaluation lab) or psychological risk (e.g., being stressed by a task that is too hard, a time limit, or an unfamiliar environment; see Figure 4.2). These risks can be reduced by careful consideration of the logistics of the evaluation and by pilot-testing of the intended evaluation tasks. Another safeguard here is ensuring that the children know that they can drop out of the evaluation session at any time without penalty. A session should be stopped immediately if a child participant is becoming distressed.

A critically important safety issue is the risk of child abuse or, conversely, the risk to the administrator of being accused of abuse. Any time an administrator works alone with a child, the risk increases that the administrator might molest or abuse the child or that the child might accuse the administrator of inappropriate behavior. Both of these occurrences are very rare, but when it happens it is very serious. Vetting of the administrators in advance is not sufficient to prevent the first of these risks, and does nothing to reduce the second. A better approach is to design

Figure 4.2

"Just go into the little room, and we will watch from out here." A usability lab can be a daunting environment for a child. Do not place a child in such an environment unaccompanied.

the study so that an administrator and a child are never left alone. A second adult in the room can act as a deterrent and, if necessary, as a witness. This might increase the cost or even reduce the effectiveness of the evaluation in some cases, but it is a price worth paying.

If it is considered to be critical to the success of the evaluation that the administrator and a child are alone in a room, one possible solution is to have a "witness" (perhaps a parent) observing through a one-way mirror and to video-record the entire session.

The safety of all participants, not just the children, can be improved by carrying out a risk assessment. Many organizations have standard procedures for doing this and standard forms that must be filled out. The major advantage in completing such a form is that it makes the evaluator think about the risks and thus is likely to reduce them. Completing such a process may also be necessary in many circumstances for legal reasons or to ensure that insurance coverage applies.

Consent

Investigators need to seek permission from children, and from adults, throughout the evaluation process. This section considers when and how to obtain appropriate consents, with special reference to situations in which children are involved. There is also discussion of the additional issues that arise when the method employed requires the use of deception.

Consenting to Take Part in the Study

All participants in an evaluation should give their consent. They should be participating voluntarily and as far as possible understand the purpose of the evaluation and their role in it. This is called *informed consent*. Even with adult participants, this level of understanding of the situation is difficult to achieve. The purpose of the evaluation might be very complex or difficult to explain. Additionally, it may not be possible to explain exactly what data are being collected and why without compromising the data.

Some philosophers argue that even informed consent is insufficient in helping a person make a valid judgment on whether to participate. They believe that "educated consent" is required. This means that the person would have to be able

Figure 4.3
Children can behave like adults in many ways, but they probably can't give informed consent to take part in an evaluation.

to judge whether the evaluation has been designed appropriately and how the results will contribute to knowledge. This level of understanding is impossible in most practical situations.

When the participants are children, things become even more complex. Young children may not be capable of understanding the purpose of the evaluation, even at a basic level. It is unlikely that they will be able to give informed consent, let alone educated consent (Figure 4.3). In most countries, and in most situations, the child's parent or guardian (or, in some jurisdictions, a schoolteacher or other responsible adult) can give consent on the child's behalf. The ages to which this applies vary among countries, but it is rarely clear-cut legally.

In some countries, the law reflects the rights-based philosophical view that children are "competent participants in their everyday worlds" (Farrell, 2005b, p. 6), who are able to understand a situation well enough to give consent themselves. Children as young as 3 years have been judged as competent to consent to medical treatment in some circumstances. Hence, in situations where the child could sufficiently understand the implications of taking part in the evaluation, it may not be legally necessary in some jurisdictions to obtain consent from a responsible adult. To be safe, however, we recommend getting the appropriate consent from a parent or responsible adult.

A good plan in most situations is to seek (at least) informed consent from a responsible adult and explain to the child at an appropriate level what is going on. Asking the parent/guardian/teacher for consent doesn't absolve the evaluator of responsibility to consult the child, too, even when there is no legal obligation to do so. Children have a right (in most cultures) to decline to take part (even if a responsible adult has given consent); their wishes must be respected. If a child wants to drop out of an evaluation session before it is completed, he or she should be allowed to do so. It is important to ensure that the child knows this before the evaluation begins.

Another issue is that children may not feel comfortable expressing their own views about whether they want to participate because they are not accustomed to being given the choice. Danby and Farrell (2005) give some fascinating transcripts of conversations with children about consent that illustrate the kinds of pressures they face. In particular, young children find it difficult to express their own opinions if they are asked about consent in the presence of a parent or of a teacher if they are in school.

Thus, if you want a child to take part in a study, ask a responsible adult for permission, and then ask the child if she agrees. Either of these consents can be withdrawn at any time. It is the responsibility of the evaluator to ensure that procedures are in place to allow for appropriate consent and agreement to be obtained and to ensure that there are procedures for them to be withdrawn.

Withdrawing agreement by the child can be a problem. The administrator is (normally) an adult and thus probably an authority figure from the child's viewpoint. Consequently, children may not feel they can withdraw or indicate in a direct way that they want to. It is thus the responsibility of the administrator to be proactive in this matter and watch for any signs of boredom or distress. If such signs appear, the experimenter should ask the child if he wants to continue and should explicitly assure him that it is okay to withdraw from the evaluation session.

Danby and Farrell (2005) give an example of a consent form that is suitable for use with young children. Our experience has been that a form that requires a signature may be intimidating rather than empowering for children, but circumstances vary and such a form may certainly be appropriate in the right situation. At least having a form to sign makes it more likely that all of the relevant issues will be discussed. Of course, for younger or less literate children, it will be necessary to read the agreement to them and to ensure that they understand what they are signing.

Deception

In some evaluation situations, it isn't practical to explain the purpose of the test in advance. For example, the evaluator might be interested in children's reactions to unexpected error messages, so explaining this in advance would make the data worthless. With such a test, it is necessary to deceive the testers or, to put it bluntly, lie to them. Some people believe that this is always unacceptable when working with children, but others feel no real harm is done if deception experiments are carried out carefully. An example of an evaluation method where some deception may be involved is the Wizard of Oz technique discussed in Chapter 12 and in the case study in Chapter 16.

A policy that should be defensible in most situations is that deception in an evaluation involving children is justifiable when all of the following conditions are met:

- The data to be obtained are genuinely valuable.
- There is no feasible way, within practical constraints, to collect the data without deception.
- The real purpose of the evaluation, and the nature of and reason for the deception, is explained to the responsible adult, who is giving consent in advance of the work if at all possible or immediately afterward.
- The real purpose of the evaluation is explained (in suitable terms) to the children as soon as practicable after the end of the session.
- The participants are given the chance to withdraw retrospectively. It is possible that, had they known the true purpose, they would not have consented to take part; consequently, they should be allowed to say that they don't want the data collected from them to be used.

In our experience, children themselves are not concerned about deception of the type described here; it is more often their parents and guardians who worry on their behalf. Perhaps children are more accustomed than we would like to admit to being misled by adults!

Covert Observation

Sometimes as part of an evaluation, it would be nice to know how users would behave if they weren't being observed. It is often the case that a child who knows

Figure 4.4

Is it acceptable to watch people in a public situation without their knowledge?

she is being observed will behave differently than usual. Evaluators may be tempted to observe users covertly to avoid this problem.

Most people are aware that they are being observed when carrying out certain activities in public places. Shopping is one example, where stores watch for shoplifters (see Figure 4.4). Children are aware that they are being watched in the classroom (when the teacher checks that learning is taking place). However, it does not follow that observing someone without his or her knowledge in such an environment for another reason (such as to evaluate educational software) would be ethical. Many people (including children) in many cultures would regard this as an unwarranted invasion of privacy. Consequently, we do not recommend this approach.

Consent for Photographs and Audio and Video Recordings

In addition to getting consent for participation and data collection, it may be necessary to obtain consent separately for photographs and audio and/or video recording. It should be noted that such data are usually *personal data* in data protection terms—in other words, it is personal information about an identifiable individual.

Even if the recording is done to collect data (for example, recording an interview or videotaping an observation session), the collection of AV material raises ethical issues. These issues relate to how the recordings will be stored, used, and ultimately deleted. Often the same consent procedures can be used for such recordings as for other forms of data.

Sometimes the AV materials are collected for other reasons, such as for a record of the physical layout of an observation scenario or to provide materials for publicity. In these circumstances, it is better to treat these materials completely separately from the data and to seek consent separately. Consent for photography or AV recording should be sought in advance. It may be too late to obtain consent after the data collection starts.

A significant number of parents will not allow their children to be photographed by strangers for a variety of reasons. Sometimes one parent has taken the children and relocated to escape the other parent who has a history of violence, and does not want photographs of the children in circulation. Unfortunately, this is not a rare occurrence these days, and it is clearly important to respect such wishes. Typically, we have found that in a class of around 30 children, the parents of 1 or 2 of them will refuse consent for photographs of their child to be taken. Far fewer, typically, will refuse to allow the child to take part in the evaluation.

It must be made clear in the consent agreement how the photographs and other media will be used. Consent to take a photograph or to make a video recording is not the same as consent to use it freely. These are some of the ways photos or recordings might be used:

- Viewed privately by the evaluators to assist with the analysis of the evaluation
- Shown to the client privately to illustrate how the evaluation was done
- Shown to students in a class
- Shown to trainee evaluators
- Shown during a conference presentation
- Published for marketing purposes
- Published on the Web for public information or public amusement

An agreement to make recordings should specify the purpose of them. For all but the first use, we suggest that new consent should be sought from the child and the parent after they see the photos or recordings and that a decision then made as to whether they may be used. Mackay (1995) discussed some of the issues that arise when recordings are used without full consent. An additional concern arises when video and audio recordings of children are used: Children grow up! An 8-year-old child (and his parents) might be happy about his appearance in an evaluation session being shown to the public (in fact, most children that age would be delighted!),

Figure 4.5

Sometimes a picture can show what is needed without the children being identifiable, but at times it is important to be able to see facial expressions.

but ask the same child when he is 13 and he may be embarrassed and object strongly. We believe that consent by a child for such use has an implicit time limit, but perhaps it should have an explicit one.

Another problem is that once a video or photo has been shown to a class or at a conference, it is likely with today's technology that members of the audience have recorded it, so time limits are difficult to enforce. A safe and very cautious policy is to never use videotapes or still images of identifiable children who are participating in a study, although this can make reports, papers, and conference presentations pretty dull. Sometimes you can use pictures taken from behind without worry (Figure 4.5) or find other ways to make the subject anonymous, but this isn't always possible. A balanced policy here would be that it is acceptable to use images of children with permission from both the child and a responsible adult if the child is clearly not stressed or doing anything that makes him or her look foolish.

Inducements for Taking Part

Sometimes small rewards are given to children to thank them for taking part in an evaluation. This is not a problem as long as the reward is small and given consistently, no matter how helpful (or otherwise) the child has been! A problem can arise, however, if the reward is significant enough that it influences the child's decision about whether to take part. Children may end up participating when, without

Figure 4.6

A child taking part in an evaluation. The chance to play with a new game is a reward in itself!

the incentive, they might not have done so. Also, this may make them feel obligated to say nice things about the product being evaluated.

We have found that children generally enjoy the experience of taking part in an evaluation and that rewards are not necessary unless the evaluation requires a great deal of their time. Younger children (see Figure 4.6) like to receive a certificate, whereas older children like to hear about the overall results of the study so they can get a better idea of what they contributed to (see Chapter 7). In cases where an entire class has participated in the study, it is often more appropriate to offer a gift to the school, such as books or software. Schools always appreciate this gesture, and it should not be problematic for the school to accept such gifts. Sometimes, especially for academic research, parents or schools will go to considerable lengths to support the study just to help out or because they appreciate the exposure children might get to technology and researchers. In this situation, a guided tour of the research laboratories for the children may be an appropriate way of thanking them and their parents.

Ethical Selection of Participants

Selection of an appropriate sample of children from the population of possible participants is discussed in Chapter 6. An ethical issue can arise here if the sample is to be taken from a group of people who know each other—for example, a school class. It is likely that some of the students will not be in the target population for the product to be tested—for example, because they don't read well enough to use the product. Children will see who is chosen and who isn't and will form their own (not necessarily correct!) theories about why. If a sample is to be picked from the class, it should be by a transparently random process. Alternatively, it may be better to work with every child for whom consent has been obtained and, if necessary, discard results from the children who don't fit the target population. This strategy is also fairer in the sense that each child gets the same opportunity to experience whatever new and exciting technology is being studied.

Privacy

The participants in an evaluation have a right to privacy. No data collected in the course of an evaluation should be published in any way that allows the identification of the participant without full consent. Even with consent, the evaluator needs a good reason to breach the person's privacy. In this sense, *data* include numerical results, verbal comments, photographs, and audio and video recordings.

One way to guarantee privacy is never to collect names or any other data that identifiy an individual, but this isn't always possible. Apart from anything else, children (particularly in a school situation) tend to write their names on any piece of paper they are given, even when they have been asked not to! Also, children often strongly wish to attach their names to something that they have created, such as a drawing or a piece of writing, as a statement of authorship. Another situation when full anonymity may not be practicable is where "before" and "after" data need to be matched up in the analysis.

The next best solution when data can't be completely anonymous is to keep the evaluation data separate from the identification data, using a code to link the two. General data protection principles should also be adhered to whenever there is any possibility of individuals being identified. Only personal data that are necessary for the evaluation should be collected. The data should only be used for the purpose for which it was collected, and it should be destroyed within a reasonable time afterward. Five years is often considered a reasonable time period for work in an academic research context, since other—possibly conflicting—research data protection principles suggest that raw data relating to published work should be kept for five years in case there are questions about the data analysis. In the United States, data subjects are entitled to ask for the collected data under the Freedom of Information Act—another reason why data should be kept for a certain period of time.

Getting Advice and Permission

A problem for the evaluator who is designing an evaluation is that he or she may be too close to the situation to see all the ethical problems it raises. It is always useful to get the views of someone else—particularly someone with relevant experience.

In most large organizations involved with evaluation and other research involving children, there will be an ethics committee that advises on good ethical practice and, if necessary, refuses permission for procedures considered unethical. This can be a useful safeguard for evaluators, but it does not remove their responsibility! A proposal isn't necessarily ethical just because an ethics committee has approved it. Also, in some organizations insurance coverage may not be valid for the evaluation if ethical approval hasn't been obtained.

Most ethics committees will require the completion of forms that describe the evaluation procedures in some detail. Unfortunately, such forms and processes may be considered burdensome or even pointless by evaluators (Allen, 2005) because they seem overcomplicated and overcautious. One problem is that such procedures, in an academic context at least, may be designed to cover a wide range of activities. However, it can be argued that having to go through this process makes the evaluator think about the ethical issues, and this ultimately is the purpose of the process.

Exercises

Here is a fictional scenario to consider. We are not recommending this as a design for an evaluation!

Charlie is designing a writing application to help young children compose written text on a computer. It is a specially adapted word processor. One area that is particularly problematic for the children is correcting their typing errors. Charlie has implemented two possible error correction methods, and he wants to find out which one is better. Here is a description of the proposed study: The evaluation will take place in a local school, using an entire class of 30 children, aged 7 to 8. Fifteen of the children will test each error correction method. The children will be removed one at a time from their class and asked to type a fixed piece of text on a laptop keyboard. To ensure that they all make a reasonable number of errors and that they all make similar ones, the keyboard interface has been "fixed" to generate errors. The children will see text on the screen that already has typing errors and will be led to believe that they made the errors themselves. They will then be asked to correct the errors, using one of the two error correction methods.

A full log of all inputs from the keyboard and mouse (with timings) will be kept for later analysis. Of course, the children might also make their own typing errors, which they can also correct, but data will not be collected from these. The whole session will be recorded on video so that the children's reactions can be analyzed later.

1. What questions should an ethics committee ask about this proposal?
2. What changes might they make?
3. Can this test actually be done ethically?

Further Reading

Ann Farrell's thought-provoking book, *Ethical Research with Children* (2005a), covers a wide range of issues in ethical work with children. It concerns research in the social sciences, so it covers issues that are unlikely to be relevant in evaluation studies (for example, research on sensitive issues like child abuse). But it also covers most of the problem areas that could occur in the domain of this book. Views are presented from different philosophical schools of thought.

Two volumes on research with children and young people, collected by Fraser et al. (2004) and Lewis et al. (2004), are also good reads. Lewis et al. is a collection of case studies that raise a range of ethical issues, with commentaries by the researchers involved.

The book chapter by Malcolm Hill (2005) is an excellent summary of the issues discussed here, and it contains an extensive list of references.

Wendy Mackay (1995) provides lots of thought-provoking examples and practical advice regarding video-recording. Most (if not all) of that discussion is directly relevant to making and using video recordings of children during an evaluation.

CHAPTER 5

PLANNING THE EVALUATION STUDY

This chapter presents the preliminary steps for an evaluation study and continues to the stage at which the study has been crystallized and captured. An evaluation plan clarifies and outlines the evaluator's decisions about a range of issues: What aspects of the product will be evaluated? Where should the evaluation take place? Who are the participants? What is the evaluation's goal, expected outcome, and final result? What methods will be used for evaluating the product?

These issues are not normally dealt with in such a neat order—it isn't that simple! In practice, some of these decisions are interdependent and must be made together. Some decisions may also be assumed implicitly by project stakeholders or, worse, may have been overlooked completely. Part of the job of an evaluator is to help clients make the right decisions and use their efforts and resources appropriately.

This chapter explains some of the reasoning and trade-offs involved in making these decisions. On the way, it introduces terminology and concepts that will be useful when contemplating and discussing evaluation studies. It presents different approaches for, and purposes of, evaluations and outlines the different criteria that might be used to formulate evaluation goals. Further, it discusses how these different approaches might be served by different evaluation methods and analysis procedures and demonstrates how any evaluation study represents a trade-off between control and the realism that a test setup can achieve.

Defining the Purpose of the Evaluation

The first step is deciding what the evaluation study is trying to achieve. Different purposes may require different approaches to evaluation, different data to be collected, and different analysis procedures. An evaluation can have several purposes; this section introduces some important distinctions.

Diagnostic Evaluations

In most cases, an evaluation is conducted to find out how to improve a product or a prototype, and its main output is a list of problems regarding interaction with a product. The goal of the evaluation here is *diagnostic*. It is not enough to find and name problems; they should be accompanied by explanations for the causes of the problems and suggestions for correcting them.

The following are example outcomes of diagnostic evaluations:

> *The icons chosen for the navigation are not well understood by the children because they don't look like navigation icons that the children are familiar with.*
>
> *The wolf character in the game was too scary for the children of the chosen age group, who did not enjoy that part of the game.*

Formative and Summative Evaluations

Evaluation outcomes like the preceding ones are more useful during the design process than after its completion. Their purpose is *formative*—the outputs help shape the intended product. *Summative* evaluations aim to document the quality of a finished product. These definitions blur in practice: A summative evaluation concerning a finished product may itself feed the design of a new product. For example, in the early design phases it may be appropriate to evaluate an earlier version of the product, or some competitor product, to identify areas of improvement.

A summative evaluation may involve comparison with a benchmark or a competitor product. A comparison between products or intermediate design prototypes with respect to some desired set of attributes can also inform the choice between different design options—for example, different ways of navigating, different input techniques, and so forth.

Exploratory, Measurement, and Experimental Studies

Questions about the product can be "open" or "closed." Open questions are those for which the range of answers is not known in advance, such as "How will children react to a robot that can display facial expressions?" This is in contrast to closed questions (where a list of all possible answers can be prepared in advance) that aim to produce numeric measures or to check prespecified expectations one might have for a product—for example, "Can children find books in the library faster using interface A rather than interface B?"

Open questions can be asked at all phases of the design lifecycle. They may concern usage patterns, unpredicted problems of use, areas of improvement, or areas of opportunities for future products. If the study starts with an open question, it will be more exploratory in nature. It will seek to uncover and explain occurrences of events, emerging patterns of behavior, and so on.

Formative evaluations are by their nature exploratory, seeking to uncover areas where the product can be improved. It is usually sufficient to evaluate just the product or current prototype. Sometimes it is useful to compare the product with another one or with not using a product at all. The contrast can help to uncover interesting events or issues relating to the product. For example, when looking at how a new messaging device is used, patterns of use with this device can be compared against earlier systems or using no messaging system at all.

When asking a closed question, the product is characterized against some criteria that follow from the design goals (see Figure 5.1). This is a form of *measurement*. Measurements are most useful when comparing to a benchmark of success or comparing two designs. For example, it is possible to test if one controller device is more comfortable than the other, or whether the text entry speed is better with a new text input device versus the keyboard. This sort of comparison can be done through what is called an experiment. An experimental study can be summarized in the form of a *hypothesis*, a clear statement in a form that can be shown true or false by gathering data.

Measurements and experiments differ from exploratory studies in at least two ways:

- To obtain meaningful measures, the influence of external factors must be minimized. For example, if assessing how easy (or difficult) it is to learn some software, it is advisable to eliminate the possibility of parents assisting children during the test. This requires control of the testing situation and rigorous procedures. On the other hand, an exploratory study may aim deliberately at exposing and understanding the influence of these factors on the product. This requires relinquishing control and letting real-world influences manifest themselves.
- Participants in experiments should be selected randomly from a particular user group they represent, whereas in an exploratory study the selection may be designed to highlight contrasts between different types of users within this group and can be very heterogeneous.

Evaluation Criteria

Here are two example outcomes of an evaluation:

> *The child participants learned how to play the game by just watching the tutorial demonstration and having one try at the game,*

> *The children found the animations shown between different game levels boring and would like a way to skip over them.*

Figure 5.1

Evaluation goals at different phases of a product lifecycle.

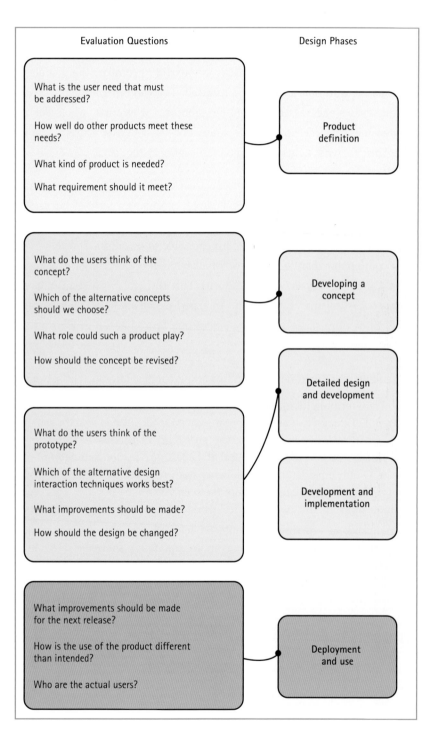

Evaluation Questions | Design Phases

What is the user need that must be addressed?

How well do other products meet these needs?

What kind of product is needed?

What requirement should it meet?

Product definition

What do the users think of the concept?

Which of the alternative concepts should we choose?

What role could such a product play?

How should the concept be revised?

Developing a concept

Detailed design and development

What do the users think of the prototype?

Which of the alternative design interaction techniques works best?

What improvements should be made?

How should the design be changed?

Development and implementation

What improvements should be made for the next release?

How is the use of the product different than intended?

Who are the actual users?

Deployment and use

The first statement concerns ease of learning, or *learnability*, which is a measure of how well or how fast users learn to use the product. Learnability is especially important for children. Adult workers can be trained to use a product that is difficult to learn but useful for their work, or they may persevere because using it is part of their job. On the other hand, children are more likely to abandon a product that they cannot easily learn how to use.

The second example is about the enjoyment experienced from playing a game. Enjoyment is not usually considered a component of usability, but the two are connected. Good usability may contribute to enjoyment, whereas low usability may prevent children from enjoying the game or using a product at all.

The preceding two examples also demonstrate a distinction between subjective and objective evaluation criteria. The first statement suggests observation of child testers. Any criterion that can be assessed with observed or logged data is often called *objective*. On the other hand, the second statement clearly refers to how children experienced aspects of the design during a test, and such a question can be answered by asking (surveying) them about their thoughts, feelings, and experiences. A goal and an evaluation outcome described in terms of opinions or judgments by test participants are considered *subjective*. It is relatively easy to evaluate subjective goals with adults by asking test participants to judge how much a product has met a particular design goal. This is not as straightforward for young children, who may find it hard to reflect on and evaluate their experiences.

It is not always possible to find objective measures for answering questions that evaluate how products support user performance or a particular user experience. For example, how much fun a game is may well be described as a subjective outcome when based on surveyed opinions, but it is difficult to observe. One can observe related behaviors of children that relate to fun, such as gestures, facial expressions, or even measures of skin conductivity that relate to the arousal of the child during the evaluation session. Finding meaningful and reliable objective measures for assessing interactive experiences is the subject of several ongoing research investigations worldwide.

Whether objective or subjective, evaluation criteria may be expressed and therefore evaluated *qualitatively* and *quantitatively*. For example, the enjoyment from a game could be evaluated quantitatively, such as "How many children mentioned that they enjoyed the product?" It could also be evaluated using qualitative data, in which case anecdotes and quotes can be listed in the evaluation to support and clarify the conclusions. A qualitative analysis can uncover crucial oversights that render a game impossible to play, or it may tease out unexpected reactions to the game story, the graphics, and so on. On the other hand, when evaluating the performance of users using two different input devices, a quantitative analysis may be a more meaningful basis for the evaluation.

When a project adopts a quantitative rather than a qualitative criterion, the evaluation becomes precise and provides a clear criterion of success rather than one that is elastic and may be relaxed under time pressure. On the other hand, a quantitative criterion may become an end in itself and create a tunnel vision effect for the design team. Making sure a child can learn to start a game and personalize its character in less than two minutes may be a valid target, but focusing on it prematurely may mean that insufficient attention is paid to fixing more substantial problems with the story line or the game controls that are crucial for making the game fun to play. The design team should strive to balance the need for a clear measure of success while ensuring that this measure is relevant to the success of the product.

Products may be evaluated against criteria that are project specific; it may require some skill and effort to formulate such criteria in an operational manner, so it is good practice to use prior art. There is a wide range of criteria defined in the literature together with relevant measures that can be used. The criteria in the next box should give you an idea of their diversity, as well as a starting point for exploring related sources.

Criteria to Evaluate Against

Usability: ISO 9241-11 defines *usability* as the "extent to which a product can be used by specified users to achieve specified goals with effectiveness, efficiency, and satisfaction in a specified context of use" (ISO, 1998). The repeated use of the word *specified* suggests that usability is not a singular, concrete, measurable criterion but a framework for measuring related aspects of the interaction with a product.

Effectiveness: The accuracy and completeness with which specified users can achieve specified goals in particular environments.

Efficiency: The level of use of resources (usually time) for reaching a specified goal.

Satisfaction: According to ISO 9241-11, satisfaction is "freedom from discomfort and positive attitudes toward the use of the product" (ISO, 1998). Satisfaction as a dimension of usability can encompass many users' perceptions, attitudes, and feelings regarding the interaction with the product. Satisfaction with the interaction can be even more important than performance. Children are much more likely to be motivated to use a product again if they get some satisfaction from it rather than if they obtain some measurable performance gains.

Usefulness: The degree to which a product provides benefits to users or helps them address their needs and goals. Usefulness concerns the supported functionality and how relevant and important this is for the users. The usability of a product affects directly how useful it is perceived to be (see Davis, 1989).

Learnability: How easy it is to reach a certain level of competence with a product; often the critical level is the point at which the user can use the product effectively without help. Contrary to adult workers, children cannot be assumed to follow a training manual, though in some cases—for example, classroom products—an instructor may be at hand to help.

Fun: This is hard to define! Carroll (2004) summarizes it well: "Things are fun when they attract, capture, and hold our attention by provoking new or unusual emotions in contexts that typically arouse none, or [by] arousing emotions not typically aroused in a given context." It could be added that the emotions should be happy ones. Carroll isn't writing about children here, and children may not experience fun in exactly the same way. Draper (1999) suggests that fun is associated with playing for pleasure and that activities should be done for their own sake through freedom of choice. In other words, "fun" is not goal related, whereas "satisfaction" is.

Accessibility: The extent to which a product can be accessed by the full range of potential users in the full range of potential situations of use. The word *accessibility* is frequently used in the context of users with disabilities and whether they are capable of using a product.

Safety: Where children are concerned, two aspects of product safety are important: whether a product has sharp edges or represents an electrical hazard, and if interactive products, such as websites, or communication tools, such as cell phones, expose children to inappropriate Web content or cause them to give personal information to strangers.

Choosing Evaluation Methods

Suppose that an evaluator wants to compare two design prototypes for an interactive toy for 5- to 6-year-olds to determine which one is more fun. Three approaches can be used here:

- Do an expert assessment of the two designs, examining whether the designs follow the rules for a "fun" product. A suitable method would be an inspection method (see Chapter 15). Unfortunately, appropriate rules or methods for evaluation may not exist or may not work well for the criterion of interest; testing the product with children may be the only recourse.

- Look for "signs" of fun in a sample of users. When it comes to children and having or not having fun, signs might be laughing and smiling, being easily distracted, showing reluctance to continue, or taking frequent breaks. One could do an observation study (see Chapter 10) in which the number of smiles is counted or what the children say while using the product is noted.

- Consider the "symptoms" of having or not having fun. Some, such as pain, cannot be observed. So a candidate method for assessing fun is *asking* children which design they think is more fun, using a suitable survey method (see Chapter 13).

In the chapters that follow, several variants of these three approaches will be discussed, each with its strengths and weaknesses. In general, it is wise to combine more than one of these approaches, triangulating the results. Triangulation may help corroborate conclusions. Potential differences between what is found with each method can help evaluators to be more critical of their findings and get a deeper understanding of how the product is experienced by its users.

Tip

Triangulate at all levels. Combine methods; involve different children, different test administrators, and different tasks; and compare your product against others.

Reliability of Evaluation Results

Compare the following statements:

> *Three out of four children preferred the stylus and seemed also to be consistently faster with the pen when compared to the speech input.*

The average time for entering an age-appropriate text presented to 10-year-olds on a piece of paper is significantly higher when they use the keyboard, compared to spoken text input.

The first statement shows a small-scale evaluation, but the numbers are clearly too small to allow generalizations. The second sentence suggests a higher *reliability* for the results. It indicates that a statistical analysis has been made, and the superior speed of the keyboard is not considered to be a chance occurrence.

Reliability is important because design teams must be assured that when an effort is invested in modifying a product, it is because more than the test participants are likely to benefit from the changes. Any study that involves people is likely to be affected by random errors in the measurements. This is an inherent part of any type of measurement and can't be avoided entirely.

Tip

Some early qualitative input by a few children may have much more impact on the quality of the product than a large, formal evaluation at later stages.

When planning an evaluation, you must weigh how important it is that your findings are reliable in the preceding sense. Ideally, one would want to have certainty for every single design decision made in the type of design process described in Chapter 3. In practice, this is usually not possible, and you must spread the resources available for evaluation over several iterations of the product design and over several design choices. As an evaluator, it is important not only that you are able to collect and then analyze data, whether qualitative or quantitative, but also that you can convey how reliable your data and analyses are and how your audience should use the results. These issues are discussed further in Chapter 8.

Field versus Lab: More Than Just a Location!

An important decision that must be made when planning an evaluation, particularly when children are involved, is where the evaluation should take place (see Figure 5.2). Typically, this means choosing between testing in either a laboratory or a field setting. Large organizations and research establishments have specialized usability-testing laboratories (see Chapter 9). Testing in the field means testing in the actual

Figure 5.2

*Testing at the lab (a)
and testing at the
school (b).*

(a)

(b)

physical and social context where children are likely to encounter the technology evaluated, such as at home or school.

Control and Realism

Choosing to test in the field or in the lab is more than a choice of location. A better way to think about it is as a trade-off regarding the degree of control the evaluator has in the testing situation versus the realism of the evaluation. *Control* might refer to environmental factors such as noise and lighting but also to practical things like knowing that the test application will work as expected and using a familiar technical infrastructure that works consistently and reliably for all participants. Control can also refer to social context. Evaluation sessions may lead to completely different results when a child's friends or parents are present. Laboratory testing can help in controlling the context and knowing exactly who will be present, ensuring this will not distort the results. More control also means a more rigorous process and a more formal setup. Giving predefined test tasks and even simulating intermediate results are ways that an evaluator might enhance control.

Evaluating in a Laboratory

When an installation can be tested only in a laboratory, designers should be cognizant of the physical and social contexts of the lab environment, as it might influence the children's experiences with the product.

Scorpiodrome (Metaxas et al., 2005) is a mixed-reality installation where children construct a physical landscape on which they drive remote-controlled cars (scorpios). The installation combines the advantages of playing with toy cars and construction kits with playing a video game. The design team's goal was to compare alternative design options to measure the level of engagement and fun that the children experienced.

As it turned out, the children became so animated, excited, and engaged that any option presented to them would not have made a difference. In response, designers attempted to degrade the game to evaluate single features but to no avail. It was clear that the evaluation setup did not distinguish the impact of coming to the lab and the novelty of taking the role of a test participant. A possible remedy might be to have the same children participate in repeated sessions so that the "newness" of both the lab and the designers will eventually wear off. Only then will comparisons between design options yield useful results.

Testing in the field means relinquishing control to ensure that conditions of actual use (relating to social context, equipment used, and physical environment) are reflected as far as possible. This realism helps us understand how a product is used

Figure 5.3

Children building the landscape and driving the scorpios during an evaluation session of the Scorpiodrome in the KidsLab.

in the unpredictable situations in real life, lending ecological validity to the evaluation results so that conclusions are likely to hold for the intended context of use rather than just for the protected environment of the laboratory.

The control–realism trade-off can be better understood as a continuum rather than a binary choice. Factors that influence this trade-off are the goals set for the evaluation, the maturity and robustness of the technology that is being tested, and other practical constraints—for example, children may have to be at school during working hours or they live far away from the lab.

Evaluating Products with Children in the Field

Testing products in the field places fewer demands on the children to adapt to the testing environment compared to testing in a laboratory. This can be particularly important for children under about 9 years of age. Practical concerns also make field testing attractive; it takes much more organizational effort to bring eight children to a lab for a day than going to their classroom for a test session. In the latter case, the cooperation of the teachers is invaluable for practical issues like getting permission from parents, making time available, helping with the selection of the children, and finding a location in the school. If teachers are able and willing to offer their time, their views on the observations and their impressions of the children can be very enlightening. Also, as they are aware of the children's capabilities, personalities, and social behaviors, they can place particular behaviors or comments in a richer context.

For some products the intended context of use is at home, where a parent will provide technical support and explanations and where software is typically used for leisure rather than as a component of the educational curriculum. It may be difficult to find participants who are willing to host a usability test in their own home, so a good compromise is to test such products in the school during after-school activities. Although the context of use may not be exactly the intended one, it is still a familiar environment and one that offers the practical advantages already mentioned.

Evaluating products and applications intended for classroom use can be challenging. Rode et al. (2003) discuss the constraints of designing interactive products for use in the classroom and propose four key constraints that must be met by such technologies; these constraints also apply when evaluating technologies in the classroom:

- The evaluation should fit within a session (this could be, for example, about 70 minutes for 11-year-old children) and support lesson goals consistent with the curriculum.
- The evaluation should have a high degree of structure, continuity, and predictability in line with the usual progress of the lesson. If the evaluation is replacing a lesson, it should still go on even in the event of technical or usability failure.
- The experimenter must adapt to the administrative and regulatory framework of the school. For example, the evaluation should fit scheduled school activities; also, note that members of the school administration may expect to be able to observe parts of the evaluation.

- The evaluator should seek to eliminate "lesson stoppers"—that is, events or materials like animations, technology failures, and so forth, that may distract children from curriculum objectives and thus derail the school day.

Goals and Testing Context

Depending on the evaluation goals, it may be necessary to adopt a different strategy. For example, if the goal is to evaluate how an almost finished classroom product integrates with other classroom activities, it may be better to avoid influencing the classroom activities and to relinquish control of the evaluation session to the teacher. If specific parts of the product need testing (perhaps some of the exercises it supports), it may be necessary to negotiate with the teacher so that the classroom activities include these exercises.

When the evaluation concerns the role of a product, the product and the participants should be exposed to a realistic usage scenario and context. Ideally, long-term field testing should be done. (A technique suitable for this is the diary method, discussed in Chapter 14.) Where this is not possible, some realism can be obtained by simulating usage contexts and allowing children to bring their own tasks, content, and preferences to the context of the evaluation.

In cases where the evaluation goal is determining how the product helps a child perform certain tasks, generalizing and interpreting the evaluation results can only be ensured when sufficient control of the test situation is achieved. Testing in the lab, or controlling (as far as possible) contextual factors in the field, may be the required strategy. Similar reasoning applies to experience-related design goals. Here, it is often more practical to conduct the evaluation in the lab. On the other hand, some experiences and performance measures may only make sense in the intended context of use, such as a wayfinding GPS appliance.

When choosing between testing in the lab and in the field, it helps to list the potential influences from the physical, social, or organizational setting and to consider how these might affect the outcome of the test. If understanding sensitivity to these factors is exactly what is sought, then field testing is the appropriate way to go. If the possibility exists that these factors may render the conclusions meaningless or unreliable, it is necessary to find ways to control them in the field. If that is not possible, a lab provides a ready solution.

The Evaluation Plan—Why Make One?

A successful evaluation is a sum of many variables and constraints that change over the course of the design phase. To manage the evaluation process, it is helpful to build an evaluation plan that defines systematically why, what, who, how, when, and where. This evaluation plan provides a shared and explicit record of the evaluation team's decisions about the issues discussed in this chapter. This record ensures that all relevant issues are well thought out, dealt with, and verified before the actual evaluation effort takes place. A sound evaluation plan ensures that the actual evaluation will run smoothly and that the obtained results can be analyzed with reasonable effort and used in a meaningful way.

The form of an evaluation plan varies from checklists to full-scale reports, depending on the needs and time line of the project. An evaluation plan is a "living" document that will be updated and refined while the evaluation is being planned out and pilot-tested. Its main contents are a context definition, evaluation goals and outcomes, choice of evaluation method, choice of location, and a profile of test participants.

Context Definition

The context definition briefly describes the features of the interactive product, indicates the target users, and details where the product is used or will be used (see Table 5.1). The context definition can be a pertinent issue of discussion with the client when evaluation is being contracted and negotiated.

Tip

Before carrying out an evaluation, spend a lot of time playing with the product or prototype to be evaluated and, if possible, let some children use the product in an informal setting before making the final evaluation plans.

Evaluation Goal

After establishing the context of the evaluation, it is necessary to clearly state its goals. It is important to make a distinction between goals of product use and goals of evaluation. For example, even though the main purpose of a product X might be

Table 5.1

Context Definition

Context	Describe	Affects Directly
What? Aspects of the interactive product to be evaluated	• The type of product it is (single-user, multiuser, collaborative, task-oriented, entertaining, educating, home use, classroom use, mobile, fixed, PC, toy, multimodal, control device, etc.) • When and how it is used or meant to be used • The stage of the product development (low-tech or high-tech prototype, fully implemented product) • The main use cases of the product	• Evaluation goal(s) • Methods and techniques • Choice of test participants • Test cases (number of cases) • Test environment
Who? Target group	• The characteristics of the user groups of the interactive product to be evaluated (their abilities and developmental stage, age, gender, cultural and socioeconomic background, energy level, expectations, fears, previous experiences, relationships, etc.) • Any constraints or characteristics that would limit the used methods or techniques	• Methods and techniques • Choice of test participants
Where? Use environment	• Where the interactive product is used (school or home environment, indoors, outdoors, lighting, noise level, disruptions, etc.) • Any limitations on where the testing can be done (internal or external validity, observational technology required, usability lab vs. field testing, etc.)	• Methods and techniques • Choice of test participants • Test environment

"learning new skill A," the evaluation of the product might focus on the usability of the user interface rather than on measuring the learning of skill A.

Stating the evaluation goal in the early stages so all stakeholders can understand it is a good idea whether you are doing a small, informal study or a full-scale commercial usability evaluation. Larger projects may have several goals; it is important to make sure those are not conflicting in terms of the requirements they place on the setup of the evaluation. If they are conflicting, multiple evaluations may be needed.

Rather than just specifying goals in abstract terms, it is important to clarify the expected outcome of the evaluation in terms of the broader project context. In commercial assignments, this description forms the basis of the agreement between you and the client and of the questions you will be expected to answer.

Here are some examples of how evaluation goals are linked to the expected outcome of the study:

Goal: "Is design A better than design B in terms of text input speed?"

Outcome: A or B has faster text input.

Goal: "What are the main usability problems of product C?"

Outcome: List of usability problems (and possible solutions to fix them).

Goal: "Which Web services do U.K. children ages 8 to 10 use?"

Outcome: Statistical analysis and report of the top 50 Web services children of ages 8 to 10 use in the United Kingdom.

Goal: "How do children behave while using online community D?"

Outcome: Report on children's behavior when visiting online community D; their perceptions of their behavior augmented with interviews of moderators of the community.

Goal: "What are the main design issues of tactile input device E for children with sight impairments?"

Outcome: Report on the issues that arise during the usage of the prototype and force feedback input system, augmented with interviews on participants' views and desires on input technologies.

Evaluation Method

Initially, the evaluation plan must record a choice and justification for an evaluation method. Chapters 10 to 15 discuss a wide range of methods that are suitable for evaluating products for children. Choosing the right method requires understanding the trade-offs between these methods. To guide this choice and your reading, Table 5.2 gives an overview of the methods discussed in this book while also connecting them to the issues discussed in this chapter.

Tip

Try to involve children as often and as early as possible in the design process.

Location and Profile

During the early stages of the evaluation plan, you must resolve three more issues: where to evaluate, who will be involved, and the participant's role. Based on the context definition and your choice of evaluation method, you can specify the users.

Table 5.2 *Evaluation Methods and Connections*

	Method	Brief Description	Strengths (+)/ Weaknesses (−)	Context
Observation Methods Chapter 10	Passive observation (structured)	Based on a structured observation guide, observers record instances of predetermined sets of behaviors.	+ Child is unencumbered by the evaluation. + Structure of the observation leads to more reliable results. − Issues outside the scope of the observation guide can go unnoticed.	Field or lab
	Passive observation (unstructured)	Observers watch children interact with the product, looking out for any behavior relating to the evaluation goals.	+ Good for uncovering unexpected issues, such as usage patterns. − Can produce data that are too diverse or too hard to analyze.	Field or lab
Verbalization methods Chapter 11	Think-aloud methods (concurrent, retrospective, picture cards)	Testers verbalize their thoughts in front of a test administrator while learning how to use a product or while watching a tape of a test session.	+ Can explain why children find the product difficult, fun, and so on. + Using picture cards can make the situation more comfortable and enjoyable for children. − Can be demanding cognitively and uncomfortable for children.	Lab
	Intervention techniques (active, post-task interview, robotic)	Test administrator questions children about their thought processes while they interact with the product.	+ Comfortable social situation for the child. + Administrator can have a lot of influence on the child. − Verbalization concerns specific questions asked by the test administrator and not actual thought processes.	Lab
Wizard of Oz method Chapter 12		A human operator simulates some part of the interactive system to give the illusion of a working system.	+ Helps evaluate something you cannot build in time or with the resources you have. − Needs at least one extra person involved (the wizard).	Lab
Survey methods Chapter 13	Questionnaires	Rating scales, ranking scales, and other types of survey instruments are handed out on paper.	+ You can ask many children at once and obtain lots of data.	Field or lab

Table 5.2—_Cont'd_

	Method	Brief Description	Strengths (+)/ Weaknesses (−)	Context
	Interviews	Questions are asked one to one with a child.	− Children not very reliable when answering questions. + Allows in-depth discussion with each participant. + Richer qualitative data can be obtained than with other methods. −Laborious, and data harder to analyze.	Field or lab
Diaries Chapter 14	Diaries	Children or their parents fill in a questionnaire regularly to describe their interaction.	+ Allows context-rich information to be gathered over sustained study periods. + Realism of the testing situation. − Punctuality of diarists worsens with time.	Field
Inspection methods Chapter 15	Heuristic method	An inspector steps through the interaction and checks whether some high-level design rules are broken.	+ Allows evaluation when involving children is difficult. − Heuristics only well developed for evaluating usability and, to an extent, fun-related issues. − Can flag problems that are not there (mishits) and can miss problems that are there (misses).	At evaluator's office
	Walkthrough methods (SEEM and personas)	An inspector steps through the interaction and asks a fixed set of questions regarding how the child reasons and experiences an application.	+ Allows evaluation when involving children is difficult. + For some cases, SEEM outperforms heuristic evaluation. − Can flag problems that are not there (mishits) and can miss problems that are there (misses).	At evaluator's office

For this first cut of the evaluation plan, you should be able to specify the characteristics of the children you want to recruit, such as their age range, interests, experience, and what makes them candidate testers of your product. Alternatively, your method might not require children at all.

Depending on whether it is a lab or a field study, and depending on the method you choose to apply, you can then specify the location of the test. Is the field a home or a school? Finally, depending on your method, you need to consider if you can do the testing alone or if you will need the help of a team of evaluators.

Summary

Often, evaluation has a diagnostic role where problems with a product and fixes are identified. In the planning phases, you must decide what your evaluation goals are and whether they will be better served by an open and exploratory study or by more precise measurements and experiments. There is a wide range of criteria against which you can evaluate your product. You may have to devise some on your own, but you should always consult the literature for well-defined criteria and measurements.

The data you collect may be quantitative or qualitative, and it may also be distinguished by whether it concerns subjective or objective aspects of use. It pays to combine (triangulate) objective and subjective data and combine methods for collecting them. Choosing where to run your test is a manifestation of a more general decision you must make regarding how much control you want over the evaluation setting versus how much ecological validity you want to achieve.

Decisions about the goal of the study, your understanding of its context, and your plans for participants, method, and location should be made explicit and summarized in an evaluation plan. You will be consulting and revising this document in the final stages of the evaluation study.

Exercises

1. Alone or with a colleague, discuss the nature of the goals for evaluation in the following context:

   You are developing an educational product for a classroom to support mathematics for small groups of pupils age 12. You have a concept of an educational application that requires a novel hardware platform that allows three or four children to interact over a horizontal surface, and you have implemented a fully functional prototype to support one lesson in algebra. Before you design more material, you think it might be good to run an evaluation. Consider the following choices:

   - Should children be involved? If so, how many?
   - Should evaluation be done at your premises, at a school, or at any location you can get the children to come to?

- What type of evaluation goal should you have at this stage if you assume that no earlier evaluation has been done before this prototype?
- Do you need to make an experiment or a measurement, or should you aim to be more open and exploratory?

2. Consider that you are developing a new text input technology for cell (mobile) phones. Specify a few qualitative and quantitative evaluation goals. Imagine different parts of the design process, starting from the first conception of the interaction technique up to its deployment.

3. Consider the following qualitative evaluation goals, and try to describe corresponding quantitative goals:

- The digital camera should be easy to learn.
- The karaoke machine should be fun to use.
- Children who are using the educational toy should be motivated to keep playing.
- The educational software should be appropriate for use in the classroom.

Discuss what would be the implications for your design project of adopting the corresponding quantitative goals.

4. You are shown a video of children enjoying themselves while doing arithmetic, using a calculator program. The calculator is operated through a "smart board," where the children can "write" numbers with their fingers, and it uses an interface that avoids some of the design flaws of traditional calculator devices. What kind of evaluation would you propose to distinguish between the following explanations?

- The whole application makes doing arithmetic fun.
- Writing with your finger on a smart board is fun.
- The calculator interface is fun.

Further Reading

For more information on experiments, read the introductory textbook by Hayes (2000). Some extensive information on planning a usability evaluation can be found in Rubin (1994).

CHAPTER 6

BEFORE THE EVALUATION

This chapter is the first of three that will guide you through the process of conducting an evaluation study with children. Taking an example from a real study, the three chapters highlight the practical considerations in planning, doing, and concluding an evaluation study.

This chapter discusses the detailed design of an evaluation, introducing and explaining the need for pilot-testing, examining the design of tasks, and highlighting the need for organization of the evaluation in advance. This chapter assumes that the goals of the evaluation have already been established, the style of the evaluation has already been determined, and the location of, and possible participants in, the evaluation have already been identified.

The discussion begins with recruitment of participants and then considers the preparation of technology and evaluation instruments before considering order and activity planning and the communication of the plans to the people involved in the study.

The PlaTUI Evaluation

As an illustration for these three chapters, a real evaluation study with children is described and used as a backdrop. The original concept behind the PlaTUI study was to evaluate three different (but similar) interfaces for playability and to discover what children thought of each of them. There were three goals: The first was to discover if the three games had any usability problems, the second was to see if children enjoyed playing the games, and the third was to capture information about the interactivity of the games by observing how children played them.

An initial evaluation plan was drawn up (see Figure 6.1), and a decision was made to evaluate the three games in a school setting, using a combination of verbalization, survey methods, and observation. A school evaluation was chosen because this would eliminate the problem of arranging transportation for the children, and it was considered to be a more efficient use of the children's time. As the evaluation was based on opinions, a choice of surveys and observations was indicated.

Figure 6.1 *Initial evaluation plan.*

Initial Evaluation Plan

Context Definition

Using three versions of the food game; one screen and mouse based, one using the tangible blocks, the third RFID based. These are all fully functional interactive prototypes. Intended to be used in museum settings, accessed by children voluntarily and played with for as long as they want to. Intended users of the three products, primary school age children - aged 5 - 10, can be played singly or in pairs.

Goals of the Evaluation

To discover if the fun experienced in one game is the same as the fun in another and to discover if fun and interactivity are related. Hypothesis: Fun is related to interactivity and therefore the more interactive prototype will see better fun scores. An extra question is to evaluate the fun toolkit further. Approach: Surveys and observations and logging time on task.

Participants

Children from local school aged 8/9/10 - Any children to participate but some sorting out during the evaluation (see methodology below)

Determining test tasks

Children will play the game to a winner in twos. They will then be encouraged, but not made, to have two more turns in order to find the best of three.

Specifying roles for adult participants

Letter to school to be sent. Four adults, three to carry out observations (one at each of the three technologies but swapping around to reduce evaluator effects), the other to manage the test environment.

Where and When to Evaluate

Local school, on two consecutive mornings in September. Need to find a room.

Methodology and Procedures

The plan is for each child to use all three. The three need to be varied. Aim for 12 pairs from each age group. Pairs will be friendship pairings (as dictated by the teacher). Children will use the three technologies in the same time. Will come in in groups of six (two to each technology)

Deciding on People and Places

In the early planning stages, the evaluator will have made a decision on location and participants, but this will generally be quite vague; for instance, location—work in the usability lab, participants—school-age children. The detailed design of the evaluation requires that these choices become realities; people and places need to be organized.

Confirming a Location and a Time

Decisions must be made about the specifics of where and when the evaluation will take place. With children, the three location choices are usually a group activity space (like a school or a nursery), at home, or in a lab. (Chapter 5 discusses the advantages and disadvantages of each type of location.) Some specific considerations about each type of space are discussed here.

For evaluations in group activity spaces, the evaluator should visit the location and meet the responsible adults well in advance of the evaluation to ensure that all the details are arranged. Schools are especially problematic spaces; rooms are often allocated on the day of the evaluation, and even then they might be occupied by other activities. Equipment that was represented one way may turn out to be something else entirely, and teachers who promised that their class would be free may suddenly remember there is a rehearsal for the school musical on the day the visit is scheduled. For all these reasons, some preplanning for these types of contingencies is essential.

Tip

When you plan an evaluation in a space that is not your own, make sure to bring everything you need!

If the evaluation is in someone's home, educate yourself about the dynamics of the household. Again, it is a good idea to visit before the evaluation if possible. Do not assume that you will be able to connect your laptop to the home network, and be prepared for interruptions from phone calls, visitors, or other unexpected events.

Testing in a laboratory is easier to control, but children need to be brought to the location and there will be logistical problems associated with this. Before the test, make sure that any adults who will be in the vicinity where the children are working know about the evaluation and know that children will be in attendance. Make sure you carry out a risk analysis and arrange car parking.

Tip

It is a good idea to visit the test location even before the pilot testing.

Figure 6.2

Letter to principal for PlaTUI.

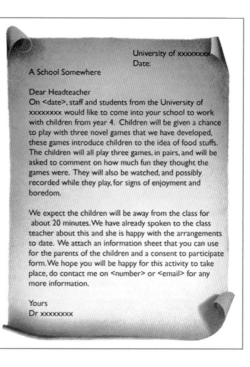

University of xxxxxxxx
Date:

A School Somewhere

Dear Headteacher
On <date>, staff and students from the University of xxxxxxxx would like to come into your school to work with children from year 4. Children will be given a chance to play with three novel games that we have developed, these games introduce children to the idea of food stuffs. The children will all play three games, in pairs, and will be asked to comment on how much fun they thought the games were. They will also be watched, and possibly recorded while they play, for signs of enjoyment and boredom.

We expect the children will be away from the class for about 20 minutes. We have already spoken to the class teacher about this and she is happy with the arrangements to date. We attach an information sheet that you can use for the parents of the children and a consent to participate form. We hope you will be happy for this activity to take place, do contact me on <number> or <email> for any more information.

Yours
Dr xxxxxxxx

Contacting a School and Recruiting PlaTUI Participants

In the PlaTUI evaluation, the work was done in a school. The school was recruited using a letter that was accompanied by an information sheet detailing the study so the school could make an informed decision about whether or not to participate in the work. These two documents are shown in Figures 6.2 and 6.3.

The information letter and the information sheet were sent to the school only after an initial phone call had outlined the planned work. If a phone call had not preceded the study, it would have been necessary to send a short letter asking for a meeting, by phone or in person, to initially discuss participation.

Besides location, it is also necessary to think about timing. The younger the children are, the more affected they will be by the time of day and mealtimes. In comparative studies that will take place over a couple of days, it is especially important to keep the time constant. Young children may get sleepy after lunch and might

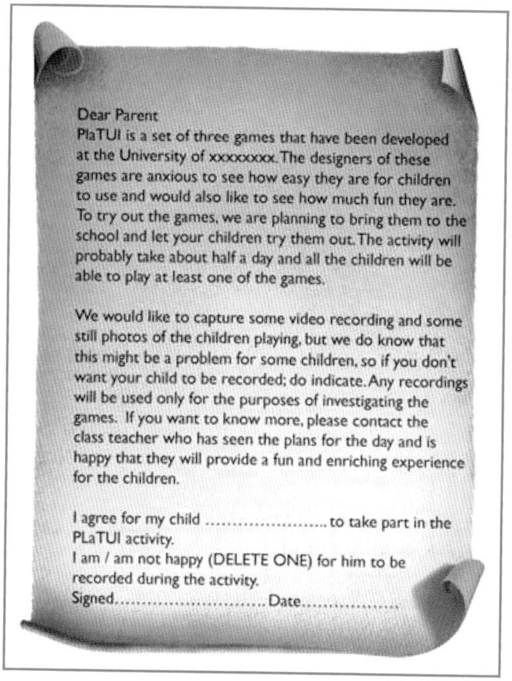

Figure 6.3

*School information
sheet for PlaTUI.*

Dear Parent

PlaTUI is a set of three games that have been developed at the University of xxxxxxxx. The designers of these games are anxious to see how easy they are for children to use and would also like to see how much fun they are. To try out the games, we are planning to bring them to the school and let your children try them out. The activity will probably take about half a day and all the children will be able to play at least one of the games.

We would like to capture some video recording and some still photos of the children playing, but we do know that this might be a problem for some children, so if you don't want your child to be recorded; do indicate. Any recordings will be used only for the purposes of investigating the games. If you want to know more, please contact the class teacher who has seen the plans for the day and is happy that they will provide a fun and enriching experience for the children.

I agree for my child .... to take part in the PlaTUI activity.
I am / am not happy (DELETE ONE) for him to be recorded during the activity.
Signed........................... Date...................

be much more alert in the morning. This factor may require the evaluation to be extended over a longer period of time. Time can, to some extent, be controlled; however, the weather is another problem! School-age children can become excitable on windy and rainy days when they can't play outside, and they may have less focus. Little can be done in these instances except to be prepared and to consider the findings from the evaluation in the light of external influences.

Selecting Child Participants

Evaluation goals and context definition, as well as the selected methodology, will have set some early requirements for choosing participants (e.g., only those who can read can participate). The selection of children for a study is invariably less straightforward than the selection of adults. Very often compromises and adjustments must be made.

For resource reasons, child participants in any evaluation are often chosen from a subset of the group of potential participants. The selection can be based on age, gender, or some other characteristic (see Chapter 1 for more information about children and their characteristics), as suggested by the evaluation plan. The goal in any selection is to obtain a representative sample of participants for the study who match the target group. Several sampling strategies (see, for example, Martin, 2005, or Coolican, 2004) are available; the most common is the division of the population into subpopulations (strata) followed by the taking of a random sample from each stratum. However, with children, and especially when carrying out an evaluation in the field, the sampling is more frequently based on convenience, especially in cases where a group of children (such as one classroom) is nominated to participate.

In addition to getting a good sample, deciding how many children to have for the evaluation is important. The more testers (participants) who are involved in a study, the more reliable the results will be. On the other hand, however, the more testers you have, the more data you have to analyze, and this can stretch project resources. Even after a sample size has been decided on, an evaluator might have to add a couple of extras to avoid problems such as children getting sick or withdrawing their consent to participate.

Recruiting children as participants must be done in a nonbiased, nonauthority-based manner. (For more discussion about the ethical selection of participants, see Chapter 4.) If the evaluation is to be fair, all children should be given a chance to take part. Children with learning disabilities or sensory or physical handicaps should be included on the same basis as the others, even if their contributions cannot be used.

How Children Influence the Evaluation Design

PlaTUI was an evaluation of three interfaces. The school that was asked to take part in the study had 31 children in the class that was most suitable for the work. The class was mixed boys and girls, and the children were ages 7 and 8. Two children in the class did not speak English as their first language. The children were told about the work and were very excited about taking part in the study. For that reason, it was decided that the evaluation study would be designed to allow all the children in the class to participate. Thus, there would be no sampling and every child would have a similar experience of the games.

It might seem surprising that the children influenced the design of the evaluation study in this way. When working with schools, flexibility is very important. Designing the evaluation of PlaTUI to accommodate all the children was a challenge, but the satisfaction from the children and the class teacher was deemed to be at least as important as discovering usability problems and gathering opinions.

Selecting the Evaluation Team

In general, an evaluation with children should always have at least two adults present. This ensures that the evaluation is managed properly, and with two adults one can focus on the test organization and the other can be responsible for reporting and note taking. In addition, should one of the administrators be unable to attend, the effect is less catastrophic—a third party will hopefully be available! Besides improving the evaluation, the addition of a second adult makes the event safer for both the children and the adults. This cannot be overemphasized: Have at least two adults present!

It is important to make sure that each role is clearly defined and communicated to all stakeholders and that each person's tasks are clearly explained. This is more detailed information than would be included in letters to parents or teachers, but it is important to record unambiguously. Materials might need to be created for some of these roles: checklists, observation forms, sheets with instructions for reading out to participants, and so forth.

Adults and the PlaTUI Evaluation

Because 31 children were to take part in one event for PlaTUI, several team members were required. The teacher was recruited to keep an eye on things and fix practical problems. Three research assistants, one postgraduate student, and one helper were recruited, who along with the evaluator in charge would be responsible for the management of the children on the tasks and the supervision of the test environment.

Preparing Technology and Evaluation Instruments

The initial evaluation plan will indicate what technology and what method(s) of evaluation will be used. At the planning stage, the technology has to be checked and adapted to the location of the study, any work (test tasks) to be done by the children must be specified, and any evaluation instruments must be prepared.

Tip

Before carrying out an evaluation, play with the product or prototype to be evaluated and, if possible, let some children use the product in an informal setting before making the final evaluation plans.

Preparing the Technology

Decide what technology will be needed well before the evaluation. Make a list and specify where this technology is, which model will be used, who will bring it to the study, whether it needs to be prepared in any way, and what software needs to be loaded. This may seem trivial, but many evaluations fall apart from a lack of this basic planning. As a backup, install any software to be tested on one extra machine or bring a spare interactive product. If the evaluation is in an unfamiliar location, do not assume a proliferation of handy electrical outlets; bring an extension cord! Figure 6.4 shows the technology (and paper resource) list for PlaTUI.

Designing Test Tasks

A test task is something you ask children to do during an evaluation. When designing test procedures, evaluators have to choose whether testing will be based on pre-defined test tasks or on free exploration. In addition, evaluators must make sure that test task design and selection is suitable for child participants' developmental stage, especially their cognitive and language skills. Sometimes, the choice of test procedures will be dictated by the availability of other resources. In the next section we describe common test procedures and consider how these need to be carefully thought through when children are the participants.

Materials and resources used during the study

3 PCs loaded with the game, one box grid and

phidget technology, one RFID kit and large box.

Smileyometer sheets for each child (attach to

observations sheet), Orders for each child pair

(issue cards with this on to the children and write

on log sheets)

Timers

Pens and Paper

4 cameras, 4 video cameras, 4 notebooks

Tripods (large ones)

Extension leads, spare batteries

Final question sheets

Figure 6.4
Technology list for PlaTUI.

Nontask-Based Testing

Nontask-based, or spontaneous, testing lets children use the interactive product freely without any predefined tasks. This approach is especially suitable when testing products with small children or even with toddlers, since the omission of instruction makes it unnecessary for them to understand written language or complex speech. Also, the children do not need to be able to follow instructions in a systematic way, so they can focus their attention on those parts of the product's functionality that they find particularly compelling.

Even though most of the data obtained by free exploration can be very interesting, this approach does have some disadvantages. The biggest problem is that the resources used and the data obtained might not support further product development in the best possible way. However, nontask-based testing might be an option—for example, during acceptance testing of a finalized product—when testers are particularly interested in how children receive the product and how well they can use it without any guidance or instructions. In addition, when used with interviews or questionnaires, free exploration can be used to evaluate fun or other user experiences. Using predefined tasks in these situations might force children to ignore possibly interesting functionalities.

Task-Based Testing

In many evaluation studies, defined test tasks are used to both limit the required resources and ensure that the data obtained during testing is valid and consistent between participants. The main purpose of test tasks is to aim and focus children's actions toward those product functions or characteristics in which the evaluators are interested.

One of the main principles when testing products with children is that the children should not be exposed to situations where they cannot function. When designing test tasks, children's language, cognitive abilities, and developmental levels must be taken into account. Carrying out even simple test tasks requires efficient use of short-term and working memory and an understanding of cause-and-effect relationships. In addition, because the test tasks are more complex, children must be able to guide and monitor their own actions in a systematic way. These requirements are quite demanding, especially for young (4 to 6 years old) children who have limited attention spans. Thus, evaluators must ensure, through pilot-testing, that the designed test setup is appropriate and can be carried out without stressing the children.

Wording Tasks for Children

In a recent study to evaluate word processors with children 4 to 6 years old, the authors used this series of simple test tasks. The test tasks were read out to the children but were also presented on a single sheet of paper.

1. Underline the word "Humpty."
2. Change "fence" to "wall."
3. Make "fall" bigger.
4. Change the color of "horses" to red.

These tasks may seem highly unambiguous, but half of the children used capitalization of "fall" to make the writing bigger. This shows how easy it is for us to create test tasks that seem clear but still need to be piloted. In the second version, which was created after the pilot study, instruction 3 was rewritten as "Change the writing size in "fall" so it is bigger (looks like it has been magnified)."

Giving Test Tasks to Children

Test tasks for children should be read to the children if they cannot read fluently and independently. Even if a child is considered a good reader, reliance on her interpreting the test task should be minimized. It is not uncommon for a child to confidently state that she can read the test tasks only to discover later that she could not understand the task. In almost all cases, it is worth reading over the test tasks. If the evaluator cannot be sure that the child understands the text task, it may be impossible to know whether errors in using a system are due to mistakes made during the reading process. It is best to state the test task verbally and also provide written instructions (maybe in simplified language).

If the test task is complex, a significant challenge for the evaluator occurs when a child asks for clarification or a rereading of the task. One option is to use automatic or computerized tasks in either written or audio form that a child can replay as often and as many times as necessary.

If a child finds the test situation too stimulating or the test tasks too broad or difficult, he may misunderstand the task, forget it more easily, or be afraid to ask for clarification. In this case, a child's unfocused behavior during a test might be unintentionally interpreted as a defect in a user interface, even though the problem really lies in the test design.

From an ethical point of view, it is important to emphasize that the purpose of the test tasks is to evaluate the interactive product and not the children. In addition, the test situation should be comfortable enough that a child feels he can stop carrying out the tasks at any point or even skip over a task. A child should never be persuaded or forced to continue.

Guidelines for Test Task Design

The test tasks should have the following features:

- Be understandable and interpretation-free. This means that a child must be able to understand easily what he or she is expected to do.
- Be noncomplex and small enough to be remembered. Usually one task at a time is enough.
- Be possible to perform without help from the test supervisor. This reduces the supervisor's effect on test data.

- Be small enough in number that children can perform them without getting tired. Make sure that the length of the test session is appropriate for the target group.
- Be pilot-tested and refined. Always test the tasks with a target group. In addition, an adult who knows the children should read the tasks to give you useful feedback on their intelligibility.

If a set of tasks that do not rely on one another is used, it is good practice to reorder them for different participants so the same tasks are not always at the end of the session when children are tired (Hanna et al., 1999). This reordering also improves the validity of the evaluation. The first task in a session should always be easy so children's initial fears are eased. It is also important that each child has enough time to complete the tasks. Some children are really meticulous in carrying out specified tasks, whereas others are quick and carefree.

Multiple Test Tasks

Van Kesteren et al. (2003) studied whether children could perform complex test tasks that each contained two separate tasks. The researchers were particularly interested in whether children of 6 or 7 could remember two tasks without help from an adult and whether the children would need to be prompted to continue their actions. According to that study, many children needed to be reminded about the task. The study also revealed that the employed evaluation method appeared to have an effect on the need to be prompted, which suggests that test task complexity is not independent of the evaluation method chosen.

Interactive Products That Contain Tasks

Test tasks are usually helpful in guiding interaction with the product, but when evaluating products with built-in tasks and predefined navigation paths, such as computer games or educational products, defining test tasks that conflict with those of the product is not advisable. In these cases, a test designer must decide what kind of test tasks are appropriate and determine if it is better to let the product guide the children's actions.

Barendregt, Bekker, and Speerstra (2003) studied a group of 8 and 9 year olds to see how using tasks affects the game play of an edutainment product. They found that test tasks become goals themselves that compete with the goals presented by the product. Interestingly, they also found that the number of usability problems found was not dependent on the presence or absence of test tasks. Thus, they proposed that test tasks are not necessarily required with products that contain built-in tasks.

No Test Tasks for PlaTUI

In the PlaTUI study, children were simply playing with the technology, so for this evaluation no prescribed tasks were used. The instructions were "Play in pairs. When you have finished the game, you can play again." However, one principle of text task design was used, that of changing the order of tasks. The children went around the activities in a route that allowed for the findings to be generalized.

Evaluation Instruments and Instructions

Consideration must be given to how data will be collected during the evaluation, who is doing what, and how this data will subsequently be analyzed. Many otherwise well-planned evaluations fail at this stage. Sometimes evaluators aim to collect too much information (especially in observational studies) and end up leaving the event with a jumble of data they can never interpret, cannot code, and that therefore have little value. It is tempting to video-record "everything" to minimize the risks associated with data capture, but collecting a lot of data is not a substitute for thinking through what you need and how you will collect and analyze it.

Here are two useful tips in this respect:

- You will only record half of what you hoped to record, so don't be too ambitious. Pilot your data gathering and pilot the analysis of it.
- You will be in a muddle on the evaluation day, so do as much as possible in advance. Write the names on the evaluation sheets, and arrange the test tasks in order, making a table that shows who is doing what when.

If the study will eventually be published in an academic journal or written up as a report for a client, it makes good sense to write up-front the method and analysis sections because this will help to clarify the final evaluation plan and encourage a focus on how the results will be analyzed.

If survey materials are being used or if children are completing questionnaires, these must be prepared. Create them well ahead of the day, but save the printing and duplicating until you are nearly ready, since small changes may have to be made. Allocate to one evaluation team member the task of collating and bringing all paper materials to the evaluation.

Data Collection in the PlaTUI Study

In the PlaTUI study, two evaluation sheets were prepared; one was to be used after each "activity," the other was to be used at the end of the day. Examples of both of these are shown in Figures 6.5 and 6.6 Be aware that the order in which the items appear on the sheets can affect the children's responses. For PlaTUI several versions of these sheets were used so the order of appearance was shuffled in much the same way as the order of participation. These variations are not shown here.

Figure 6.5

The evaluation sheet for use during the game.

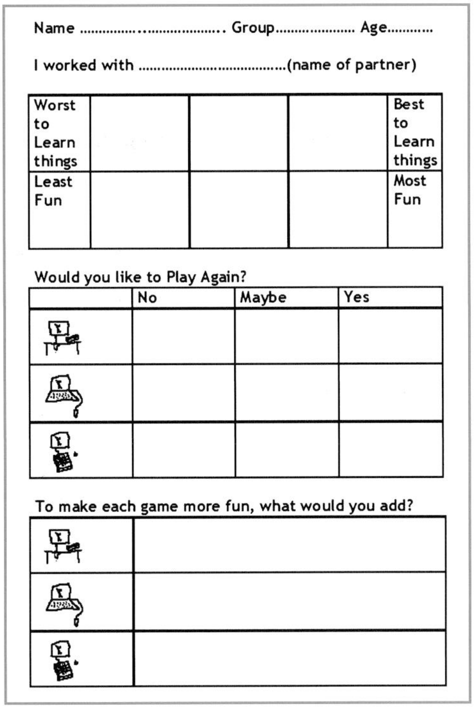

Name .... Group..................... Age............

I worked with ....(name of partner)

Worst to Learn things				Best to Learn things
Least Fun				Most Fun

Would you like to Play Again?

	No	Maybe	Yes

To make each game more fun, what would you add?

Figure 6.6

Evaluation Instruments for PlaTUI.

Planning the Day

When planning the evaluation, decisions must be made about the space required and the order that children will arrive. Plans must also be made for the adult participants in the study. You should tell them, in writing, what to do, what to record, and how to handle the data they collect. Instructions for the PlaTUI study are shown in Figure 6.7.

Space

How the space for the study is used affects the flow of events and how well the data can be gathered. It is advisable to make a map of the test space when visiting the location for the first time. It can be useful to take photos of the space and use them to decide what equipment is needed and how the furniture will be arranged or if more furniture is needed. For significant space alterations, especially in schools, the school head teacher or principal and/or a caretaker/custodian will have to be consulted.

When an evaluation is done outside the lab, the evaluation technology must be installed before the testing. This can take quite some time, so scheduling should

Figure 6.7

Instructions for PlaTUI investigators.

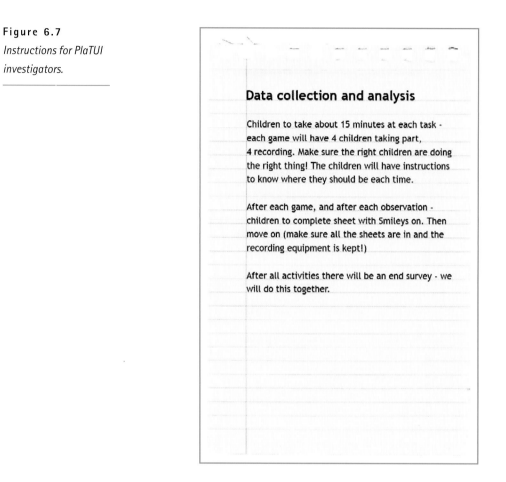

Data collection and analysis

Children to take about 15 minutes at each task - each game will have 4 children taking part, 4 recording. Make sure the right children are doing the right thing! The children will have instructions to know where they should be each time.

After each game, and after each observation - children to complete sheet with Smileys on. Then move on (make sure all the sheets are in and the recording equipment is kept!)

After all activities there will be an end survey - we will do this together.

allow time to be spent on setting up the space and rehearsing how children are likely to move around it, especially if pilot testing was done somewhere else.

Make sure all team members know where they will be situated in the area. Before the evaluation, practice with your colleagues how children will be brought to the test location, where they will wait, how they will be escorted into the space, and where they will sit while they are taking the test. Consider where video-recording and other equipment will be located so the data captured will contain all the necessary material and it will be easy to access if something goes wrong.

When a participant will be in a fixed position, such as when using gaze-tracking technology, make sure that the space is planned so the children can comfortably sit quietly for long enough.

Managing Children, Tasks, and Technology

A major consideration for many evaluation studies, especially if they are research driven, is the management of the task/child process. For instance, a study may require a child to carry out three tasks. In this situation, each child may carry out task 1, then task 2, and then task 3. This is not ideal because the child's performance on task 3 will be affected by her experiences with the previous two tasks.

Avoiding this kind of problem can be crucial, especially if you are measuring performance such as time to complete tasks, number of errors, and so forth. To counteract the effects of learning and fatigue, a Latin square approach can be used. This balances the order to make evaluations "fairer." For instance, with three tasks an ideal situation would be to have different children carrying out tasks in the following orders:

$$1, 2, 3 \quad 1, 3, 2 \quad 2, 1, 3 \quad 2, 3, 1 \quad 3, 1, 2 \quad 3, 2, 1$$

Thus, to cover all sequences the minimum number of children for the evaluation would be six. Unfortunately, when more tasks are considered or more factors need to be tested—for example, different products need to be used—the number of combinations and the complexity of the setup increase. These problems are beyond the scope of this book, but a useful text to consult is the psychology research book by Martin (2005).

Assigning Tasks to Children in the PlaTUI Study

The order effects in PlaTUI were especially interesting because as many as 31 children would be performing only three games. A decision was made to create an extra three activities by having four children observe each game as the other four children played it. Because there were three games, this still occupied only 24 children, so a seventh activity had to be planned to include some of the children.

Each group of children (there were seven groups in total) elected a group leader, and the leader was given a clipboard and a sheet of paper that showed the order in which to take the group and a space for the children to tick off completion. This sheet is shown in Figure 6.8.

Figure 6.8

Child's record sheet.

Where to next?

F	Activity	Child 1	Child 2	Child 3	Child 4
3b	Box Game	Play	Play	Play	Play
1b	Computer game	Play	Play	Play	Play
2b	Table Game	Play	Play	Play	Play
3	Box Game	Video	Draw	Notes	Camera
1	Computer game	Notes	Camera	Video	Draw
2	Table Game	Camera	Video	Draw	Notes
K	Abc Typing	Do	Do	Do	Do

If the children are carrying out several tasks or taking part in different activities, they can easily get confused. One solution is to give each child a "road map" that shows where to go next. Another good idea is to give each child a "passport" that is stamped as the child performs each activity or completes a task. This helps the children see their progress and makes the evaluation fun!

Training Evaluators and Pilot Testing

Having planned all the details, the next stage is to prepare the team and test out the plan. Evaluations should always be piloted. There is only one downside to pilot testing: It takes an extra day. Pilot testing allows the evaluator to do the following:

- Check that the equipment works.
- Time how long the evaluation will take (per child) and overall.
- See if the chosen recording methods work.
- Discover if the test tasks are workable.
- Find out if the right information is being recorded.
- See if the instructions (to the children and the administrators) are clear.
- Determine if the children can cope with the chosen evaluation method.
- Find out if the children (or the administrators) need any training.

- Investigate what the best layout of the space will be.
- See whether extra adult helpers will be needed.
- Rehearse and act according to the plan.

The pilot test should take place about a week before the real evaluation. Prior to it, if any adult participants need training in the techniques or methods to be used, ensure that this is carried out. Then the pilot test can be used to check that they are proficient. Children who participate in the pilot test are generally not the same ones doing the real study. It is not always necessary to have children who are doing the pilot test exactly match the sample who will be doing the real test, but where possible the children should be the same age. A good pilot test will have at least two or three child participants to make sure that what is observed is not unusual.

Communicating the Details

Having tested that the evaluation works and made any necessary adjustments, the only remaining task is deciding how the details will be communicated to the child participants and the adults. At this stage, an action plan for the day will be produced, the details of the event finalized, and permissions and consent gathered from the children who will be taking part in the final study. An example of an action plan for the PlaTUI evaluation is shown in Figure 6.9. Note that this action

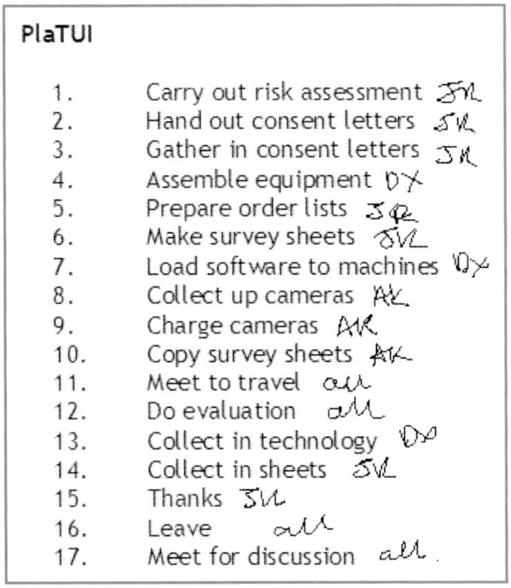

PlaTUI

1. Carry out risk assessment
2. Hand out consent letters
3. Gather in consent letters
4. Assemble equipment
5. Prepare order lists
6. Make survey sheets
7. Load software to machines
8. Collect up cameras
9. Charge cameras
10. Copy survey sheets
11. Meet to travel
12. Do evaluation
13. Collect in technology
14. Collect in sheets
15. Thanks
16. Leave
17. Meet for discussion

Figure 6.9
Action plan for PlaTUI.

plan includes a risk assessment and details about who is doing what. When an evaluation study is planned to this level of detail, the chance of it going well on the day is significantly increased.

Next Stages

Having decided on the details that cement the evaluation plan, the next stage is to carry out the study. No amount of planning can guarantee that the event will go off without a hitch, but careful attention to detail pays dividends at the next stages. The safest thing to do is to pilot your study, plan and prepare all you can in advance, and leave some margin for the unexpected.

CHAPTER 7

DURING THE EVALUATION

The big day has arrived, and, well prepared, the evaluators either eagerly arrive on site to carry out their planned activities or await the children's arrival. This is where it can all go horribly wrong! There are many anecdotal stories about video cameras not being turned on, batteries running out, children doing incorrect things, and software refusing to download; however, with careful planning, such things can mostly be avoided.

This chapter is a practical guide to what should be done on the day of the evaluation. It discusses setting up the location, giving instructions, managing time, and dealing with difficulties. Lots of things will be going on as well as the many tasks to think about (see Figure 7.1). The chapter concludes with an outline of what needs to be done to conclude the day.

Arrival and Setup

Considerations for the day of the evaluation begin before the study takes place. The primary concern of the chief investigator should be to ensure that any children who are taking part in the study are attended to. This might mean paying attention to very practical things like buying beverages, reserving parking spaces, or signposting restrooms. With drinks, it is generally safest to provide only water, and with car parking, reserve it well in advance so the children don't have to walk a long way. In some cases, children may be walking to your venue from a local school. This takes careful planning to determine a safe route, estimate the time needed for the walk, and recruit adults to help with crossing streets and roads.

Figure 7.1 *On the day there are lots of things to think about!*

Preparing the Evaluation Team

The evaluation team must be prepared as well. In an ideal world, they will all arrive well rested and with a positive mindset. Where the evaluation is part of an individual's research degree or is being carried out the day before a usability report is due, the evaluation team may be quite stressed. It is important to always keep in mind that whatever the evaluation aims to achieve, even if it all goes wrong it is not the end of the world. It is also unlikely that any failure will be the fault of the children, and even if it is, never blame *them*!

Setting up the Space

It generally takes between 30 and 60 minutes to set up an evaluation space, so it is a good idea to arrive with time to spare. Make sure you tidy up the area before the testing begins. Tape power cords to the floor, and put away video camera bags and your personal belongings.

Figure 7.2

One of the three PlaTUI interfaces showing how cables and wires were kept away from where the children were working.

Space in the PlaTUI Evaluation

In the PlaTUI evaluation, the space had to be arranged by moving tables and chairs, finding electrical outlets, turning on laptops, and setting up the programs to be evaluated. In addition, the children's response sheets had to be placed at the different locations, the recording equipment had to be shared around, and pencils had to be placed at each task location.

Tip

If a lot of furniture must be moved around, as is commonly necessary in school locations, ask the teacher if the children can help.

Introductions and Instructions

In an evaluation, much of the mood is set at the very beginning, when the children and the evaluators come together. What is said at this point by way of introductions and instructions can have a significant effect on the evaluation study as a whole. It is worth considering how the outsider (the child in a lab, the adult in a school) feels at the start of an evaluation.

Children in Adult Places

When children are the outsiders (i.e., brought into adult spaces), they should be made to feel safe and comfortable. Here are some key things to consider:

Allay fears. Make the children feel comfortable with their surroundings, warn them if there will be a great deal of activity at a certain time, give them an idea about what will happen at the location, and take them on a short tour of the building where the study is taking place.

Make friends. Introduce everybody to each other, and do something fun together before the testing. Play a game, discuss hobbies, or tell a story. Try to aim for natural communication.

Ensure their comfort. Tell them where the restrooms are, and explain what they should do if they need to use them (young children might need to be accompanied by an adult). Give the children an idea of when they will be able to leave, and inform them about when, if at all, they will be served food or a drink.

Keep them safe. Tell the children what will happen in the event of a fire alarm. Tell them where to go or what to do if they get lost.

Doing Research with Children in Industry

Libby Hanna, Hanna Research & Consulting, LLC

What is the key difference when working with children in industry? Speed! We need the data by yesterday! There is no time to study children in their natural habitats. On rare occasions when there is, researchers will be pulled in during product concept development and will get to do all kinds of cool ethnographic and participatory design techniques with the children. Those times are great, but for the most part we're coming in on the fly to do a reality check with no time for getting off-track.

> *Example:* To do a study on how well children can draw onscreen using standard input devices, why not let children draw whatever they want? Because they may choose to draw an elaborate scene with mermaids and waterfalls that would take them half an hour. Or they may draw circle after circle after circle, and then want to color them all with different colors. Sure, that would be more fun, and you'd have lots of data on how that particular child drew lots of little lines and curves, but if you have to compute an average across a group of children, then all you really need is two minutes of their time ("Draw a house just like this one"), and then you can get all your data in one day.

Here are some of my latest priorities for doing studies with children:

Go ahead and be like a schoolteacher; it works

When children are with you for a very brief period of time, both you and they will be more comfortable if there are clear expectations and familiar roles. Don't ask them to suddenly be buddy-buddy with you (although some kids will instantly bond). I use all the basic teacher techniques:

1. Give instructions as statements rather than questions ("Go ahead and figure out how to start the game" instead of "Can you figure out how to start the game").

2. Don't ask "Okay?" after telling the children what to do (unless it's okay with you if they say no).

3. Expect children to work with you without parents in the room (unless that's part of your research design or if either parent or child insists on it).

4. Watch them like a hawk! As soon as they get restless, you can prompt them or move them on to something else (otherwise they might find something else to do on their own).

5. Believe what they do, not what they say. Make sure you set up the study to be able to watch them doing things rather than just talking about them.

Don't worry about measuring if the children like the product or not

There will always be those on the product team who want to know if the children "like" their product. They ask, "How can we tell if they really enjoy it if they're in this sterile lab and you're only giving them a few minutes on each task with the product?" The answer: It's not realistic to evaluate appeal of a product for children until you're pretty much done with it (or have a very solid demo). Children don't have the patience to put up with buggy or flimsy prototypes, and they can't abstract a game concept from the nuts and bolts of trying to play it. So the kind of evaluation we mostly do is all usability. Can they understand the goal? Can they figure out the game play? We can get that information in the lab in one or two days of trying it out with kids. (But see the next paragraph for a possible worksaround to observe engagement.)

From about 6 years of age up, pair children with friends

Having two friends working together to figure something out (make sure they're really friends) encourages them to talk during the study. And if you're lucky, you might also get some indication of whether they're having fun with the product and so can appease the anxious product designers. This way you can leave the two children in the room together and observe them on their own. With children younger than 6, you should plan to be sitting next to the child in the testing room.

Give parents something to do in the observation room

Ask parents to fill out a very brief questionnaire about their observations of their child with the product. This helps parents appreciate being apart from their child and feel useful, and it gives you additional feedback on the product (focusing on the child's use of it, not the parent's opinion, though that will come into play).

Go overboard on screening criteria

You want to be sure that the only things children are struggling with in the lab are the things you want to test. So go ahead and require that they're familiar with all the rest, they've used the relevant input devices before, they're in certain grades of school and so are at predictable reading levels, and they don't have special needs. Yes, of course, we want the product to be appealing and usable to a huge range of children. But when trying to come up with an "average" response from a small number of children, you'll have nothing if you don't constrain the sample to begin with. Even a sample of only 5-year-olds will give you a huge range of abilities and experience.

Test the youngest end of the targeted age

If the little children can do it, you can be sure the older ones will be able to do it, too. For usability testing, we try things out with the bottom year or two of the target age. If the product marketers are saying, "This is for 6- to 10-year-olds," then test with 6- and 7-year-olds. The 10-year-olds won't want to play with it anyway.

Give up on perfection

Finally, when trying to improve products for children in industry, you have to give up on trying to make them perfect. Product teams work under incredible pressure from budget and schedule constraints. Often products for children are price conscious, and budgets are even tighter than usual, so there's little room for big changes once a product is in development. Focus on working with product teams to understand what can be changed to make it better. Even adjusting some wording can make a big difference in usability.

Adults in Children's Places

As an adult in a child's place, it can be uncomfortable. You might want to recruit a child to show you around. When arriving in a child's place, find out how the place functions and what happens at lunchtime and between lessons. In a school, be very careful about assuming that you can go into the places that teachers occupy. Wait to be invited into the staff room, and don't use the kitchen facilities without asking first!

People who are not used to children's spaces can find them quite scary! The noise levels of schools can be a surprise, as can the levels of activity. Children appear to be everywhere and all over the place. In high schools, children may seem alarmingly large or may even appear threatening.

Tip

Visit the children's spaces in an informal capacity before committing to assist in or undertake an evaluation.

Children and Instructions in the PlaTUI Study

In the PlaTUI evaluation shown in Figure 7.3, the children were in their own school, so that was very safe and comfortable for them. The children were told the adults' names and advised that they could use first names. They were also informed that their teacher would be in the room the whole time and they should ask her if they needed to use the restrooms.

Some of the adult participants were new to the school. One had not been inside a school since he was a boy! *Before* the study the adults were shown where the restrooms were and told how the school operated.

Giving Instructions

What is said before the evaluation starts is crucial to the smooth management of the event. The participants, both adults and children, need to know the procedure for the day and instructions that are specific to the evaluation. Take care to speak to individual children as shown in Figure 7.4.

In most cases, the adults should already be well briefed, but last-minute instructions may still be necessary, especially with regard to the use of space and time. This should be done before the children arrive.

Figure 7.3
Children during the PlaTUI evaluation.

Figure 7.4
Give the children clear instructions. This may mean speaking to each child individually.

CHAPTER 7: DURING THE EVALUATION

Instructions for Adults in the PlaTUI Evaluation

In the PlaTUI study, the adults were told that their task was to manage the children, ensure that all the children got a turn, make sure that the recording equipment was shared, and, once all the children had played with the technology, have the children complete the survey sheet. They were also told to make sure that each new group that came to them was in the right place!

Children's instructions need to be clear and unambiguous. Anything that is really important may need to be repeated, and it is helpful to check that the children understand what they need to do. Where groups of children come alone or in small groups, they should receive consistent instructions. In these cases it is sensible to have these in written form.

Managing Time and Space

The time taken for an evaluation will vary from case to case, but a general rule is that young children should not normally be expected to focus on a single task for much more than 20 minutes. If children have to do several lengthy or complex tasks, consideration should be given to how this should best be managed.

Keep an eye on the clock. Parents may arrive to pick up or drop off a child. All the children may have to complete a set of tasks in the fixed time available. Where evaluations take place in schools, the study also must accommodate timetables, playtimes, and mealtimes. Appoint a time keeper, or use a kitchen timer. Do not rely on the clock on the computer or your cell phone because they may not be easily visible, and you may not notice time slipping away.

Often, an evaluation takes place in a small room, maybe a lab, and the children arrive singly or in pairs. In these situations, room must be allocated for children to wait, children who are waiting will need something to do, and the adults who accompany the children must be made comfortable. In complex evaluation set-ups, it is helpful to have an extra facilitator just to manage the waiting and moving activities.

Managing Time and Space 121

Working with Schoolchildren

In schools, a common method is to take children, singly or in small groups, from a class. It is useful to speak to their teacher before the evaluation to determine how the children will be brought to the evaluation. A good plan is to have the teacher allocate the children into groups before the evaluation starts and number them so that, for example, when group 1 returns to the classroom, group 2 knows to go to the evaluation. This saves a lot of time and minimizes disruption to the children's regular activities. When possible, children should not be left waiting around for evaluation activities because this makes them restless.

When each child (or group of children) comes to the evaluation, do the following:

- Introduce yourself and any other evaluators.
- Find out the child's name.
- Explain what is happening.
- Explain that they can leave at any time if unhappy.
- Explain the text tasks.
- Carry out the evaluation.
- Thank the child.

Sometimes a child will arrive at the evaluation in good spirits but then become unhappy. In this case, the child must be allowed to return to his or her earlier activities. If there is a child in the evaluation who has some learning disabilities or sensory or physical disabilities, that child should still be allowed to participate as much as possible. The results from his or her interaction can always be discounted afterward.

Monitoring the Tasks

It is important to keep a close eye on what happens during the evaluation. Many evaluations require different test tasks to be done by each child, and that gives the evaluator a lot to focus on. Preparation and checklists are essential where the evaluation is complex. In Kano et al.'s (2007) study, children copied text phrases into a computer, and these text phrases varied among participants. To ensure that the evaluation went smoothly, sets of test phrases were printed out on paper, numbered for use, and laid out in the room before each new group arrived at the evaluation.

A list of children was maintained against the numbered test tasks, and automated key logging was used. These precautions helped the evaluation to run smoothly.

Dealing with Problems on the Day

It is seldom that an evaluation study involving children goes off without a hitch. When things do go wrong, the evaluator must be able to think quickly on her feet. In this section we discuss some common problems in evaluations and offer some solutions.

I planned for 24 children, but 3 were sick on the day of the evaluation. If 24 children were needed to cover all the possibilities, then there is no good solution to this; one possibility is to reschedule the study. In most cases, 21 children looking at a product will be ample! In general, a good plan is to always assume some children will not attend and design the evaluation to limit the effect of no-shows.

I forgot to press the record button on the video camera. It happens. The only real fix for this is to do the work again. To make sure the same mistake doesn't happen, write PRESS RECORD on the instruction sheet. It is helpful to have one adult participant focusing on just the recording.

One child in the class was unable to read and write. If in a school, the teacher probably knew this already and may have warned you. In this case, the child should have been accommodated and given help to carry out the evaluation, and not made to feel different. If many children could not read or write and you did not anticipate that, you need to return to the planning phase.

A child wants to quit in the middle of the evaluation. Again, you will miss one participant, which might affect your data analysis. If this happens with more than one child, you should perhaps take a look at the way you are carrying out the evaluation. Is the setup pleasing for children? Is there something more interesting going on in another classroom? Is the evaluation period too long or the setup too demanding?

The children are not doing what I want them to do. This can often happen when more than one child is in the test space. Children might not focus on the task; they might start doing something completely different, such as playing with the video camera or disturbing the other children. There are a few ways to prevent this from happening: Plan the activities so that there is less opportunity for disruptions, divide the children into smaller groups, separate parallel activities in separate spaces, and recruit enough adults to facilitate activities. Discuss with the teacher if there are more energetic pupils who have problems concentrating on such activities, and consider having smaller groups for these children. Remember that children are curious about you, the other children who are doing the evaluation, the setup, and the technology.

Problems in the PlaTUI Evaluation

In the PlaTUI evaluation, several difficulties occurred on the day. Two of these were technology related. The first was that the power supplies in the school were inaccessible due to gym equipment having been placed in front of them. This was remedied by some energetic climbing and stretching! As a result, the room layout had to be changed from the original plan. The second was that the children used the cameras for videoing, and the cameras ran out of memory! The fix for this was to have one of the evaluators designated as the "camera person," and when the children found the cameras full, they ran to her and had her delete the unnecessary files. Some useful data was lost, but at least the children could still use the cameras.

For the children, one problem occurred when one child became upset at not having had a turn with either the camera or the video camera. One of the adults present let this child use her mobile phone as a camera. In hindsight, a spare camera would have been a good idea. One child in the study was newly arrived in the country and had difficulty understanding the tasks. This child was helped by others in the class. It was then not clear if the results were the child's own, but the impact of this was slight. It was deemed more important to make the child feel included than to worry if the work had been fully understood. In the analysis of the results, this child's work was disregarded.

Children had some difficulties working out where to go next. This was supposed to be easy because they had a sheet with all the possibilities on it (see Chapter 6) and it was assumed that this would be easy to follow. The descriptions of the activities proved less clear than we had hoped, and four groups arrived in one place at one moment. To counter this, the administrator who was managing the activity checked the children's "route" sheets to confirm that the right group was in the right place.

Closing the Evaluation

The evaluation ends, and, depending on the sort of work that was done, there will be many outputs, probably including a great feeling of relief, a messy room, and a mound of paperwork or videotapes.

Leaving the Area Tidy

Critically, the evaluator must leave the evaluation area as it was found. This can be a distraction from the "serious" work of collecting all the equipment and data, but nevertheless it must be done, and ideally an extra pair of hands will be recruited to deal with this. This way you leave a good impression, and you are likely to be welcome the next time you want to do an evaluation.

Saying "Thank You!"

For any kind of evaluation, it is polite and wise to thank all the participants, stakeholders, and gatekeepers as soon as possible after the evaluation exercise is completed. Taking care in this small activity is a good idea because the participants' help might be needed again, either for more work related to the study in hand or for a future study.

Approaches to thanking will be different for different participants. If the study took place in a school, it is usually appropriate to thank in person the children and any school staff directly involved. It is also polite to write a letter (no e-mails please!) to the school's head or principal, especially because he or she will be delighted to receive a gracious thank you note that can be displayed for prospective parents to see! In general, adults (including parents and teachers) can often be thanked by phone or letter, but it is better to thank children in person. It is often possible to thank children immediately at the end of the evaluation, but if this is not possible, a special trip back to evaluation location might be necessary to deliver your thanks.

If rewards have been promised, they should always be delivered. In general, children don't expect a reward; they are used to doing tasks for adults, and they seem to be more than happy with a certificate stating how helpful they were. It is nice to print color certificates with fancy fonts and personalize them with the child's name. Figure 7.5 shows a sample certificate. These are easy to produce, and they make a great impression on younger children.

Figure 7.5

A sample certificate as used by the Child Computer Interaction Group at UCLAN.

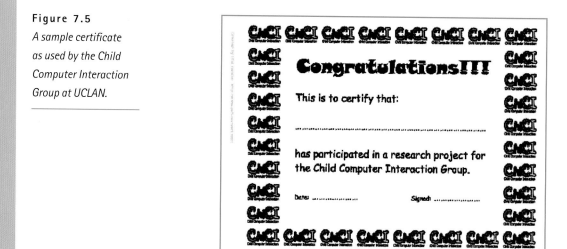

Teachers, helpers, and children should all be thanked, and, where possible, the participants should be given information about what they have contributed. This may be sent after the results have been analyzed. The next chapter looks at the analysis of results and considers what needs to be done after the evaluation.

CHAPTER 8

AFTER THE EVALUATION

Once an evaluation study is completed, there is still plenty to be done. Some of this work must be done on the day of the evaluation, and some activities must be performed in the days and weeks following. First, the data must be sorted out and coded, and then the evaluator can start to consider the findings from the evaluation. This process involves some reflection and action and a more analytical mindset. After that, the "raw" data must be handled carefully, particularly if it is not anonymous, and it will need to be destroyed in an appropriate way when it is no longer needed. This chapter examines these functions, beginning when the evaluation has concluded and ending when the findings have been reported.

Getting the Data into Shape

The products of the evaluation, in their untreated form, constitute raw data. Raw data can exsist in a variety of forms, including questionnaires, interview notes, observation notes, videotapes, or electronic logs. Raw data generally need some attention before they can be interpreted and used. Figure 8.1 shows some raw data from the PlaTUI study. The PlaTUI study also included raw data as photos, notes, drawings, and videos that the children had made themselves.

In many cases, a study will result in raw data in several formats, and these data may be stored on several devices. As soon as possible after the evaluation is concluded, the raw data should be collected, checked to ensure that they have been both unambiguously recorded and tagged with dates, times, and names (if not anonymous) or codes (see Figure 8.2). The data in the figure are tagged with a code for the child, a specification of the task to which they relate, and a date (day) marker.

If untagged items are found at this stage, it may be possible to reconstruct what they were and what they represented. As time passes, however, this becomes more difficult. It can be very annoying, for instance, to carry out a set of pretests and post-tests, only to discover later that you can't tell which is which or which pretest goes with which post-test.

Figure 8.1

Raw data from PlaTUI.

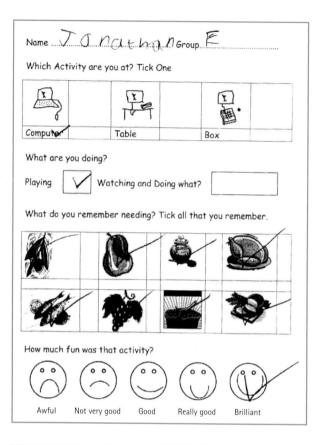

Figure 8.2

Image of tagged data.

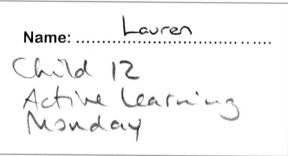

Having ensured that all the data have been tagged and sorted, you then need to make some sense of them. The following process must take place so the evaluator will end up with useful, sorted, coded, secure data:

- *Translate* the children's writing into something meaningful.
- *Transcribe* paper responses into a digital format.
- *Anonymize* the data and any digital copies.

- *Code* the data, especially qualitative data.
- *Analyze* the data for similarities, trends, and oddities.

When translating data from children, be very careful to keep the original data so they can be referred back to. Devise a sensible system for linking paper and digital documents; folders with dates as names are quite common. Coding and analyzing data requires some expertise, so these are discussed in a little more detail in the next section.

Coding and Analyzing the Data

Analysis is the process of taking data and discovering what story they tell. Generally, the process of coding and analyzing data is different for quantitative and qualitative data. Although a detailed coverage of analysis procedures is beyond the scope of this book, the following subsections give a brief outline of the important aspects for these two data types.

Coding and Analyzing Quantitative Data

Generally coded as numbers, quantitative data can appear deceptively simple. First, each "portion" of the data should be inspected. A good way to inspect data is to graph them. This can highlight outliers, data that are not normal, and trends. If two sets of data are being compared, graphs can present averages and standard deviations and scatter plots can present correlations. If two sets of data have similar averages and similar standard deviations, this might suggest similarity. If two sets of data appear correlated when graphed, this might suggest a relationship.

These similarities and relationships can be discovered by inspection but generally are only confirmed with the use of statistical tests. Statistical tests are a way to verify whether a result found is "statistically significant." This means that a statistical test has been carried out on the data that shows that the results are unlikely to have occurred by chance. A wide range of statistical tests is available, allowing these calculations to be done on a variety of forms of data and on different experimental setups. (The details of all these tests are beyond the scope of this book. Readers who are interested in the appropriate use of statistical tests are encouraged to refer to Martin, 2005.) With modern statistical software packages, it has become very easy to apply different tests. Readers are warned against applying tests haphazardly, since results of applying tests incorrectly are misleading despite their "scientific gloss."

Tip

It is worth spending some time with the data to try out the analytical tools with a small part of what you have before continuing to full analysis phase.

Presenting Summaries of Quantitative Data

Results can often be summarized simply with data and some associated statistical measures. Mean scores and measures of standard deviation are often worth calculating. The former gives a helpful summary of the findings, and the latter indicates the spread of the results. For example, you may wish to report the average time to perform some specified task, the median number of errors in carrying out such tasks, proportions of tasks completed successfully, and so on. Similar statistics can be computed for subjective measures—for example, average ratings of enjoyment, ranking of preferred items, and so forth.

Example of Using Quantitative Data

If you present numeric data, your audience will usually generalize your conclusions for the target population, even if that isn't what you meant! Reporting that children entered words in a dictation program with only 5 percent errors is interpreted differently from claiming that all five children you tested got between 1 and 5 words wrong when entering the same 40-word-long text. Even better, you can add a disclaimer to your result saying that readers should not jump to conclusions about how fast other children can enter text using the dictation program.

Despite their precise nature, numbers derived from evaluation studies should be interpreted with care. While an evaluation is not necessarily an experiment (and usually it is not), its output should never be presented as a generalization outside the context of the evaluation when the evidence provided and the analysis are not sufficient to support such inferences.

Analyzing the PlaTUI Results

Some of the results from the PlaTUI study are summarized in Table 8.1. The table shows the raw data for 12 children for one part of the evaluation (36 surveys were looked at from a total of 174 for the whole PlaTUI evaluation). In this form, it is difficult to see what the results mean. The number of spoiled (incomplete) results was quite high. When these data were coded 5 = Brilliant, 4 = Very Good, 3 = Good, etc.), the results could be examined to see how the three games compared. The results are shown in Figure 8.3.

The visualization in Figure 8.3 makes it appear that the computer game was the one preferred by this (small) set of children. However, care must be taken here because of the missing data from the other two games. It may well be that this visualization tells an incorrect story. If the average (mean) scores per completed sheet are calculated for the results, they would be as follows:

- Table   4.3
- Computer   4.75
- Box   4.78

Now the computer game doesn't seem quite so impressive! Even these results are not convincing due to the number of missing scores and the small number of papers considered.

Game	Awful	Not Very Good	Good	Very Good	Brilliant	Spoiled
Table			3	1	6	2
Computer				3	9	
Box			1		8	3
TOTALS			4	4	23	5

Table 8.1

Number of children selecting specific scores for the three PlaTUI games.

Figure 8.3

The PlaTUI data presented visually.

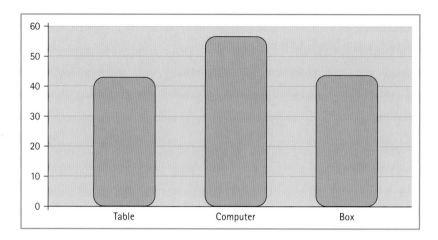

Analyzing Qualitative Data

Often, user quotes are inserted into the evaluation report that demonstrate how the product is experienced. Qualitative data could also include descriptions of situations in which difficulties were encountered or where surprising results were found, photographs and screen shots, or even video extracts illustrating (usually) problematic aspects of the interaction.

Tip

Do not be tempted to select "cute" quotes or funny behaviors of children during your test. Rather, check that what you choose to highlight portrays adequately your understanding of how children experienced the product during the evaluation.

Despite its imprecision or anecdotal nature, qualitative data can be a striking and persuasive way to demonstrate the results of an evaluation study. A vivid record of the reactions and emotions of a child who is bewildered and puzzled by a "child-friendly" interface may be more convincing than a long report or argument by an expert or a statistical analysis that shows that children perform poorly with this interface.

Apart from this illustrative purpose, qualitative data can also stand on its own as the basis for answering open questions in the evaluation—for example, understanding different usage patterns, gut reactions, finding usability problems, and so forth.

Qualitative data can be analyzed with different degrees of rigor. Unfortunately, if sufficient care is not exercised, it is only too easy to pick the funniest moments or most peculiar interactions or to simply fall into the trap of seeking evidences confirming your own presuppositions. Proper and "rigorous" qualitative analysis can guard against this trap. (A treatment of qualitative data analysis is beyond the scope of this book. Readers are encouraged to seek specialized texts, such as Miles and Huberman, 1994.)

Even without delving into such methodology, you can do a lot to avoid misuse and misinterpretation of qualitative data. Contrary to numerical data, where a rigorous procedure should reach a certain conclusion independently of the analyst and his or her disposition, qualitative data rely on the analyst making sensible and sound interpretations. To analyze this type of data, it is important to adopt an open mind that is truly inquisitive instead of looking for facile and impressive conclusions.

Example of Misinterpretation

It is quite common for an evaluation report to contain statements like "All subjects liked our system" or "They would like to take it home." For adults, often the price they would be prepared to pay is mentioned. Such statements should be treated with skepticism. Although we would like to be able to report these statements back to the designers or product developers, it is often the case that the test participants say these things simply to be polite .

In cases where you want to demonstrate with qualitative data that a design goal has been met, it is important to review all your evidence—transcripts, videos, handwritten notes—for both confirming and disconfirming evidence. This can be done with varying levels of rigor, depending on the purposes of your analysis. Without expanding too much on the topic of qualitative data analysis, suffice it to say that avoiding checking against your own biases when reviewing qualitative data is a slippery slope that is best avoided!

Qualitative analysis of the data often exposes images and recordings of the testers to the public. This may include people on your development team, or it may end up being published. See Chapter 4 for a discussion on ethical use of data.

Reporting Results

In most cases, the findings from an evaluation will need to be reported. The report will vary according to the needs of the person for whom the evaluation was carried out. Before constructing a report, it is essential to be clear about its purpose. Seely (2002) suggests that a report has three purposes: to inform, to record, and to persuade, and any individual report will contain a certain proportion of each. This is normally true for a report on an evaluation study. The author or authors will be doing some combination of the following:

- *Informing* the readership of what has been found as a result of the evaluation study.
- *Recording* relevant background information and what the investigators did.
- *Persuading* the readers to take actions as a result of the findings.

A good report writer considers the needs of the readers in the design and content of the report. So a good start is understanding who the readers are likely to be!

Know Your Audience

An evaluation report will generally be prepared for one of three distinct audiences. These are developers and clients, researchers and academics, and participants. The report needs to be written with the audience in mind.

Developers and clients will want to know what needs fixing. They will be mostly interested in results rather than methods, although the method is still important. The report will be read by designers and developers who need to act upon the report's findings and recommendations, as well as by managers who will be looking for an overview. Sometimes an evaluation study uncovers a lot of problems. These must be reported, but it can make the report look like a laundry list of defects, which may not be encouraging to the people who must use it. Evaluation studies also find features that work well and that users like; these points are often forgotten when the report is written. It is a good plan to include both good points and bad points in the report. Start with the good points, because evaluators like to know that they got some things right!

Academic audiences tend to be more interested in the rigor of an evaluation, with the results often being secondary. They like to know how well the evaluation methods worked.

It is customary in evaluation studies that involve adult users to provide feedback—a summary of the findings for those who helped with the evaluation. However, when the evaluators are children, particularly the very young, this may not always be a useful exercise. The team needs to consider whether children would understand what was being said if a summary of findings was reported back to them. Where children might not benefit from feedback, the school or the parents that facilitated the evaluation study might be glad to have a summary of the findings.

Structure and Style

The report can be written, perhaps as a research paper or a technical report, presented on a poster, or given orally. In some instances, two or more of these methods will be used. Whatever method is used, the report will generally include sections that cover the same general elements:

1. Executive summary or abstract
2. Background
3. Method
4. Results
5. Discussion and/or recommendations
6. Conclusions (and maybe suggestions for further work)
7. Appendices and possibly references

Each of these sections is described briefly below. It is interesting to note that the structure is similar for each of the preceding report styles, so, for example, a poster for a conference, a confidential report to a commercial client, and a paper written for an academic journal will all have the same sections. They vary, however, in length, detail, visuals, and writing style.

The Executive Summary or Abstract

An *executive summary* appears in a report of an evaluation study in a commercial situation, and an *abstract* appears in its place in a research report for publication. They each serve a similar role. Each is a summary of the report, so it is usually best to write it last, even though it normally is the first section of the report.

The executive summary is a brief version of the report that is intended for readers who have a general interest in the content but don't need a lot of details. These would include the managers of the designers and implementers who will have to

Figure 8.4

Abstract for PlaTUI.

This paper describes a study of three computer games with children. The study compared the three games to see how the children played with them and children were asked to comment on the how much fun they had playing the games. The results indicate that the children enjoyed all the games. The paper discusses how the experimental set up affected the results and three recommendations for similar studies are made; cut price reporting techniques, visualisation of game play and competitive evaluation methods.

act on the findings and recommendations. Such a summary needs to stand alone and to make sense when read independently of the report. In general, executive summaries do not exceed a couple of pages.

An abstract is also a summary but for an academic paper. It is typically shorter, usually no more than one page. It also needs to summarize the whole paper and must make sense when standing alone, but its purpose is a little different. Researchers will read abstracts to assess whether they need to obtain and read the entire paper. The abstract must summarize the methods used and, particularly, the findings.

Tip

Write your abstract to convey what you did, why you did it, who took part, and what you found. Figure 8.4 shows an abstract for reporting the PlaTUI evaluation. Researchers will see that, despite the results of PlaTUI being unconvincing (with respect to finding out which game was preferred), the abstract still promises some valuable insights on, in this case, evaluation studies with children.

The Background to an Evaluation

Following the executive summary or abstract, the first part of the report proper should set the scene and provide a context for the rest of the report. For a report on an evaluation study, a vital part of this section is a description of the product being evaluated, including its intended market. Pictures can be very useful here. A screen shot or photograph can often say more about a product than the equivalent space filled with words. In the case of a product under development, a discussion of rival products and their competitive features is often relevant as well.

Another topic to cover here would be a summary of other evaluation studies that have already been done (and reported elsewhere) on this product. In the case of a research study, this section would include a review of the literature on the particular issues that the paper covers—for example, the type of product or the evaluation method.

The final topics that must be set out in this section are the scope and the purpose of the evaluation study being reported. In the case of a commercial evaluation, these will have been agreed on in advance, but they should still appear because not all of the readers will have been involved in the scoping of the project.

Methods

This section describes what was done during the evaluation study. A good description here enables the reader to form a judgment about the rigor and validity of the work that has been done and to understand its limitations and the validity of the findings. Specifically, this section should cover the evaluation methods and techniques that were used, the location and layout of the rooms and laboratories, the users (if any were used; not all evaluations need them), how many users participated, how participants were chosen, what rewards were given, how consent was obtained, what tasks were done by the children, why they performed those tasks, and any other details of the logistics and timing of the study that might be relevant. Often it is difficult to decide exactly what to include here. There is the risk of the report becoming too cumbersome. A useful test for the Methods section of an academic paper is that a reader should be able to replicate the study, using only the information included in it. This is also a good test for other types of evaluation reports.

Illustrations are useful here, too—for example, a plan or photograph of the room layout. Avoid using recognizable photographs of children, however innocuous the image seems to you unless (1) you really can't make your point any other way, and (2) you have specific consent from a responsible adult, as well as consent from the child to use the picture in this way. Usually, you can illustrate your point with a photograph taken from behind the child or one that conceals the child's face (see Figure 8.5).

Results

Presenting the results of the evaluation must be done with care. Readers may be overwhelmed if *everything* is included. Charts and tables are normally a good way to present results. It often helps to present data in more than one way, if space allows.

Figure 8.5

Photo from the report of PlaTUI showing the setup without children's faces.

Discussion and/or Recommendations

This is the most important section of the report for most readers, particularly if they are the developers who need to act on its contents. This information is the reason they are reading the report. In fact, some readers will skip straight to this section, omitting all the "background" material that precedes it.

Tip

Since readers may skip straight to the results and recommendations, be sure that this section makes sense.

Sometimes a special stand-alone version of this section is produced just for developers. This is known, not surprisingly, as a Recommendations Report. A critical prerequisite for a useful recommendations report for designers and developers is that the findings from the evaluation studies are organized sensibly; converted into specific, implementable recommendations; and ranked in importance. Developers need to know which of the problems identified are critical and which are minor irritations.

Conclusions

Commercial evaluation reports may omit this section and end with the recommendations. For publication purposes, a summary of the main findings and their importance is needed, as well as perhaps a discussion of possible future works that stem from these findings.

Appendices and References

Appendices to the report should contain material that isn't essential to understand the report but would be useful to readers with a particular interest in certain aspects of the study. For example, it would often be appropriate to include a blank questionnaire in an appendix in the case of a questionnaire-based study or details of tasks that were set for user tests.

The report should refer to other studies to allow readers to judge whether the methods used were appropriate and to give them a starting point for further reading. In academic texts, it is usual to cite references using either a name and publication date (as is done in this book) or a reference number, and to list the references with complete information at the end of the paper. For more information on how to format references in academic publications, see Murray (2004).

Some commercial reports use the academic conventions just described, but usually such reports contain comparatively few references, and it is easier (for the reader) to use footnotes for information about the references.

Oral Presentation of Results

Often, especially when the report is for a commercial organization, it is usual to do an oral presentation before a written report is produced (Courage and Baxter, 2005). An oral presentation can make it easier to explain issues that would be hard to explain in writing (Courage and Baxter, 2005). For example, usability issues can often be very well illustrated with a video. Most oral presentations are accompanied by a visual presentation that has been created with specialized software. These tools can be used creatively to illustrate your findings, including the use of images, video clips, and animations.

Some Cautions

Whether oral or written, reports of evaluations with children need special consideration, relates to two concerns: clarity and care. Writing about children requires clear language so readers can understand what was done, with whom, and in what context. These are the important points to include:

Age: In most cases, ages should be reported in actual rather than school years, which differ from country to country. Similarly, it is better to avoid terms like *college, high school,* or *kindergarten* without explaining their meaning.

Location: Do not assume that your readers know what happens in a nursery school or a school playground. Describe, in a few words, what "unusual" activities would be "usual" in that place.

The report may reside in the public domain for some time, and it may be read by people for whom it was not initially intended. A common approach with slides used in presentations is to place them on websites. Care must be taken to protect the children and the data. Here are three requirements in this respect:

- *Don't tell* anyone more than they need to know. It is okay to say in an oral presentation that Sam couldn't work the mouse. The audience doesn't have to know that he had just been in the hospital to have his tonsils removed!

- *Don't post slides* for presentations with pictures and videos unless you have permission to do so. Remove these before the presentation goes to the Web. Replace them with descriptions of what was there.

- *Minimize problems* by removing anything from written reports that could cause embarrassment or harm to the child later. Blur pictures where it makes sense; if giving the name of a school, don't give its address!

Care of Data

It is important to safeguard the data gathered during an evaluation and the media on which they are stored, for three reasons. First, some of the material may be commercially sensitive. The team owes to the client a duty of care, and probably a legal duty as well, to look after this material. It is possible that a confidentiality agreement has been signed relating to this, but the duty of course remains even if there is no formal agreement. Such material needs to be kept under lock and key until the report is finished, and even for a period after that, to allow for follow-up questions. After that, it should be destroyed or given to the client. Sometimes clients are not aware of the ethics, so make sure they know what they can and cannot do with the data and how it should be handled.

Second, some material may be about identifiable individuals: the children involved in the study. Questionnaires may have names on them, or photographs or videotapes may have been taken. Even if this material does not appear to be sensitive, it is still personal data and must be treated as such. Such data is covered by data protection legislation in many countries, and there may be regulations about its storage and use.

Third, the data is needed to complete the report! Even material that isn't about identifiable individuals or isn't commercially sensitive must be handled with care purely for pragmatic reasons. Data must be safely stored. Agreements with the clients or local legislation may specify what is required. If not, a sensible minimum security system is to keep the data in a locked storage area with a system in place for signing material out and in when it is being used.

How Long Should Data Be Kept?

A conflict exists between the desire to keep data and raw materials for possible further analysis or to answer questions and the desire to destroy sensitive and personal data when the analysis is done to protect both the children involved and the interests of the clients. Consequently, there is no simple answer to the question of how long data should be kept after a study. Ideally, the consent agreement (see Chapter 4) should specify how long the data will be kept so everyone is aware of the situation in advance.

It is standard practice in many research organizations to keep data for five years after the first publication of the results to allow challenges to the findings from the academic community to be addressed. But in the case of a commercial evaluation, this kind of time scale would be overcautious. In reality, data should be kept for only as long as "necessary." How long that is depends on the circumstances, but it should be agreed on in advance with all relevant stakeholders.

It sounds like an easy thing to dispose of data once the time has arrived. However, it may not be that simple, especially in the case of electronically stored data. Apart from deleting files from a computer directory, it may be necessary to overwrite the medium (e.g., the disk) to ensure that deletion has taken place or to trace and delete automatically made backups.

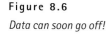

Figure 8.6

Data can soon go off!

Tip

Take technical advice and establish a system for storing, backing up, and deleting data at the appropriate times. Ensure that the technicians involved in the deletion processes understand the importance of following the procedures.

Reflecting on the Process

During analysis and reporting, it is a good idea to reflect on the evaluation activity, especially if it was part of a research project and may have been designed to discover a particular solution. In the reflection of PlaTUI, the evaluation team spent some time considering how the study design affected the evaluation and focused particularly on the difficulties that working with the entire school class had brought to the study. Some notes that were made during the reflection are shown in Figure 8.7.

A notebook can be invaluable for jotting down what worked and what didn't and for keeping ideas for any future activities. The following questions can assist in reflection:

- Did the evaluation yield any surprises?
- Were there any technical problems that could have been avoided?

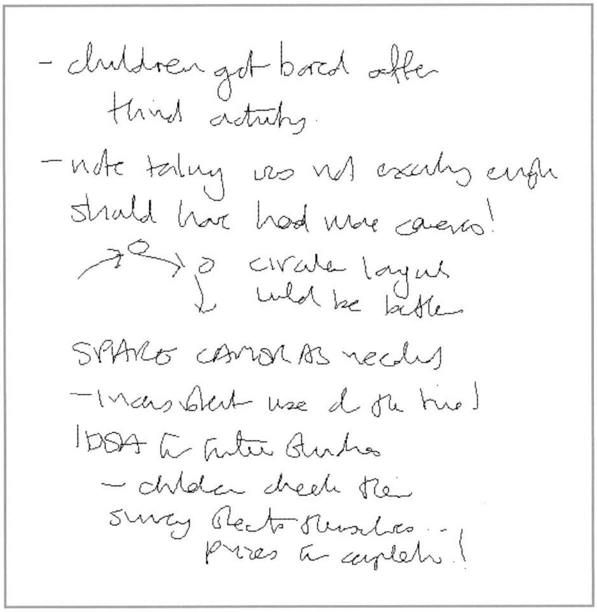

Figure 8.7
Reflecting on PlaTUI.

- What worked well?
- Was the activity appropriate for the children?
- Was the evaluation method appropriate for the children?
- Were the children fully occupied?
- Did the teacher or parent have anything really useful to say?

Make notes of the thoughts you and other evaluators had both immediately after the day and later on. This will ensure that the next evaluation will be even better!

Summary

The preceding three chapters have walked you through the process of carrying out an evaluation. While a particular example has been given in each, the general principles are portable to other situations and different contexts. The remainder of the book concentrates on describing specific evaluation methods. Evaluators will need to bring together best practice from the methods chapters with the practical tips given in Chapters 6, 7, and 8 to ensure that their evaluations take place with minimal possibility of error and frustration.

PART 3

METHODS OF EVALUATION

CHAPTER 9

RECORDING AND LOGGING

This chapter describes a range of technological solutions to the problem of recording interaction between children and products. These technologies are normally used alongside, or as part of, the evaluation methods described in subsequent chapters. The technologies covered include automated logging of interactions, video and audio recording, and gaze tracking.

Automated logging involves recording the user's inputs to a system in a way that is not intrusive so that the user's actions can be examined or analyzed later. Video and audio technologies have obvious applications for recording users' reactions in observation studies, but they can also be used in interviews as an alternative to simultaneous note taking and in usability tests as a convenient method of recording task completion times. Gaze-tracking technologies can be used to record (with varying degrees of accuracy) where users are looking as they perform tasks.

Automated Logging

Logging can be done at a number of levels. At the lowest level, user keystrokes and mouse movements can be recorded, or the evaluator may be interested in higher-level actions, such as which pages of a website are visited and for how long. For low-level logging, in a typical PC setup user inputs that might be logged could be a mouse movement, a mouse click, or a key press. Usually each input is recorded in a text file along with a timestamp. Higher-level logging is done in fundamentally the same way; it is just that a record is made only of a subset of the users' actions. Sometimes the system's outputs to the user are recorded as well, usually in the form of a video recording of the screen display. System-generated events (such as processes starting or ending) may also be logged.

Such recordings are useful because the user's actions can be replayed in real time (or at a different speed, if required) so an evaluator can discover what the user did—with either a video recording of the user's screen or the record of the user's inputs as the input channel—and so can "redo" the user's actions. This latter approach doesn't always work. For example, the user may be interacting with a system (such as the Web) that cannot be guaranteed to behave in an entirely repeatable way. Alternatively, or in addition, the file of recorded user actions can be analyzed without significant replaying—for example, by counting the occurrences of certain actions of interest.

Recording the Data

Normally, the user's actions are recorded in a text file or in a more structured form (a spreadsheet is a common format) to make the analysis easier. The files can become large, particularly where interactions are recorded in detail, such as when logging mouse (or other pointing-device) movements, gestures, or other multimodal interactions.

Screen output is normally recorded as a video, using one of the standard codes used in other video applications. Full-screen resolution isn't necessarily required. Nevertheless, file sizes can become very large if lengthy interactions are logged.

Software for Logging

Although logging is relatively easy, analysis and interpretation of the results can be hard work. Fortunately for the evaluator, software is available to help with both logging and analysis. Techsmith's Morae (see *www.techsmith.com/morae.asp*) and the Noldus Observer XT (see *http://www.noldus.com/site/doc200703006*) are examples of commercial products that can assist with logging user inputs, screen outputs (efficiently compressed), and relevant system events. They also include tools to assist with the analysis of the resulting recordings and with the presentation of the results.

Practicalities

A worthwhile logging system is transparent to the user, meaning that the evaluator can capture the data without informing the user. But this kind of electronic eavesdropping would clearly be unethical, in the same way as observing users without informing them that they are being watched (see Chapter 4). Children should be told that their actions are being recorded even though this knowledge may make them self-conscious and affect their behavior. As discussed in Chapter 4, the explanation should be at a level commensurate with their age.

A practical issue to be considered is that not all applications can be logged with the same ease. There are two problems. The first is that to capture the data the evaluator must have access (either directly or through logging software) to the low-level operating-system functions that receive the user inputs. Sometimes this isn't possible—for example, with dedicated devices such as handheld games or electronic toys.

Tip

When a prototype is being built for an evaluation, it may be possible to build in data-logging routines without too much extra effort.

The second problem is that capturing the data requires some processing and disk storage time, particularly if the screen output is being recorded. In cases where the logging software runs on the same processor as the application itself, it may affect the performance of the application being evaluated. For many applications the processing time for logging will be insignificant, but for video games or other processor-intensive graphical applications, the delays caused by the recording process can affect the appearance of the application for the user, thus working against the purposes of the evaluation.

Video and Audio

Across a range of methods discussed in the subsequent chapters, it may be helpful, or essential, to capture moving images or voice recordings of participants. A video record of the user's interactions can be invaluable in analyzing an observation session; an audio or video record of an interview can be very useful too.

The Technology

For evaluation studies, one requirement is usually to capture on video children's behavior, such as facial expressions, body language, or hand gestures. Small and inexpensive cameras may be sufficient for doing this. In some cases you will need a higher resolution, and for screen-based interactions you might want to have this footage mixed with a synchronized stream of video of the screen content. Until recently this required an expensive and bulky infrastructure as would be installed in usability laboratories. Currently it is possible to have a portable setup involving a

Figure 9.1

A minimal observation lab: a laptop computer with the Observer XT software (Noldus Information Technology) and a camcorder connected by a FireWire cable. It can be used for live behavioral observation and video recording and subsequent detailed annotation of the recorded video.

digital video recorder and a laptop; an example is shown in Figure 9.1. This allows almost any room to be converted temporarily into a basic usability laboratory, which makes the availability of observation technology one of the less important factors in deciding whether to test in a laboratory or in the field (see Chapter 5).

Some cameras have built-in microphones, but these are not usually of the highest quality and for some studies are inconvenient to use. With desktop evaluations, it is easier to have a separate microphone that can be placed independently of the camera position. Choosing suitable microphones may be harder than choosing the cameras. The choice depends on the task and the environment where the recording is to be done. Some types of microphones record ambient sound from all directions, whereas others are directional, meaning they pick up sound from one particular direction and minimize background noise from other sources. An ambient microphone may be good for recording activity in a small evaluation lab, but recording field work—in a classroom, for example—might be better done with directional microphones.

If the aim is to record audio only—for example, when interviewing—where video would be superfluous, a handheld sound-recording device can be used. Devices that record in MP3 format are very practical because this format can be used by most audio software tools.

Setup and Use in Usability Labs and Elsewhere

During the 1980s and 1990s, it was common for organizations that were developing or researching interactive systems to establish special-purpose "usability laboratories." These facilities vary in size and technological sophistication. Possible setups for a usability laboratory are described by Dumas and Redish (1993). The basic setup consists of an area where participants test the product, an observation room from which one can view the testing area through one-way mirrors, and video-recording equipment. The technology installation in such laboratories involves controls for the cameras, mixing of signals from different cameras, and recording equipment.

Usability Labs for Children

When working with children, some adaptations to a usability laboratory are helpful, or a special-purpose laboratory can be set up. An example of the latter is the KidsLab at the Eindhoven University of Technology, whose design is in line with the recommendations made by Hanna et al. (1997) for usability labs for children. This lab consists of a main testing area separated from an observation room by one-way mirrors. It has furniture that is appropriate for children younger than 9 and adult-sized furniture that can be used for older children. The decoration is colorful and pleasant, and curtains have been placed to conceal the one-way mirrors when appropriate. Care has been taken not to go overboard with childish decorations or toys. Figure 9.2 shows a view into the testing area during a test session.

The lab has three cameras, with remote-controlled pan, tilt, and zoom, mounted high up so they do not face the child directly. Two directional microphones have been placed far from the child (one is visible on the top shelf at the very top of Figure 9.2); these are sufficient to capture the children's voices. The observation room is equipped with mixers for the audio and video signals arriving from the cameras and the PC. Sometimes the observation room is used as a waiting room for parents, siblings, and teachers who escort or accompany the test participants. The room mirror allows the parent to observe the child without interfering with the experiment and to be nearby if needed.

Placing Cameras and Microphones

In a purpose-built laboratory the cameras and microphones can be wall or ceiling mounted, safely out of the children's reach! Using cameras with remote-controlled motors for moving and focusing is much easier than having to climb up every time

Figure 9.2

The KidsLab at Eindhoven University of Technology.

they need adjusting. The temptation to use the motors to move the cameras during a session should be avoided, however, as even very quiet motors can cause a distraction. The aim in placing cameras is that there should be one showing the user's facial expressions and one, or even better two, showing the user's posture and what she is doing with the keyboard, mouse, or whatever devices are being used (see Figure 9.3). It is very useful to do a pilot test of the setup, with a child of the appropriate size, to check that the children are in the shot before the real recording starts. It isn't usually necessary to have a camera filming the computer screen (if there is one) since the display can normally be captured directly.

Tip

Remember that children are more active and restless than adults. They may stand up and continue with the task when you had assumed they would be seated. It may be necessary to zoom the cameras out further than you normally would with adults, just to keep them in the shot!

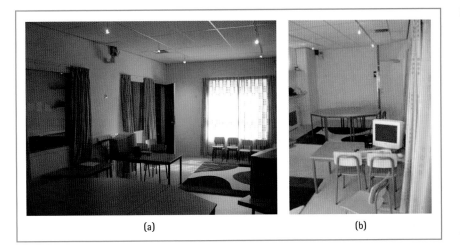

(a)   (b)

Figure 9.3

Views of the testing area of the KidsLab. Notice the ceiling-mounted cameras at the corner of the room and above the desk with the PC. A directed microphone can be seen on a shelf under the ceiling-mounted camera.

Tripods for video cameras are very useful, but a full-sized tripod can take up a lot of space and poses a tripping hazard for active children. The camera is probably at more risk than the children! It is often better to have a smaller tripod and to mount it on a table or shelf where it will be out of the way. Temporary adhesive (e.g., the puttylike substances marketed as Blu-Tack, Fun-Tak, or BlueStik) is very useful for fixing the tripod to the surface it is resting on.

Lighting

For the observer to be able to pick out facial expressions and small actions from the video recording, the children must be in reasonably good lighting. Ceiling lights may be fine if they are in the right place (that is, in front of the child rather than behind her, where they will be casting a shadow over her face). If the room lighting isn't ideal, it may be possible to take advantage of reflective surfaces to improve the lighting on the subject. It probably isn't helpful to set up special lighting in front of the subject, as this will be distracting.

Cables and Power Supply

Most video cameras can be run from batteries or from electrical outlets. Batteries reduce the number of potentially hazardous trailing cables, and the position of the camera isn't dependent on the availability of power sockets.

Tip

Take along a spare battery pack for the camera *and* a power cable just in case!

Ethical and Practical Issues When Working with Children

Always remember that video and audio recordings of people constitute personal data. In principle, a child can be identified from the audio track even if his face isn't shown. Appropriate consent is needed before recordings are made or shown (see Chapter 4).

When children are being recorded, they often take an interest in the equipment. It is sensible to start the session by explaining what is being recorded, pointing out the camera or cameras and demonstrating the microphones. In a usability lab you can show the children the observation room and, in particular, the monitors that are normally present to display the image that is being recorded (see Figure 9.2). If this isn't done, the children are likely to notice things during the session and become distracted from their task or activity. In any case, it is only fair that they should understand, at an age-appropriate level, what is going on.

Tip

If children seem anxious about the cameras, it may be helpful to allow them to try recording something themselves and viewing the recording.

Investigators might be tempted to hide the cameras and microphones to avoid the delays caused by explaining and demonstrating the equipment and to avoid the behavioral problems described in the following paragraph. Parents and guardians might well give consent for such a course of action. But we believe that this would be unethical, and we can't recommend it. Even young children deserve to know when they are being recorded. There must be a very good reason to justify "covert surveillance," and interaction evaluation is probably never a good one!

Many young children are fascinated by cameras and microphones. Generally they like to be recorded, and they often want to see or listen to the recording afterward. Some children (particularly older ones) are very self-conscious in front of a camera and become very static, whereas others become hyperactive and want to perform. They will get very close to the microphone and may yell into it. If the microphone looks like the kind that singers use, they will pick it up and sing into it. Or they will move very close to the video camera and make faces.

However, the novelty soon wears off, and after a few minutes the children almost always forget that the recording equipment is there, even though they are aware that it is still recording, and they get on with the task. Once the first few minutes of a recording session with children are over, we have experienced few problems.

Drawing attention to the equipment in any way during the session—for instance, by moving the camera or adjusting its settings—is best avoided. This reminds the child that the equipment is there, and it can start off another bout of performing for the camera.

Tip

Don't have a camera operator. Having someone holding the video camera or constantly moving or adjusting it attracts showing-off behavior, from younger children in particular. Set the camera running on a tripod and leave it alone.

Gaze Tracking

Gaze tracking (or eye tracking) is the process of working out and recording what the users are looking at from moment to moment as they carry out an activity. This record can be very useful in helping to work out what the user is doing, how, and why. A wide range of technologies is available for gaze tracking; different technologies are appropriate for different situations.

Gaze-Tracking Measurements

Early observations of a subject's eyes enabled researchers to conclude that the gaze point does not move smoothly across text when reading, or across a scene when viewing it. The gaze point is moved rapidly, then the gaze is fixed for a time, and then it moves on to another point. These movements are called *saccades,* and the stationary points are called *fixations.* There are only about three fixations on a typical line of text when an experienced reader is reading. Saccades are typically 30 to 50 milliseconds long; fixations are longer. The length varies a lot, according to how much information needs to be processed. Interestingly, people are usually not aware of the locations of their fixations; if asked after a gaze-tracking session what they looked at, they may well be wrong.

Figure 9.4

A heatmap of a web page obtained using the Tobii gaze-tracking system. Red and yellow areas are those viewed frequently and for long fixations, green are viewed less, and the rest are hardly looked at by users. Source: Gaze-tracking image courtesy of Tobii Technology AB. Website screenshot courtesy of BBC.

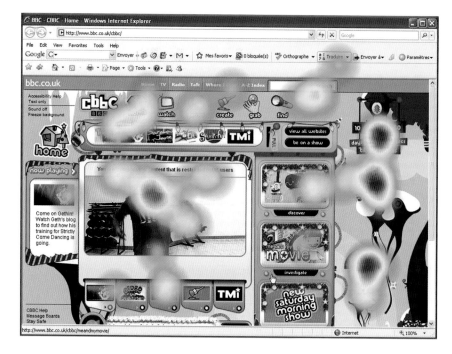

Gaze-tracking technologies attempt to measure the position and duration of the fixations. It is usually possible to conclude that an unusually long fixation (or repeated fixations on the same object) is caused by the object being especially interesting or especially confusing. Both of these are relevant in user interface design and evaluation. Also of interest are points that are not fixated on when the designer felt that they should be—for example, onscreen instructions. If users don't look at the instructions, they are either unnecessary or in the wrong place.

Outputs Produced by Current Systems

Figure 9.4 shows a "hotspot," or "heatmap," image that tells you which parts of a screen image a user (or possibly a number of users) is focusing on over a period of time. It is easy to see from such an image which parts of the screen image attract users' attention and which don't. Figure 9.5 shows a "gaze plot" for a single user for a brief period, perhaps a few seconds. It illustrates the sequence and length of fixations. The gaze plot can show the effort needed to locate information.

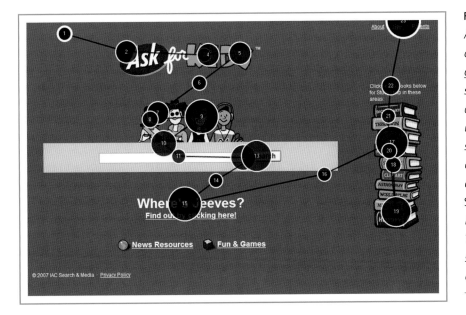

Figure 9.5

A web page "gaze plot" obtained with the Tobii gaze-tracking system shows positions and durations of a single user's fixations. Lines show the saccades. The circles' size indicates duration of fixations. Source: Gaze-tracking image courtesy of Tobii Technology AB. Web site screenshot courtesy of Ask.com.

Example

Santamaria (2003) described the use of gaze tracking in the evaluation of a children's website with children age 8, using a retrospective think-aloud protocol. Gaze plots (see Figure 9.5) were recorded while the children interacted with the website; afterward, they were shown the plots. These showed where they had been looking during the interaction, and, of course, where they had *not* been looking. Using the image as a mnemonic, children were able to discuss why, for example, they were looking at one part of the screen when the designer had hoped they would be observing something else—for example, a message.

Gaze-Tracking Technology

Gaze tracking can be done by fixing markers directly to the eye. These techniques can be traced back to Javal (1879; cited in Richardson and Spivey, 2004), who was interested in the physiological processes of reading. Direct-contact methods with contact lenses are still used in some situations because they provide the greatest accuracy.

But the intrusive nature of these methods means they are hard to justify for interaction evaluation, and we certainly can't recommend them for use with children.

Current eye-tracking technology relies on the fact that when a light is shone on the eye's pupil it is reflected in four different ways from different parts of the eye's structure. It reflects from the front of the cornea, the back of the cornea, the front of the lens, and the back of the lens. These reflections are called the first, second, third, and fourth *Purkinje images*, named after the nineteenth-century Czech physiologist who discovered them. These images each behave differently with respect to head and eyeball movements. The dual Purkinje method (Crane and Steele, 1985) uses two of these reflections (the first and fourth). Comparing the positions enables the gaze point to be followed even when the head is moving slightly.

Tracking the reflections in both eyes also helps, usually because, if the user turns her head or puts her hand in front of her face, one eye may be illuminated by the light source and be in the range of the camera but the other may not.

Hardware for Participants

For many potential applications of eye tracking, the ideal system would allow tracking of the gaze point while the subject could move his head freely. There are two ways to achieve this: Either the camera (or cameras) viewing the eyes must move with the head, implying that it must be mounted on a helmet of some kind, or the position and orientation of the head must be continuously recorded by fixed desk-mounted cameras and combined with observations of the eye positions (which can be done using the same cameras) to calculate the gaze direction and thus what is being fixed upon.

Head-Mounted Systems

Until recently, head-mounted systems were of limited use, particularly for children, because the size and weight of the cameras, and the fact that they needed to be linked by cable to recording equipment and computers, meant that freedom of movement was significantly restricted. Nevertheless, they had their uses, particularly in situations where the user was seated and wearing a helmet anyway—as pilots do, for example. Today, cameras are smaller and lighter, and wireless communication technology is also small enough to be mounted on a helmet with the cameras, making it possible to dispense with cables.

However, wearing a helmet covered with electronic devices is a very unusual sensation for children, and it is almost certain to interfere with normal behavior. So

Figure 9.6

A desk-mounted gaze-tracking system.

although they would work in a technical sense, we can't recommend the use of head-mounted systems with children in evaluation studies.

Desk-Mounted Systems

The alternative approach is to place the cameras on a desk or another surface fairly close to the area in which the subject will be looking. In the case of a screen-based application, the cameras are usually best located on the desk immediately underneath the screen (see Figure 9.6). These systems have the major advantage that the user isn't physically constrained or encumbered.

In practice, tracking through complete freedom of movement is unlikely to be achieved, as multiple cameras would be needed to keep the eyes in view, but major steps have been made in the direction of allowing free movement. Furthermore, if the head does move out of range temporarily, it is possible to quickly pick up the tracking again when it moves back into view. Some systems can also track the gaze of more than one user at a time, which is particularly useful for work with children, who often work in pairs or groups when using interactive products.

Usually gaze direction can be followed over a fairly wide range, covering, for example, a desk surface (with keyboard and mouse) as well as a screen. Systems can be set up with 3D models of the environment in which the test is taking place so that they can calculate what objects are being looked at during any particular time. This type of technology is practicable for use with children; it is nonintrusive and does not seriously constrain movement, so naturalistic use of a product can be analyzed.

Figure 9.7

*The nine calibration
target points.*

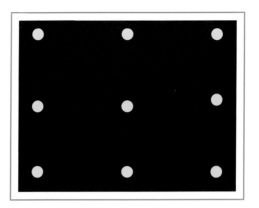

Setup and Calibration with Children

When working on gaze tracking with children, it would be nice if they could simply walk up to the system and begin the task in a natural way. Unfortunately, this isn't possible. All of the methods described in this chapter can be quite accurate in measuring the *relative* position of a gaze fixation, compared to other fixations by the same person. But all of them suffer from the problem that the *absolute* gaze point can't be established with any accuracy except by setting up the system for the individual user so there are reference points with which to compare the observations. This process is called *calibration*. The procedures vary according to the technology in use, but they all take up some of the user's time. For current systems, calibration time is on the order of minutes.

Typically, for the system to have some reference points from which to work out the actual gaze position, it is necessary for the user to focus on a number of points in the target area for several seconds each. Often this is done by displaying a colored spot on a contrasting background. This is repeated, usually, for nine different screen positions (see Figure 9.7). This can severely test a young child's patience, and it may be impossible to get a very young child to cooperate with this calibration at all. Sometimes with young children, the calibration test is reduced to five points (in the corners and the center) or even just one point (in the center), but this leads to loss of accuracy. Another partial solution is to replace the target spot with an amusing animation that will attract a child for long enough to perform the calibration. This option is included with many current commercial systems.

Using Gaze Tracking with Children

Using these video-based systems is an expensive option; the hardware and software aren't cheap, and the person calibrating it requires at least a day's training and a good deal of practice to make the process run smoothly. Read, Kelly, and Birkett (2006) report some informal testing of gaze tracking with children. They note that it became more difficult to follow the gaze path as time passed, presumably due to the children becoming tired or bored with the task. It would be a sensible precaution in view of this finding to keep tasks short where children are involved or to allow significant breaks during data gathering.

All gaze-tracking systems are prone to periods of data loss—gaps between fixations that are too long to be saccades. These may be caused by the eyes being occluded or shaded, the head moving out of range, or limitations of the technology. Desk-mounted video-based systems usually have a data loss of 10 to 15 percent. A study of on-screen reading by young children using the desk-mounted Tobii 1750 system (Renshaw and Dickenson, 2007) found a data loss rate of 18 percent on average, only slightly worse that one would expect with adults.

Further research, and more practical experience, is needed to get the best out of gaze-tracking systems when used by children, but the difficulties do not appear to be insurmountable and many potential application areas are available. For example, many gaze-tracking studies of the use of websites have been performed with adults (Nielsen, 2007; Nielsen and Pernice, 2007); these have led to a better understanding of web page layout. Children also use the Web extensively, and probably not in the same ways as adults. Gaze-tracking studies would be very helpful in optimizing children's website layouts.

Summary

Logging the activities of children while they use software products is an attractive option for usability studies. These methods are unobtrusive and can often run alongside other evaluation activities. Some methods need special treatment when used with children but, in general, the use of these methods is relatively straightforward although care must be taken, especially when recording children, to ensure that the logging method does not interfere with the interaction of the child with the product.

Further Reading

Duchowski (2007) is a comprehensive study of gaze-tracking technologies and applications. The article by Poole and Ball (2006) looks more specifically at uses in evaluation studies.

CHAPTER 10

OBSERVATION METHODS

Observation is invaluable when it comes to evaluating products for children. Observing children who test a prototype or product can provide new insights to designers and can provide solid evidence to support design recommendations or other conclusions based on your evaluation. It can have a profound impact on your project when you or, better, several members of your development team witness how children experience the evaluated product.

In the context of usability engineering and interaction design, observation is often approached rather informally, and related textbooks omit clear methodological advice for setting up and executing observations. Implicitly, a particular type of observation is assumed by default, where the experimenter as a usability expert is on the lookout for behaviors that could be related to usability faults. In these cases, a lack of explicit planning and structure can lead to problems: Observers may fail to notice aspects of the interaction that are the most useful and crucial for the design team and the records made may be incomplete or ambiguous.

This chapter discusses approaches to observation that are applicable for evaluating products with children. It then discusses in more detail a particular form of observation called *structured observation*. Participant observation, specifying the focus of an observation, and coding schemes are also touched on. A specific example of a coding scheme is presented.

Types of Observation

Generally speaking, the term *observation* refers to an examination of a phenomenon that results in a description suitable for the purposes of a research or evaluation study. In the case of evaluation, the phenomenon studied is the use of the product, whether simulated, actual, spontaneous, or staged for the purposes of the study.

Observations can be direct or indirect. Direct observations rely on the senses of the observer, who might watch or listen to how children use the product evaluated. Indirect observations are those where records of use are created through technology, such as logs of user interactions, logs of eye gaze, and so forth (see Chapter 9).

This chapter focuses on direct observation and on observation that is supported by audio and video records; in both cases, similar issues arise for preparing materials, training observers, and recording observations.

Realism in Observation Studies

Chapter 3 discussed the tension between trying to achieve realism in a test session versus trying to control the various factors that you don't want to influence the outcome of your evaluation study, such as other children, unplanned interruptions, environmental noise, and technical problems. This same tension extends to observation studies. Observation can be conducted in the field, where children use the technology or in the lab where advanced observation facilities or technical support is available. In both cases, you may be observing a use of the product that is very close to actual use. You may also choose to observe a highly structured and controlled use of the product. This way you can manage or minimize the impact of contextual factors on the outcome of the evaluation.

When it comes to observation, the realism of the situation observed and the validity of the findings are greatly influenced by one important parameter of your study setup, namely, the interaction between the observer and the participants. As an observer interested in testing a product, you will, more often than not, want to limit interaction with the testers to the minimum necessary so you can be reasonably sure that you are not influencing the conclusions of the evaluation. In some cases, though, this may not be feasible or desirable.

Participant Observation

Especially when product use is embedded in daily activities or social interactions between members of a group and is very much dependent on context (e.g., a text-messaging application for teenagers), mere observation and analysis of manifest behaviors are not sufficient to understand motivations, thoughts, and social relations within groups of people. Observers in such cases often choose to engage with participants and embed themselves in a group, turning themselves and their discovery process into observation instruments. This approach is often referred to as participant observation, a method that is closely associated with ethnography.

Participant observation is popular as a technique for working with adults, especially at the opening phases of a design project when attempting to understand the situation in which you plan to introduce a technology. It can be very useful when the goal of your evaluation is to evaluate the role of a product (see Chapter 3), the usage patterns that are likely to emerge, how and which conventions are formed, and, more generally, the social aspects of the product's usage. Participant observation is less applicable for analyzing user experience at a more cognitive and sensorial level or for evaluating user performance.

Participant observation with children can happen, for example, at a school or youth club. In these cases, the participant observer needs to embed herself in the social group studied or even in their associated online communities. For ethics reason, the participant observer should tell the children and the parents her role and goals. Participant observation requires a lot of time and effort and is best thought of as a research method rather than a method you might readily apply in the context and lifecycle of a design project.

Passive and Naturalistic Observation

The opposite of participant observation is passive observation, which requires that the interaction with the participant is minimized. Passive observation during the evaluation can help minimize potential influence on the tester. When evaluation is conducted in a lab, this might mean retreating to a separate observation room where the participant cannot see the evaluator or at least avoiding reactions to the interactions of the tester, such as appreciation, surprise, or disappointment. Taking care to be passive, even when not separated by one-way mirrors, can help protect the validity of your findings.

Naturalistic observation is when a passive observation is carried out in the field while the observer tries to minimize his influence on the situation. For example, you may want to have your educational application used and therefore evaluated within a classroom. Observing unobtrusively how children in the class go about their activities while, among other things using your product is an example of naturalistic observation (with the exception, of course, that the product itself constitutes an intervention in the children's classroom activities).

The Evaluation of pOwerball

An example that illustrates the pros and cons of different observation techniques is pOwerball (Figure 10.1), a tabletop-augmented reality pinball game designed to encourage children with mixed abilities to play together (Brederode et al., 2005). Children played the game without receiving any specific tasks from the evaluator. The evaluator acted as both technical support and facilitator during the experiment, instructing children when to start and taking care of observation equipment and the game itself.

The observer was not completely passive during the game play, and children interacted with him—for example, to ask to play once more or to receive instructions in the beginning and explanations about the video recording—but they were mostly oblivious to him during play.

The evaluation of pOwerball focused on whether the game was fun and whether social interactions happened as part of the play—for example, to coordinate actions but also to comment on the game. Children reacted positively to the game, and there were clear observable signs of many of the desired behaviors. It was also clearly visible how the augmented reality features were largely ignored by the children, which went against the expectations of the design team regarding this technology. This latter result led to significant changes for the next version of pOwerball, where the tangible interface favored by the design team was replaced by a touch screen and traditional buttons.

This positive evaluation of the game did not answer unequivocally the overriding question for the designer: Does this game support social interaction between children? To answer this question, a longer-term naturalistic observation could evaluate the game use in context and its impact on social interactions between children over time. For example, it could examine a series of questions: Do children come back to the game? Do they interact more or in other ways compared to when playing other multiplayer games available to them?

Figure 10.1
From the evaluation of pOwerball, a tabletop-augmented reality game that aims to encourage social interaction among children.

Structured Observation

A direct observation can be structured or unstructured. An unstructured observation starts with open questions where the observer tries to identify and record interaction aspects in a holistic way. In this context, *holistic* means including rich descriptions of context without a priori limiting of the range of events or behaviors recorded. The advantage of unstructured observation is its open-endedness; you allow the evaluation to surprise you and are open to new discoveries. In practice, though, lack of focus can cause some problems. It can lead to a low number of observations and low reliability of results between observers because each observer influences data collection with her own mindset, knowledge, and experience. The observations recorded also may be many but irrelevant or contrived and may not serve your evaluation goals. They may be very difficult to analyze because they are too numerous and too diverse.

In the remainder of this chapter, we focus on a more structured and reliable form of direct and passive observation that is called structured observation. These are the steps for planning and performing a structured observation:

- Determine the focus of your observation.
- Develop observation guides and forms.

- Recruit and train observers (if necessary).
- Carry out the observation.
- Analyze and interpret findings.

Tip

Even if you are low on resources and have little time, make sure you have an explicit and well-defined focus for your observations during a test.

Determine the Focus

The outcome of any observation study depends crucially on what you are looking for; this is the *focus* of the observation. For example, if you are looking for how children learn to use a product that is new to them, you are likely to notice completely different things than if you are looking for, say, how much they enjoy, and how comfortable they are, using an interactive device. Having a focus means being selective and observing specific events, activities, and behaviors. Having a focus makes it easier to keep within time and resource constraints. Observers can make more numerous, more detailed, and more reliable observations when they have a specific focus.

The focus of the observation should follow from the goals of the evaluation study. It should aim to uncover evidence that will help answer the questions driving the evaluation. Usability evaluations often focus on errors that users make, such as misunderstanding the workings of the interactive artifacts presented to them. Unfortunately, this focus is typically not stated or deliberated upon, and many related textbooks typically omit any relevant discussion. Although it is often appropriate to adopt the preceding aspects of the interaction as your focus, you are better advised to choose the focus while taking into account the project context and the goals of the evaluation. (See Figure 10.2.)

The evaluator must make a plan of what events to observe and what utterances to record according to the goals of the evaluation. Earlier chapters discussed how, when interacting with a product, a child may assume and combine several roles: learner, player, and user. The focus of the observation should then be set accordingly to behaviors, events, and speech relating to these roles.

Signs that children are having fun are when they continue to use a product or become oblivious to their environment. Happy exclamations, leaning forward, and

Figure 10.2

Observable signs of collaboration between children during the evaluation of aMAZEd (Al Mahmud et al., 2007). This tabletop-augmented reality game involves sensing psychophysiological measurements. Observations focused on the children's behaviors toward and verbal responses to the tangible elements, the bluff that was inserted in the game rules, and the use of the sensing devices.

Tip

In the formative stages of the product design process, look for signs of both design defects or problems and things that are working well.

smiling are also signs that the child is enjoying himself. Signs of a child not having fun can be sighs, frowns, fidgeting, distracted behaviors, or disturbing other children. Even the absence of any emotion should be noted as a potential problem with either the product or the evaluation setup.

To assess the educational value of the product, the goals of the evaluation are influenced by the pedagogy behind the product—for example, whether the intention is to

Setting the Focus of Observation on the Basis of Pedagogy

At the University of Sussex in the United Kingdom, researchers explored the educational potential of tangible interfaces (Price et al., 2003). With tangible interfaces, interaction with the computer happens by manipulating physical artifacts rather than through standard interactive devices such a button, keyboard, or mouse. The application was called *Hunting the Snark,* where children used the tangibles to explore a game world and hunt an elusive virtual game character, the Snark. (See Figure 10.3 on page 174.)

Children tested the game in the lab, and researchers analyzed video recordings of the play, observing the children's actions, interactions, gestures, and oral responses. These were coded on the following five aspects that characterize "playful learning," which is the pedagogical approach the researchers had adopted.

Exploration through interaction. Children were seen trying out different uses of the tangible objects. Through trial and error, they inferred causal relationships between the behavior of the interactive objects offered to them. By comparing cases where children succeeded in developing an understanding of the game world to those where they failed, the need to match experiences within the game and experiences from the real world was identified.

Engagement. The researchers observed and recorded exclamations of excitement, evidence of anticipation for the appearance of the Snark character, and signs that the children were captivated by the game.

Reflection. Spontaneous verbal interactions and discussions between children during the game or at the end of the game indicated that they were trying to understand what happened and why. The more ambiguous and abstract representations used in the game led to more varied and creative interpretations.

Imagination, creativity, and thinking at different levels of abstraction. An analysis of the children's reflections and comments on the game showed that they were able to describe the game at different levels of abstraction, sometimes focusing on the Snark's emotions and other times describing higher-level attributes such as precociousness or mischievousness.

Collaboration. The observers found evidence of collaboration encouraged by the features of the game by looking for signs of children taking individual responsibility for some parts of the interaction, handing over responsibility to other children, or verbally coordinating their activity, taking turns, and assuming roles.

help teach particular skills or simply to foster specific social behaviors. Observation can then examine whether the test participants exhibit desirable behaviors.

Develop Guides and Forms

The observation guide should be developed by the evaluator, but it may be helpful to involve in its development someone with expertise at the particular age of the children (e.g., a teacher or, at the very least, other members of the design team).

The guide can be as simple as a list of aspects of the interaction that constitute the focus of the study set by the evaluation team. With some hierarchical organization of topics, this focus can easily include 15 to 20 items. Such a rich and detailed focus may require more effort for the observation and can be excessive in the context of iterative testing. In this case a more concise observation guide should be made with only 3 to 5 topics.

It is good practice to define clearly the content of each category in the observation guide, give examples, and update the observation guide between observations to eliminate inconsistencies and ambiguities. You may find it useful to adapt an existing

Figure 10.3
(a) Using the Snooper (implemented on a handheld device), two boys browse the physical space around them for virtual objects that allow access to activity spaces where the virtual Snark character can be found. (b) Girls feed the Snark with RFID-tagged "food" items. The Snark's likes and dislikes are expressed by an animation in the "pond." Source: *Sara Price, Knowledge Lab.*

(a)

(b)

observation guide that has been used in a similar study or to use one of the codes discussed later in this chapter. The observation guide details two types of information: (1) the categories of events that must be noticed with a definition or example and (2) the information that the observer must record when observing a specific type of event.

Whether observation happens live during the evaluation or later when watching a video recording of it, it should be easy to create the notes. If notes are kept on

Shorthand	Explanation	Example
DSTR	Distraction: The child engages in other activities than the evaluation requires.	• The child requests to go to the restroom. • The child plays with the lab equipment or furnishings instead of performing the evaluation. • The child looks around to examine surroundings.

Table 10.1

Example of Elements of a Code Description

paper, some shorthand notation should be provided, and the observation guide should include a summary of the codes used. For example, the observation guide might include an entry like the one in Table 10.1 describing how to code cases where the child is distracted.

The category of behaviors under "distraction" could belong to the higher-level categories of "boredom" or "lack of engagement," which would include other similar descriptions. The codes in Table 10.1, as well as most codes discussed in this chapter, are qualitative. Alternatively, coders can be asked to record quantitative data that indicate numerically the observed level of some behavior of interest. For example, in a classroom setting, you may be characterizing the level of involvement of a single child or a group of children, using a numeric scale. In both cases, coders must be trained to learn how to use codes reliably. What changes is the type of inferences you can draw from your observation afterward and how these support the goals of the evaluation (see Chapter 4).

When focusing on usability, it is typical to code only the occurrence of events that portray that a usability problem has occurred. This is called *event sampling*. However, when evaluating other aspects of a product, like fun or learning, it may be more appropriate to characterize the behavior observed over a time interval. This is called *time sampling*. For example, you may wish to characterize the type of interactions between children for every minute during the game play or the level of concentration and engagement with a classroom learning product every 5 or 10 minutes.

In both cases it is important that the codes do not miss any events or behaviors that are important in relation to evaluation goals. Sampling over time can provide an overall indication for the prevalence of certain behaviors. When evaluating social interactions between children playing together, for example, event-based sampling will help you capture all occurrences of a predefined set of social behaviors, whereas time sampling might be more suitable for understanding how prevalent these behaviors are during the entire play session.

Recruit and Train Observers

If the evaluation includes several long sessions, or when minute details of the interaction are investigated, it can be difficult for a single observer to do the coding alone. This can be because of the sheer amount of work. Working on video might mean that every hour of a recorded session could take 5 to 50 times as long to code, depending on the level of detail of the coding. Another motivation for including coders might be the speed or complexity of the coding that requires attention to more issues than one person can handle at one time. Especially when evaluating the product at the level of detailed interactions, like speech or gestures, events unfold very fast and one coder may find it difficult to maintain focus on all types of events of interest at once.

In general, multiple coders can split up the task of coding either by working in parallel while looking for different (sub)classes of events or by splitting the whole workload vertically and coding individually different sessions or different parts of the session or on different sets of children. For example, one way to split the task horizontally is for one to focus on fun aspects while the other focuses on, say, the difficulties relating to a recognition-based interface, such as a gesture recognizer.

When splitting the coding vertically, the coders must rely on a shared understanding of the coding scheme and use it consistently. Good training and practice with coding a session that the evaluator or some other expert has already coded can help achieve correct and reliable coding.

In cases where you need some guarantees regarding the accuracy of the coding, you should include checks to assess intercoder reliability. To achieve consistent coding, plan a few "checkpoints," where different individuals code the same portion of the material and exchange notes. If you have a video recording of a session, you may want several coders to code specific parts and discuss inconsistent decisions. During this process you may calculate the following reliability metric:

$$Intercoder\ Reliability = \frac{Agreements}{Agreements + Disagreements}$$

Agreement would mean that the same event or observable behavior has been coded with the same code by the two coders. *Disagreement* means that one has not coded it at all or has given it a different code. Some texts on qualitative research methods suggest that this metric should be about 70 percent with little training and should improve to over 90 percent with more training (Miles and Hubermon, 1994). These numbers should be used only indicatively. In practice, you may not have the luxury of training until you reach sufficient reliability between coders. It is important to understand that this metric is too simple to capture some of the trivial cases of agreement between coders, and for most research purposes a more accurate calculation is done using Cohen's kappa coefficient for agreement between coders. More detailed calculations are beyond the scope of this book, but see Siegel and Castellan (1988).

Carry out the Observation

When direct observation is done "live" rather than afterward from a video recording, the observers must devote their full attention to observing, coding, and recording their codes. This means that the facilitation role should be played by a different individual who will receive and take care of guests. In a laboratory setup, the observer will typically sit behind a one-way mirror so the child is not distracted or nervous from being observed. Otherwise, it is wise for the observer to stay out of sight and even be ready to answer a question from the child regarding the kept notes. At the start of the session, the facilitator should explain why the observer is keeping notes and that the child should not pay attention to that person during the test.

Tip

Using special-purpose observation technology (see Chapter 9) equipment can save you a lot of time.

In some cases the task of the observer is very challenging, since events will unfold very quickly and the simple act of noting an occurrence of an event may stop the observer from noticing other events of interest. Prior practice with the coding scheme is valuable in such cases. Special-purpose applications that allow efficient coding of events can be helpful (see Figure 10.4).

In cases where the events of interests are sparser, the observer may have enough time to reflect and note during the evaluation. In a design project involving tight

Figure 10.4 *One tool that supports coding observations either in real time or from video is Observer XT. The video window where the video recording can be viewed and the coding scheme used to annotate the video are shown here. This provides an event log that is synchronized with the video material and other sources of sequential data, such as physiological sensors.* Source: *Courtesy of Noldus Information Technology.*

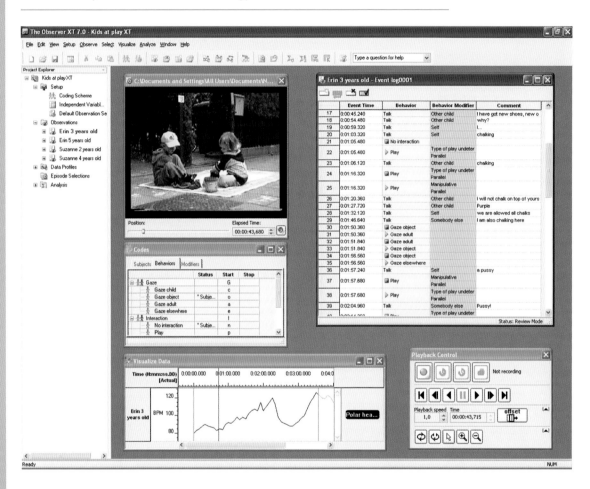

iterative loops, it is very likely that you will not be interested so much in obtaining and analyzing a coded record of the test session as in understanding what is happening and reflecting on necessary improvements to the product. In these cases, rather than meticulously creating large coded transcripts, a few observations based on your high-level focus structure will be what you and your team need to move to the next iterative circle.

Observing the Observers

This vignette comes from a recent evaluation session conducted by students in interaction design. The students who designed the game had meticulously arranged their evaluation process, tasks, and interview techniques, even using some quite advanced methods. The lab was carefully set up and the script well prepared.

During the test, and while one team member was acting as the facilitator, two team members who were on standby for technical troubleshooting kept hovering close to the children, exclaiming in clearly audible whispers and gesticulating vividly every time the children engaged in the behaviors they hoped to observe. Though the children did not engage in any interaction with them directly, it was blatantly clear to them what the design team wanted to see and how they could please them. As is often the case in such situations, children were very positive about the game and gave superlatives in every way they could.

If unchecked, this type of interaction can help get a favorable evaluation conclusion that may give a pleasing but misleading sense of closure and can be a waste of money (and time) for someone who wants to know how to improve a product.

As an observer, you should be attentive, thorough, and, especially if you are a member of the team who designed the product, emotionally distant from your creation. You must be receptive to things going against your expectations, and you should be careful not to let your expectations and beliefs about your product filter through your behavior in a way that could influence test participants.

Analyze and Interpret Findings

The results of the evaluation are presented in two ways:

- *Qualitative*—including the observations of the team and the recorded behaviors of the test participants.
- *Quantitative*—including the number of instances of different categories of observations.

The purpose of analyzing observations will be, eventually, to suggest recommendations for improving the product or questions that must be resolved from other types of analysis. When considering the quantitative results, summaries of the data must be created. At this stage, audio/video excerpts from the test session may be selected for documenting the conclusions from the observation team so they can be shown and discussed with project members.

Observations and summary descriptions refer to the observable behaviors manifested during the evaluation. In most evaluations, you will need to make the transition from observations of indications or manifestations of problems with the prototype or product to recommendations for design improvements.

Codes for Body Language and Engagement

An interesting observation study of children's behavior during the use of educational multimedia products was conducted by Mota and Picard (2002). They developed a technology for automatically measuring the level of student engagement based on sensing pressure patterns on the seat of a chair. As part of this research, human coders were asked to code body language.

The coding scheme was developed based on an earlier theoretical model of body motion. Its development was iterative until the three coders could code reliably and consistently. Codes for scoring body posture were sitting on the edge, leaning forward, leaning forward right, leaning forward left, sitting upright, leaning back, leaning back right, leaning back left, and slumping back. Mota and Picard reported an overall agreement of 83 percent using Cohen's kappa.

To compare body postures with level of engagement, they asked three experienced teachers to evaluate the level of engagement based on video of the children obtained from three different angles, a screen capture of the game, and text indicating the level of difficulty. Mota and Picard found that teachers could label reliably the affective states of high, medium, and low interest, taking a break, and bored. Teachers obtained an overall agreement of 78.6 percent using these codes. (See Figure 10.5.)

Figure 10.5 *The teachers' coding interface allowed playing synchronized video footage from two angles and the game screen capture. Teachers could see the game level of difficulty on a color-coded time line, browse through the movie (through the banner at the top), and code affective states using the colored affective labels at the bottom of the screen.*
Source: *Courtesy of S. Mota.*

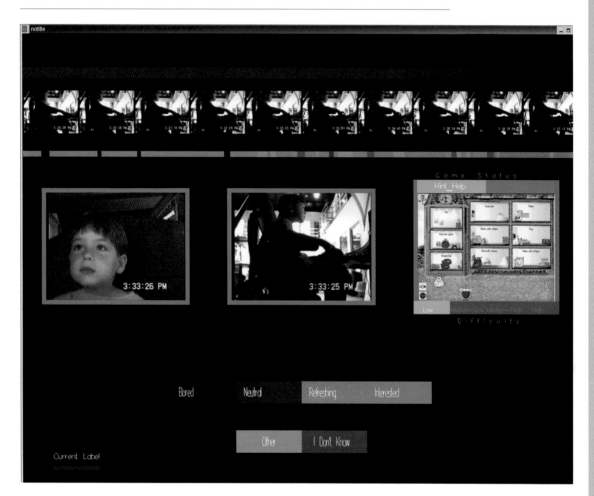

Using Standard Coding Schemes

You may already suspect that developing your own code and going through the steps just indicated are perhaps more than you want and more than you have the resources to do in the context of one evaluation study. Especially in the case of multimodal interaction, coding could be a very intricate process, and it may be

Table 10.2

Coding Scheme for Evaluating Products with Children

Code	Short Description	Definition
Breakdown of indication types based on observed actions with the game		
ACT	Incorrect action	An action is omitted from the sequence. An action within a sequence is replaced by another action. Actions within the sequence are performed in reversed order.
EXE	Execution/motor skill problem	The user has physical problems interacting correctly and quickly with the system.
PAS	Passive	The user stops playing and does not move the mouse for more than five seconds when action is expected.
IMP	Impatience	The user shows impatience by clicking repeatedly on objects that respond slowly, or the user expresses impatience verbally.
STP	Subgame—stopped	The user stops the subgame before reaching the goal.
Breakdown of indication types based on verbal utterances or nonverbal behavior		
WGO	Incorrect goal	The user formulates a goal that cannot be achieved in the game.
WEX	Incorrect explanation	The user gives an explanation of something that has happened in the game, but explanation is not correct.
DSF	Doubt, surprise, frustration	The user indicates: • Not sure whether an action was executed properly. • Doesn't understand an action's effect. • Effect of an action was unsatisfactory or frustrating. • Having physical problems in executing an action. • Executing the action is difficult or uncomfortable.
PUZ	Puzzled	The user indicates: • Doesn't know how to proceed. • Unable to locate a specific function.
REC	Recognition	Recognition of error or misunderstanding: • The user indicates recognition of a preceding error or misunderstanding.
PER	Perception problem	The user indicates not being able to hear or see something clearly.
BOR	Bored	The user verbally indicates being bored. The user nonverbally indicates being bored by sighing or yawning.
RAN	Random actions	The user indicates verbally or nonverbally performing random actions.
HLP	Help	The user cannot proceed without help; either asks for it or researcher must intervene to prevent serious problems.
DIS	Dislike	The user verbally indicates a dislike of something.

difficult to develop coding schemes to capture, for example, combined verbal and para-verbal behaviors such as body language. The development of the code itself requires the integration of specialized knowledge about speech or human movement, among other factors. In these cases, it is advisable to consult recent research literature to find a suitable coding scheme that can give you reliability between coders and examples of good coding practice. It is beyond the scope of this book to examine the range of coding schemes available, since they tend to rely on specialized theories and are application domain specific.

Tip

Even for a small-scale study, make sure different coders are coding in a similar way by training them on a small part of the data.

Table 10.2 shows a coding scheme that helps code usability problems and fun problems observed during the evaluation of interactive products for children. This scheme was developed by Barendregt (2006) as an adaptation of the Devan scheme (Vermeeren, 2002) for coding behaviors observed during a usability test. It is possible to adapt this scheme for different application domains, but this should be done carefully. The current scheme was developed iteratively until a satisfactory reliability was achieved (Cohen's kappa coefficient of 0.87 for coders coding an a priori agreed set of incidents). The scheme covers both nonverbal behaviors and utterances, so it can also be used for coding verbal data obtained using the techniques discussed in Chapter 11. An example of using a specialized scheme for coding human movement can be found in the case study in Chapter 17.

Summary

Whether carrying out a naturalistic observation or a tightly structured observation, it is always the case that watching children interact with technology is valuable. In structured observations, with easy-to-use coding schemes, intricate and very useful data, which can be used to justify changes and support hypotheses, can be obtained.

In this chapter, we pointed out some of the pitfalls and some of the special measures needed when observing children. Careful preparation, concern for the well-being of the children, and piloting of coding schemes will all result in better observation studies.

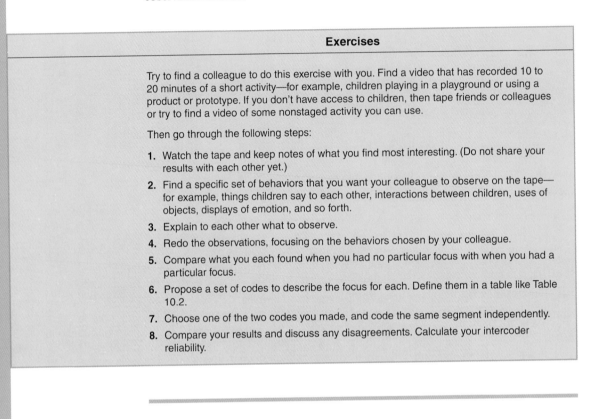

Exercises

Try to find a colleague to do this exercise with you. Find a video that has recorded 10 to 20 minutes of a short activity—for example, children playing in a playground or using a product or prototype. If you don't have access to children, then tape friends or colleagues or try to find a video of some nonstaged activity you can use.

Then go through the following steps:

1. Watch the tape and keep notes of what you find most interesting. (Do not share your results with each other yet.)
2. Find a specific set of behaviors that you want your colleague to observe on the tape— for example, things children say to each other, interactions between children, uses of objects, displays of emotion, and so forth.
3. Explain to each other what to observe.
4. Redo the observations, focusing on the behaviors chosen by your colleague.
5. Compare what you each found when you had no particular focus with when you had a particular focus.
6. Propose a set of codes to describe the focus for each. Define them in a table like Table 10.2.
7. Choose one of the two codes you made, and code the same segment independently.
8. Compare your results and discuss any disagreements. Calculate your intercoder reliability.

CHAPTER 11

VERBALIZATION METHODS

Whether testing a product in the laboratory or in the field, observation of testers alone cannot reveal how they experience interaction. Child testers may be brave in the face of severe usability defects or may persevere with a boring game, perhaps because they hope to please the test administrator if they perform well. The administrator may be unaware of their thoughts and feelings.

This chapter describes a range of techniques that encourage, prompt, or require children to talk about the interaction with the product. As we shall see, children may be talking to themselves, to a peer, or to the adult administrator in a context that is staged by the evaluator to encourage and facilitate verbalization. This setup may involve different degrees of structure and control in obtaining verbal data.

Most of the techniques discussed in this chapter originate from usability testing with adults, but verbalization is one of the areas where testing with children differs substantially from testing with adults. Techniques vary according to how taxing they can be for the child tester and how natural and comfortable the test situation is for the children. This chapter discusses the techniques available and the potential trade-offs between them.

Types of Verbalization Methods

The terms *verbalization data, verbal protocol,* and *verbal data* are used interchangeably to refer to a record of things testers say during usability testing. Verbalizations can be elicited, or can be spontaneous, with children "talking back" to computer characters, commenting or making exclamations, or asking for help. The administrator can obtain verbalization data either by explicitly instructing testers to verbalize their thoughts or, more subtly, by creating a situation in which verbalization happens more or less spontaneously. Verbalization data can indicate the feelings and thoughts of the child and can help capture the mental processes of the child during testing.

Verbalization techniques fall between the observation techniques discussed in the previous chapter and the survey techniques discussed in the next. In contrast with survey techniques, verbalization techniques make sense only in combination with an observation method. Usually, verbal data are obtained on the fly during experimental usage of a product and are intended to reflect the thought processes of the child as interaction with the product unfolds rather than being a post hoc judgment.

Think–Aloud

Think-aloud for usability testing requires test participants to verbalize their thoughts concurrently while they interact with the product under test. The administrator of the test supports this verbalization by reminding the tester to keep talking throughout. A record of what testers say while testing a product uncovers usability problems and can provide some insight into how the user understands and experiences the tested product.

In the last 20 years, think-aloud has been established as a standard practice in the usability testing of products for adults. It has been touted as "the most valuable" usability-testing method (Nielsen, 1994b). In some popular handbooks for usability testing—for example, Dumas and Redish (1993)—think-aloud is even assumed as the default testing practice. It seems that most usability practitioners use some variant of think-aloud for testing prototypes, not least because think-aloud has become an essential component of curricula in human–computer interaction.

The many versions of think-aloud differ in the way participants are encouraged to talk and what they are expected to talk about. Think-aloud as a method for studying thought processes originates from cognitive science. Think-aloud or "thinking out loud," as it is sometimes called, was developed originally for studying problem-solving strategies. It is suited to interaction evaluation because, to a large extent, interaction with a product to achieve a specific goal can be considered problem solving, especially with complex interactions.

Ericsson and Simon (1980) provided a treatise on the concerns of the cognitive scientist for obtaining valid accounts of users' thoughts. Their article is much cited in the context of evaluation methods and has significantly influenced usability-testing theory and practice. The essence of their argument is that information obtained by think-aloud can only be considered a valid record of thinking processes if the verbalizations concern only current actions and goals and, in obtaining these data, the task does not interfere with the tasks studied. Thus, think-aloud must be obtained before test participants filter, transform, or reflect upon their interaction with the product tested. To avoid such cognitive processes and thus ensure the validity of the verbal data obtained, Ericsson and Simon provided the following guidelines for the conduct of think-aloud:

- The administrator should not interfere with the test and should retreat as much as possible into the background. Consequently, it is often the case in usability testing that the administrator takes a passive role and refrains from helping testers or from explaining things that are puzzling testers.

- Encouragement should be given in a neutral manner to participants to talk (e.g., "keep talking"), without engaging in a conversation with the participant and without betraying any thoughts about the evolution of the test.

Adapting Think-Aloud for Children

Applying such advice for testing products with children poses several problems, particularly when younger children are involved. For children, thinking out loud is difficult for several reasons:

- Children may find it hard to express their thinking clearly because their language skills are still not fully developed.

- Thinking aloud puts extra cognitive workload on the test participant, who, in conjunction with testing the product, is required to provide a running commentary. Children are even more likely than adults to refrain from talking exactly at the moments when they experience difficulties (which are the ones you probably want to focus on).

- Many children are shy toward adults and will find it all the more difficult to verbalize their thoughts when trying to learn to use an unfamiliar product. Think-aloud aggravates this problem when an apparently unresponsive adult requires the child to "keep talking" rather than guiding, explaining, and reacting to the child's own comments.

- Think-aloud is a peculiar social setting for a child, who may be accustomed to situations where the adult asks questions with an implicit understanding that there is a right and a wrong answer or where the adult will advise and instruct.

- It appears to be easier for adults to slip in and out of the role of a tester, which presumes that the product and not the tester is being tested. In our experience (unless children have been involved throughout a design process), child testers tend to act as if their performance is what is being tested. Like everyone, children don't like to make mistakes in the presence of others who make them feel inadequate. Faced with difficulties they may freeze, not daring to explore the system or resorting too easily to the administrator for help instead of trying to figure out things themselves. Not interacting with them socially to put them at ease, encourage them, and coax opinions may make this worse.

Boren and Ramey (2000) talk about some of these problems in the context of usability testing for adults. They discuss how the rigorous process suggested by Ericsson and Simon is problematic and how usability-testing practice does and should depart from what would be advisable for doing good cognitive science.

Much of the usability-testing literature on think-aloud with adults seems to recommend inviting a more reflective type of utterance that would be frowned on in a cognitive science context, since encouraging such utterances flies against the methodological advice of Ericsson and Simon (1980, 1993). Related texts suggest a more dialogical demeanor by the administrator, which allows more social interaction and more guidance to offer. This is especially advisable when asking children to think aloud.

Can Children Think Aloud?

Think-aloud is not only used in usability testing but has been applied in research with children in educational settings (e.g., to investigate second-language comprehension or mathematical problem solving). Variants of think-aloud have also been used as educational techniques. For example, the technique of "self-instruction" involves a think-aloud process in which the adult verbalizes his thoughts as he tries to solve a problem. Children as learners then follow this example by verbalizing their thinking, first in a guided way and then independently, until the thinking process becomes internalized and tacit.

Very few studies of children thinking aloud for the purposes of evaluating products have been published. This may be a direct result of the difficulties of think-aloud for children (just mentioned), which discourage evaluators from using the technique, but it may also be because of the relatively little emphasis on designing for children on the part of the usability engineering and human–computer interaction community. A decade ago, Hanna, Risden, and Alexander (1997) published a set of guidelines with regard to the testing with children based on their practical experience with testing at Microsoft. They suggested that children had to be around 13 or 14 years of age to think aloud.

Today, this is considered a very conservative estimate, and more recent studies have shown that younger children are also capable of thinking aloud. One such study on usability testing by Donker and Markopoulos, (2002) established the feasibility and effectiveness of think-aloud as an evaluation method for children as young as age 7, provided that a relaxed and dialogical form of think-aloud is adopted. The following section discusses some of the problems of getting children to think aloud and suggests some practical ways to address these problems.

Getting Children to Think Aloud

Testers (the children) must be instructed on how to think aloud and must be guided through the test by the person administering it. This guidance should have a threefold aim:

1. To motivate the child to think aloud
2. To teach the child how to think aloud
3. To put the child at ease

In our experience, children are enthusiastic test participants but this enthusiasm can be tempered when the test process requires effort and sustained commitment. The administrator can motivate the child to think aloud by stressing how important it is for the design team to understand how the child thinks or feels about the product—for example, because it helps the administrator determine how other children might feel if they use this product or play this game.

Once you have motivated the children to participate, you have to teach them how to do it! Teaching testers to think aloud can be done in one or more of the following ways:

- If several children are participating in the think-aloud, a group training session can be a very efficient way to show children what they are expected to do. Trying out think-aloud in a group will help the children to be aware of the difficulties everybody else is experiencing.
- Immediately before the session, the administrator may perform a small example of think-aloud, showing the desired form of think-aloud and even counter-examples (Dumas and Redish, 1991).
- The administrator can provide small warm-up tasks (Ericsson and Simon, 1993) where it is easy to do think-aloud, such as arithmetic exercises, solving a puzzle, and so on. During this exercise session, the administrator can provide encouragement for the child to speak and perhaps ask questions to indicate the types of things the administrator would like to hear.

Here is an example of an initial training script:

> *I want you to try this computer product for me. I can see what you do, but I don't know what you are trying to do or what you think about it. I want you to say aloud the things you are thinking of when you are using this computer. I will show you what I mean with this library website. (Then you perform an example of a think-aloud.) I am looking for a book in English. I see a box that seems to be for choosing the language. It says "All Languages." I will click on the arrow because I hope to see what languages I can choose from.*

Then you can give this counterexample:

> *It is not enough for me if you just say the things I can see you doing anyway, like "I click on the language"; "I click on English"; and so on. So if I ask you to explain what you do, it does not mean you are doing something wrong but that I want you to remember to explain to me what you are trying to do and whether you like it or not, and also let me know what you don't understand.*

Learning how to think aloud is difficult and, combined with the difficulty of interacting with an unfamiliar product, may demotivate or dishearten children. Practice helps, both with think-aloud and with interacting with the administrator. Children who have participated in earlier test sessions with think-aloud or earlier stages of a design process can find it easier than newcomers to appreciate what is expected from them and are more likely to be at ease with the design team.

Tip

When aiming to get verbalization data, it is better to recruit children testers who have helped you before or who have done think–aloud before.

Interacting with the Child during Think–Aloud

Having decided on a think-aloud protocol and trained and motivated the child, the evaluation session has to be planned and carried out. The first decision you have to make as an evaluator is whether you will stay with the child during the test. Traditional think-aloud procedures often suggest that the administrator sit in a separate room, observing the tester through cameras or one-way mirrors. The rationale for this is that the presence of the administrator may influence the subjects in their behavior or influence the content of the verbalization, possibly encouraging the testers to make this content more socially acceptable to the administrator. Given this, when testers appear to produce adequate data without much prompting during the testing sessions, it may be better to leave them alone during the session.

Although these caveats still apply for think-aloud with children, in our opinion it is better to sit in the room next to them to make them feel at ease and be there to help when appropriate. Avoiding help and social interaction can, as just discussed, make the child feel uncomfortable. Rather than being a passive observer, sitting slightly behind the child but in his or her view and being prepared to help when the child is in trouble can make the whole experience less stressful for the child. This is especially important for younger children and for systems that are still in the early stages of development and so likely to cause problems.

Child testers are not likely to follow the procedure set out by the administrator as accurately as adult testers might. After a few minutes, they may forget to talk or they may turn immediately to the administrator for help rather than apply themselves to understanding how the interaction works or daring to experiment with the interactive product. Sometimes children lose motivation to complete the test; in this case, the task of the administrator is to keep the child engaged, watch for situations that might cause stress to the child, and provide help where necessary.

The administrator must also check whether children have accomplished their test tasks, help them stay on course in carrying out the tasks, and adapt the test plan on the fly to cope with any problems that may arise.

Some gentle reminders may be enough to get the child to think aloud when she falls silent. Questions like "Can you tell me what you are thinking?" or "Can you tell me what you are trying to do?" will result in a more interactive way of thinking aloud. Some of the more interactive ways of doing a think-aloud have different names, such as *active intervention* (discussed later in this chapter).

More often than not, the child will ask the administrator for help or for confirmation of his intended actions or suppositions about the product. For example, he might ask, "What will happen if I click here?" or "Do you exit by pushing this button?" This puts the administrator in a dilemma that must be resolved. (See Figure 11.1.) Not providing guidance or confirmation (as is typically advised for tests with adults) may make the test session more representative of actual use situations,

Figure 11.1

"What happens if I click on him?" Aware of the presence of the administrator, the child hesitates to try what she believes is a reasonable way to proceed.

where we might assume that a child will not be able to ask an adult for help every time he has a question.

On the other hand, the tester is responsible for the child's well-being during the test and so has a duty to avoid frustrating or upsetting the child. It may well be that the child perceives the whole situation as a test or a challenge and will be very uncomfortable when things start to get difficult.

In recent attempts to get children aged 9 to 12 to think aloud, the administrator found herself saying, "Try it," throughout the usability test to encourage the children to proceed with their intended, and sometimes verbalized, interaction plan. Simply being flexible—or even abandoning the role of the passive observer and demonstrating how to proceed to help the child regain confidence—may be a more practical way to go. If such attempts fail, and the child is unhappy, the administrator should be prepared to abandon the test.

Tip

Prepare and pilot your help protocol: Plan your behavior toward the child in such a way that you do not provide excessive guidance but still create a comfortable situation for the child.

Although it is difficult to predict and prescribe how and when a child might need encouragement and/or support during a think-aloud session, a general rule of thumb is that the administrator should consciously try to create a comfortable, relaxed atmosphere so it is easy for the child to talk. In a recent research study that compared think-aloud during interaction with interviewing the child after each task, very often children would be more talkative and think aloud more when they were not expected to (when doing a post-task interview), possibly as a result of feeling more familiar with the more dialogical nature of the post-task interview protocol. Contrary to the strict think-aloud of Ericsson and Simon (1993), it is our view that getting children to verbalize their thoughts depends on how much the administrator can make them feel confident and relaxed.

Variants of Think-Aloud

Here we present a few techniques for obtaining verbalization data that address some of the limitations of think-aloud discussed in the previous sections. A common element in the following techniques is that they have all been tried and tested with adult testers and are applied with modifications for child testers. Later in this chapter we consider methods developed especially for child testers.

Retrospective Think-Aloud

The original form of think-aloud discussed in the previous section can be characterized as concurrent: The verbalization is obtained *while* the tester is interacting with the product. Another possibility is to obtain a record of the interactions of the user, such as a video recording of the test session, and have the children watch themselves interact with the products and comments on their actions. This technique is called retrospective think-aloud.

This procedure has several advantages. Compared to a concurrent think-aloud, participants do not have the extra workload of verbalizing their thoughts during the test session. Arguably, the test session itself is closer to how a child might interact with the product in practice, so one could claim a higher validity for the findings of such an evaluation session. Finally, during the retrospective think-aloud the administrator can replay interesting incidents and pause the video to allow for discussion.

This procedure also has some clear disadvantages. Testers might not be able to recall their actions during the usability test and may find it difficult to explain them

Tip

Think–aloud is quite taxing, so keep it short! If necessary, ask different children to work on different parts of your product.

later. This problem might be accentuated when the session is longer or the children younger. Thus, a good tip would be to only use this variant of think-aloud for older children and to do it for small sections of video at a time, such as 5 to 10 minutes. Currently, no research has been reported as to the optimum procedure for retrospective think-aloud for different ages of children. In the absence of such guidance, it is necessary that the administrator be conservative and use short test sessions but also that the testing process is fine-tuned with pilot testing.

Comparative studies of concurrent and retrospective think-aloud for adult users have shown that the former tends to give a more refined record of moment-to-moment interactions that detail what they saw and what they were doing (Bowers and Snyder, 1990) and reveal problems at a very operational level (Ohnemus and Biers, 1993). Retrospective think-aloud gives more explanatory accounts of the testers' actions that describe their goals at a higher level, and the interaction defects found using retrospection are at a correspondingly higher level. It is likely that similar results will hold for children, but the main concern of the administrator is less on fine-tuning the types of problems observed than on whether the comfort and well-being of the child during the test situation may outweigh marginal improvements in the number and types of problems found.

Retrospective verbalization may be necessary for products that do not allow concurrent verbalization. A clear example where concurrent think-aloud is not possible is speech interfaces, where the verbalization would interfere directly with the control of the application. Other, more extreme cases can be outdoor games that involve vigorous physical activity, where some of the assumed context for testing does not hold (e.g., there is no lab, and the administrator cannot be next to the child throughout the game).

The Picture Cards Method

The picture cards method (Barendregt et al., 2006) is useful for obtaining verbalization data from younger children who may not be comfortable thinking aloud or

Figure 11.2

The illustrations on the cards in the picture cards method indicate, respectively, boring, don't know/don't understand, fun, difficult, takes too long, childish, silly, and scary.

interacting with adult administrators. The core of the method is to give cards to child testers, with each card featuring one of a fixed set of illustrations. Every illustration corresponds to one specific type of experience that the administrator wants the child to flag and verbalize about. The cards are spread out on a table next to the child before the test. During the testing session, the child is asked to place a card in a box every time she experiences the corresponding feeling during the interaction. If the administrator does not understand why a particular card is used, he can ask the child for an explanation.

The cards and the physical act of moving them are intended as a motivation to report problems. The illustrations on the cards act as reminders of the types of things the administrator wishes to find out. Figure 11.2 shows the eight illustrations used to represent eight categories of problems that the evaluation aims to uncover. Barendregt chose these illustrations from online picture libraries used to teach nonverbal autistic children to express themselves by exchanging the cards.

The illustrations represent the following eight categories of verbalizations the administrator may want the children to make to evaluate a game:

- The game is *boring* because it is too easy.
- The game is difficult to use because the child *does not know or understand* what to do.
- The child enjoys himself and experiences something as *fun*.
- The child considers carrying out an action *too difficult*, even though he knows what to do.
- The child considers something as taking *too long*.

- The child considers some aspect of the product *childish*.
- The child considers something *silly* or *strange* when it is meant to appeal to the fantasy of older children.
- The child considers something *scary* when it is meant to appeal to the fantasy of older children.

The categories of verbalization solicited with the cards are not arbitrary. They were selected to correspond to the types of problems one could associate with ease of use and fun, based on the task–action cycle of Norman (2002) and the four aspects of fun in computer games developed by Malone and Lepper (1987); see Chapter 5 on inspection methods to find out more about these theories.

The picture cards method was developed for the evaluation of games, although it may be difficult practically to apply this method to computer games that require the child's concentration or even physical interactions because the child may not be able to divert and refocus attention between the cards and the game. It may, however, be appropriate for other (nongame) software, such as text editors, search engines, and educational applications where usability and fun may be equally relevant.

The method has been shown to work at least as well as think-aloud (Barendregt, Bekker, and Baauw, 2007) in terms of its efficiency in uncovering problems. Its benefit lies in the fact that child testers enjoy this method more. Experience with the method is still very limited, as it has only been evaluated by its inventor. The benefits it provides may not extend to older children.

In practice, it may be appropriate to use other illustrations and even a different set of categories for problems the children should report. In the evaluation of the method reported by Barendregt et al. (2006), children hardly used the "scary" and "childish" cards (see Figure 11.3). This could be because the product she tested was appropriate for the age of test participants and no instances of these types of problems occurred.

Barendregt suggests that it may even be enough to ask children to point at a particular icon printed on a page rather than place a card in a box, thereby eliminating the need to construct special-purpose cards and making the card selection easier. These adaptations are interesting simplifications of the technique but have not yet been tried out. They seem promising if you consider their similarity to using cards during interviews to focus the children's attention (see Chapter 13 on survey methods).

Figure 11.3
Evaluation with the picture cards method.
Source: *Photo courtesy of Bart van Overbeeke.*

When setting up an evaluation, it may be safer to stay with the categories presented here and even use the same illustrations, since these have been tried and iteratively improved. It might be necessary to create a different set of cards for cases where specific kinds of verbalizations are to be invited or to eliminate some of the cards if they are clearly not applicable—for example, the card for "scary" may not apply to evaluating a search engine for children.

The cards should be large and thick enough so that the children can pick them up easily. Barendregt et al. (2006) settled for 2″ × 2″ cards that were about one-eighth inch thick. Smaller or paper-thin cards may be difficult for children to pick up, and this could distract them further from the main task.

Other Variants of Think-Aloud

Spontaneous utterances of children during a test session can also provide valuable data. This type of verbal protocol has been called "voluntary think-aloud" by Donker and Reitsma (2004). Strictly speaking, it falls under the description of a structured observation, as discussed in Chapter 10, rather than a verbalization technique.

Expect the Unexpected!

Wolmet Barendregt

Working with young children when you aren't used to them is always going to produce a lot of surprises. During my research, I have done many tests with children between 5 and 7 years old. Of course, I always prepared the tests by having an introduction and a protocol of how to behave during the test, but more often than not, my careful preparations were undermined by unexpected behavior of the children so that I had to improvise and restructure. Children can be more scared and insecure than expected, or they can be much more trusting and open than you might sometimes want.

Their reactions may be more extreme that we expect
As an example of a very insecure child, I especially remember one of the first tests that I ever did with a young girl. After the introduction to the test, I asked her to play a computer game and to try to think aloud. The first action in the game was to select a difficulty level and then confirm the selection by clicking a fish that was nodding "Yes." The girl was completely at a loss for what to do. She just stared at the screen for a long time. After a while, I felt that I had to ask her whether she knew what to do; immediately, she started crying. Only by taking the mouse from her and helping her through the first parts of the game could I convince her to try playing again. I could not use the data from the part that I helped her with, but she enjoyed the testing experience in the end, and I even got some data about the later parts of the game.

Luckily for me, most other unexpected situations occurred with children being extremely trusting and open instead of scared.

They may say very unexpected things . . .
During my experiments with the Problem Identification Picture Cards (PIPC) method, I did some tests at a school. A boy came to participate. I introduced the method and the game we were going to test. We had just started the test when he said, "My friend cannot do the test because he is ill. He is in hospital having an . . . operation." I did not really want to discuss the topic with him further, so I just acknowledged him, but it is hard to know how to respond to such openness.

They won't understand the "scientific method"
Another girl was also talking about one of her friends. The friend had been with me before, and the girl kept asking me how many cards her friend had

used, whether she had used the same cards, and whether they had used the same number of cards. I tried to avoid saying much about the other girl's test, but I can imagine that it still influenced this girl's behavior in some way.

They may be surprisingly keen to help

One of the girls in the PIPC experiment was really enthusiastic about working on the computer with me. After school she came to me with her mother, asking whether she could come again. Of course, I did not really have any use for another test with the same girl, but I agreed that she could come again at the end of the week. On Friday she came to play with the game again. She had made a large number of drawings for me, and she chatted happily about different topics. I took the opportunity to ask her more informally about the method, and she told me that she thought that the "scary" card was not useful since there were no scary things in games. Although I still think it possible that there are scary things in games, I was happy to be able to discuss the method with her, since it made it clear to me that she had understood the purpose of the test.

They will do something you hadn't planned for

Also during the PIPC experiments, one girl made interesting use of the cards that express fun. She put more and more cards in the box when she found something very funny. After a while, she had put almost all of the "fun" cards in the box, and she started to wonder what we should do if she used up all the cards. I showed her that I was taking notes of all the cards that she used. Together we decided to take some cards out of the box and reuse them, since I had already recorded when they were used. It had never been my intention to put more cards in the box to express magnitudes, but she wanted to share her enthusiasm in that way so I just went along with that.

As a conclusion, I can say that one should expect the unexpected, be prepared to improvise, and maybe even be prepared to make some of your data useless by responding naturally to the children. Take a lot of time for each session, and try not to get frustrated when you cannot gather as many data in a short time as you had hoped. I am grateful for the opportunity I received to work with these wonderful children during my experiments. As you can see, the number of positive experiences really outnumbered the more negative experiences, so I hope that this description of a few of my experiences makes other researchers relax and enjoy their work with children as well.

Donker and Reitsma adopted this approach in an extensive evaluation study with 70 kindergartners. They obtained very few utterances (fewer than one per session on average), which illustrates how unnatural think-aloud may be for children. Despite this scarcity of comments, they were a useful complement to observed behaviors in helping identify unanticipated problems with the interaction.

Dialogue between the Administrator and the Testers

The problems surrounding think-aloud have led to the development of several techniques in which the administrator interacts more thoroughly with the tester to probe her thoughts, attitudes, and experiences during the test. Some well-known examples of such techniques developed for adults are *active intervention, post-task interview, question and answer,* and *cooperative evaluation.* The differences between them are often only slight, relating to the nature of the questions the administrator should ask in what is essentially an interview that is intertwined with the testing of the product. In this section, we discuss two of these approaches that have been adapted for children.

Active Intervention

With active intervention, the administrator is more involved, probing the tester with questions, suggesting directions for the interaction to proceed in, and asking directly for interpretations and opinions regarding the various interactive elements.

In the case of the child tester, this might mean that the adult asks the child what he liked or what he imagined some interactive component might do. In such cases, the relationship between administrator and tester is more akin to what children are familiar with from their daily encounters with adults, such as teachers and parents. Seen in this way, the testing situation may be more comfortable for the child than think-aloud. The intervention of the administrator helps the child stay vocal and helps the test session focus on aspects of the interaction that are most interesting for the evaluation team.

A disadvantage of these more interactive forms of obtaining verbalization is that it is easy for the administrator to inadvertently lead the child in a particular direction, focusing on known problematic areas of the interface while ignoring other unexpected sources of problems or even eliminating difficulties with the product altogether. At the very least, they break the flow of natural interactions with the product. As a result, the testing session is further removed from actual use than would be the case with more passive behavior from the administrator.

No sufficient research evidence exists for how well active intervention fares compared to think-aloud. A preliminary investigation by van Kesteren et al. (2003) is encouraging but not conclusive.

Post-Task Interview

A restricted form of active intervention is conducting post-task interviews. A post-task interview involves asking questions about the interaction after small chunks of user activity. Clearly, the size of these chunks may vary. If one waits too long before asking questions, one can hardly consider the data obtained as verbalization. For small tasks, a post-task interview helps obtain commentary from the tester while the experience is fresh in her mind.

Donker and Markopoulos (2002) compared think-aloud with post-task interviews for children age 9 to 12, and this comparison was repeated more extensively by Baauw and Markopoulos (2004). One result that was found in both studies was that children would report fewer problems in their responses to the questions than they would report during a think-aloud. Girls reported more problems than boys. However, when comparing the number of problems spotted via a combination of these utterances and help requests, the two procedures (think-aloud and post-task interviews) fared similarly, especially when problems discovered by observing the child were included. It seems that the choice of protocol should, once more, not be dictated by concerns of efficiency of the method but rather by practical considerations regarding the test setup and the comfort of the child tester.

Robotic Intervention

A novel verbalization technique that is still under development is to use a "social robot" as a proxy of the test administrator. A social robot can be defined as one that exhibits some human-like affective and social behaviors. The administrator can withdraw out of sight from the child and operate the robot remotely. The motivation for doing this is that the child can relate more easily to a playful and toy-like robot than to an adult administrator and can be more uninhibited in talking to it.

Figure 11.4

Active Intervention through a social robot. (a) Introducing the robot to the testee. (b) Interacting with the robot and the tested software. (c) Running the robot and the observation behind the scenes.

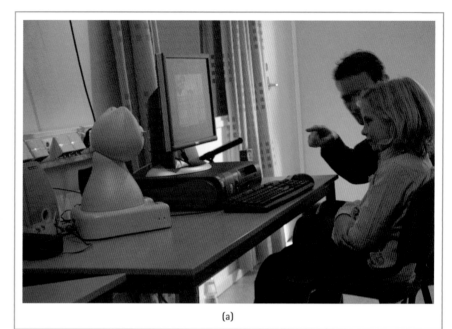

(a)

(b)

Figure 11.4

Cont'd

(c)

Currently, a simple robotic (the Philips iCat robot) is used as a proxy for the administrator who operates it from the observation room. Through a graphical control panel, the administrator can invoke simple preprogrammed humanlike behaviors (facial expressions, turning its head to look at the child, etc.). The interviewer's voice is transformed so it is not recognizable and can be attributed to the robot. These are the procedures for the evaluation:

- The administrator introduces the setup and explains that the robot is there to offer help and to ask questions.
- The administrator withdraws to the observation room, from which all of the child's interactions are observed through cameras and one-way mirrors.
- The evaluation session proceeds as in standard evaluation sessions.
- The administrator applies an active intervention protocol through the robot.
- The administrator also applies the help protocol through the robot as needed.
- The administrator returns to the room to debrief the child.

Currently, the development of this method is aimed at identifying the most useful combination of functionalities for the robot—for example, meeting the child's gaze, showing empathy, and so on. However, such sophisticated technology may not even be necessary. Early trials with relatively simpler solutions have been found to be feasible as well. More specifically, a speaker was inserted inside a fluffy animal toy, allowing for a very similar protocol to be executed and for an evaluation session to be run (Verschoor, 2007).

The first experiences with this method have been very positive:

- The children were very comfortable and enjoyed the interaction with the robot.
- With the current implementation, the administrator of the test had a heavy workload (only one person managed the robot and interacted through it with the child in these trials).
- The children provided limited spontaneous verbalizations to the iCat but felt very comfortable answering its questions.
- The robot seemed to resolve the problem of other verbalization methods in which children become hesitant to try things out and ask the administrator for help. It seems they will ask for help only when they are truly stuck.

Interaction between Testers

Another way to obtain verbalization data without forcing the tester into a monologue is to stimulate a dialogue between more than one tester, usually pairs. These techniques create a very natural context for verbalization and have been studied quite extensively regarding their applicability for child testers. This section discusses constructive interaction, an established technique that has been adapted for child testers, and peer tutoring, a technique developed by one of the authors especially for obtaining verbal data from children.

Constructive Interaction

Interaction, codiscovery, or codiscovery learning (O'Malley et al., 1984) is a technique introduced for testing with adults where two test subjects collaborate in trying to carry out test tasks with the system under test. A record of their conversation provides the verbal protocol from which the testers' usability problems, feelings, and attitudes can be identified. Nielsen (1994b) argues that *constructive interaction* would be very appropriate for testing with children. Experiences so far indicate that this can indeed be the case for older children who have acquired some skills in cooperating and working as a team.

Constructive interaction can be very fruitful when the two testers are learning to use a product for the first time. Their discussions can portray very well the formation of a mental model of the system and potential sources of errors or difficulties.

Practically, this method creates an informal and natural social context. It avoids the difficulty of training the child to think aloud and the complexities of carrying out a think-aloud. On the downside, it requires recruiting pairs of children rather than only one child, and it requires some attention to keep them focused on testing rather than on other kinds of interactions.

There have been several attempts to use constructive interaction with children, but few authors have reported how well this technique served their purposes. The main difficulties arise at younger ages, when children find it difficult to cooperate. Problems like one child trying to dominate or trying to do everything by herself, children competing at tasks rather than cooperating, or one child being drowned out or intimidated by children who are boisterous or speak loudly are all possibilities.

Even at ages where children are expected to cooperate in terms of their development stage, children often compete with each other (Markopoulos and Bekker, 2003; Van Kesteren et al., 2003). It seems that the social skills that allow adults to be effective testers in codiscovery sessions are not yet in place for younger children. Research is still sparse on this topic, but it seems that more structure is necessary to support the cooperation between younger children. This line of thinking has led to the development of the peer tutoring technique discussed in the next section.

Experiences with codiscovery performed by girls in their early teens seem to be more successful than those with younger children or boys. The relationship between the pairs of children testing seems also to be a very important factor, with children who are friends being more likely to perform well in the codiscovery session (Als, 2005). When a pool of children is participating in a series of tests—for example, when a whole class is participating—it is a good idea to ask a tester to choose whom she would like to work with. In general, if the dynamics between the two testers work out, constructive interaction can be more fun for the children who participate.

Peer Tutoring

Peer tutoring is a verbalization method based on the idea that one child teaches another child how to use the software being evaluated in a social context that is familiar to them (Höysniemi, Hämäläinen, and Turkki, 2002, 2003). The method has been specifically designed for testing of interactive products with children. The peer tutoring is based on observing whether children are able and willing to teach each other to use the product that is being evaluated. In addition, the method provides information on how children use the system and how they communicate about the product. The peer tutoring approach involves at least one tutor, a tutee, and a test supervisor who guides the collaboration.

Tip

Make it clear that children will not be criticized if they have problems using the product.

The peer-tutoring method differs from the codiscovery learning and participatory design methods in that it is not based on the idea that two participants work collaboratively on a given task and explore a system together. Rather, the task of the tutor is teaching, and the task of the tutee is to act according to the tutor's instructions. Peer tutoring usually consists of four phases: (1) introducing the test setup and the tutor–tutee roles, (2) training the tutors, (3) tutors teaching the tutees, and (4) the final interview.

During the tutoring session, Höysniemi et al. (2003) suggest that the test administrators do not teach or instruct the tutees but ask questions if the teaching situation requires adult intervention. The question-asking protocol combines both interviewing the tutor and providing help for him in the teaching situation. The question-asking protocol is simple and effective. Two categories of questions are used:

1. Questions that help tutors teach a tutee to carry out given tasks—for example, "Can you explain to Paul how to send an e-mail?"
2. Comment-related questions—for example, the tutor says, "It is very tricky." Then an adult asks, "What is tricky?" Then the tutor replies, "It's very tricky to find the button to send an e-mail."

When answering a question, the tutor provides product-related information based on the tutor's own experiences and observations, using language similar to the tutee's.

In a child–adult relationship, the differences in the levels of knowledge and authority affect the nature of the discourse between the child and the adult (Damon and Phelps, 1989). Peer collaboration provides tools for communication and equality. "Children have certain advantages over adults in teaching peers. They may more easily understand the tutee's problems because they are cognitively closer" (Gaustad, 1993). Rogoff (1990) also implies that children are likely to treat the situation differently if they are in charge of it rather than being given a task by adults, which is the case in traditional usability testing.

Peer tutoring provides us with information about the learnability and teachability of the system and what kinds of instructions children use when teaching one another. The researcher–child communication requires careful planning before the testing. Younger children in particular need help teaching other children, which requires some adult intervention. Since the test situation is not completely adult-free, it is important to make sure that the researchers behave informally and make space for the children to interact with each other. Since children are more active in the testing situation, researchers can stay more remote and adult intervention is diminished.

The communication in traditional usability testing is likely to be asymmetrical between adults and children. The peer tutoring approach encourages children to verbalize their thoughts naturally and spontaneously. One benefit of peer tutoring is that the peers speak the same way as the adults and children, which also holds true in other collaborative usability methods. Also, children are more relaxed communicating with adults when a peer is in the test space. The tutor–tutee communication is highly valuable when analyzing how well children have learned the required skills to use the product, how they perceive the interaction, and how much and what types of instructions are suitable for children.

Like all methods, peer tutoring has its drawbacks, one being that tutees, often considered less capable than tutors, tend to resist being tutored by their peers (Gaustad, 1993). This problem can be minimized by not using tutors who are much more skillful than tutees. The communication between tutor and tutee can become unbalanced; tutors speak much more than their tutees. As with many other qualitative evaluation methods, the peer tutoring approach also requires a lot of work in organizing the test sessions and analyzing the video material.

Also, as van Kesteren et al. (2003) comment, "The researcher should be aware that if the tutor forgets how the task works (and they sometimes do), the tutor-tutee situation changes somewhat in that the children will work together, as is the case during codiscovery." This requires researchers to plan their actions beforehand and choose how to guide the situation toward the peer-tutoring model.

Depending on the product being evaluated and the test setup, the tutors can take over the task completely and not allow their tutee to complete the task. It is important to explain to the tutors that they can only explain and show but not do the tasks themselves while teaching. Also, a careful test space design helps to tackle this "taking-over" behavior. One option is to situate the children so it is not easy for a tutor to operate the software.

Methodological Issues of Verbalization Methods

Verbalization methods cannot be assumed to capture precisely every step of the thought process in problem-solving tasks, but they are clearly suitable for understanding children's difficulties, misconceptions, and subjective experiences while the interaction unfolds. This section gives an overview of some of the research results regarding how well verbalization techniques work and some of the practical issues facing the evaluator in considering how to recruit child testers and how to analyze verbalization data.

Advantages and Disadvantages

This chapter has presented a range of techniques for obtaining verbalization data. To differing extents, these techniques share some advantages and disadvantages. One clear advantage is that they directly help during the test session to obtain detailed and contextualized commentary on preferences of the tester that may be hard to obtain with an interview or a questionnaire.

What sets these methods apart from the methods discussed in preceding chapters is that the thoughts that would otherwise remain unobserved are directly accessible to the evaluator, although not all methods discussed in this chapter can claim to support this aim equally well. Another important advantage is that opinions and expressions of emotion are obtained in the context of interaction and can be related to very specific aspects of the interactive product.

Also, in addition to the information gathered from observing children's interactions with a product, verbalizations can provide extremely persuasive evidence when considering whether and how to redesign an existing prototype, since software developers and product managers get to hear it from "the horse's mouth."

One disadvantage of verbalization techniques (with the exception of retrospective think-aloud) is that the tester, as well as interacting with the product under test, also has some interaction with the administrator or another test participant. This secondary interaction that is introduced by the evaluation technique may influence the course of the interaction and may mean that the interaction that unfolds is not representative of actual use. Different directions of interaction may be taken than a child would attempt alone, different performance times will be achieved, and perhaps even different numbers of errors will be made. If the emphasis is on measuring the performance of the child to complete some tasks, verbalization methods might not be appropriate. This is especially so with the methods involving dialogue with the administrator or with a second test participant.

Performance

Several studies have been conducted that compares the techniques discussed in this chapter or with other methods, such as inspections, surveys, and observations. It is beyond the scope of this book to present all this research, especially as it is still far from being conclusive. At this time, the comparisons that have been made usually concern specific ages, settings, and applications, so substantial research is still needed to elaborate the trade-offs on account of the performance of each method.

Given the studies to date, some of which have been cited throughout this chapter, it is interesting to note that one cannot expect large differences in performance per session for any given method. To illustrate the point, we present the results obtained in a recent study conducted by one of the authors that compared post-task interview and think-aloud and that was reported briefly in Baauw and Markopoulos (2004).

Figure 11.5 shows the number of problems identified through verbalization data, by post-task interview and think-aloud, when these were applied to evaluate a website for children and an educational computer game. Reading the curves in the figure, one may think that 6 or 7 test participants are enough to uncover most usability problems. Nielsen (1994) has suggested that 3 to 5 subjects are generally sufficient for uncovering about 80 percent of the problems. Subsequent research has questioned this assertion, for which little empirical evidence had been provided. It seems that a larger number of users, say 8 to 12, may indeed be needed.

Number of problems uncovered through utterances of children obtained with think-aloud and post-task interviews. The counts include requests for help by the children. The testers were 11 boys and 13 girls, age 9 to 11. Each child tested both applications using both methods (order of methods was counterbalanced).

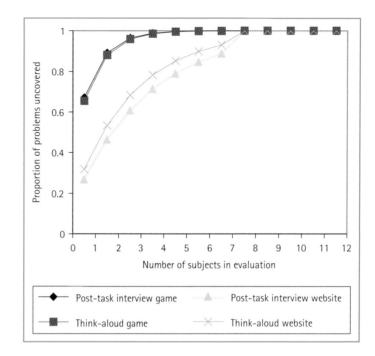

The figure clearly shows that similar numbers of child testers uncovered a similar number of problems with each method. Even in studies where differences have been found between methods (these two or other verbalization methods), it should be noted that these differences are rather small. In light of this, one may consider primarily practical concerns in selecting methods rather than optimizing the number of problems uncovered.

If difficulties recruiting children arise—for example, because they must be brought to the lab by a parent—testing individually may be more efficient than the other approaches that require two or more children.

Comparisons of think-aloud with codiscovery show that, per session, codiscovery may be more efficient in uncovering problems, but overall more data can be obtained per participant if they work independently. As yet, little is known about the types of problems that may be easier to uncover through verbalization with a pair of children as opposed to a child verbalizing individually. The findings of Als, Jensen, and Skov (2005) suggest that acquainted pairs of children will help uncover most critical usability problems per session and most unique problems. Since their study was based on 13- to 14-year-olds, who resemble adults in their behaviors as testers, it is not clear whether this also holds true for younger children.

Constructive interaction may be a good choice when there is easy access to children and the priority of the administrator is to obtain better yield per session and to create a testing situation that is more comfortable for the children than traditional think-aloud.

Peer tutoring solves most of the problems of the other methods for obtaining verbal data—for example, it creates a natural context and it can make good use of each tester. It introduces challenges regarding the ability of each child to teach her peers. For preschoolers, a friendly adult aided by picture cards seems the most promising approach.

Another methodological concern with verbal data is its validity. When children name something as a problem, is it really one, or are they just trying to provide the input they assume the administrator needs? So far, none of the methodological studies in this field has found evidence of children identifying fake problems to please the administrator or, conversely, hesitating to mention problems to avoid displeasing the administrator. Nevertheless, this is a very hard issue to tackle and one that must be kept in mind when explaining to the children the purpose of the evaluation in the introductory stage.

Tip

Don't stick to your chosen method, but be ready to switch when things go wrong.

Much of the discussion in this chapter on the use of verbalization techniques for testing products with children has focused on the relative performance of the methods (e.g., in terms of number or types of problems found) and on the feasibility of the approach for children. The reader should not overlook some essential differences between the methods discussed that pertain to their validity and the kind of information they help uncover.

Spontaneous think-aloud or post-task interviews, or even peer tutoring, cannot claim to produce a record of a child's thinking process. In some cases, apart from identifying usability or fun problems (as much of this chapter has discussed), the evaluator may be interested in understanding the thought processes underlying interaction—for example, how prior knowledge is used in the context of interaction, how different information displays are comprehended, how decisions are made, and so forth. This could be the case when evaluating a product that aims to support learning. Then the original and most pure form of think-aloud may be the only way to obtain valid data.

In contrast, in the more interactive forms of obtaining verbalization data, such as active intervention, post-task interview, or codiscovery, the interaction with another child or the administrator transforms the thought processes themselves or reveals only the points of interaction with the conversation partner, not the thought processes in between.

Which Children Should You Test?

Research has been done to determine which children are the best candidates for usability testing. This type of research has focused mostly on verbalization techniques where one could expect that children would vary in how well they can perform the different procedures discussed in this chapter.

Donker and Markopoulos (2002) found that girls report more problems than boys do. This was confirmed also by Baauw and Markopoulos (2004), but in that case it was found that when both requests for help and observations were considered, there was no difference. In general, the various studies in this domain show no conclusive evidence that either boys or girls make better participants. Barendregt (2005) found that children who exhibited critical and extroverted personality characteristics identified more problems.

For the potential gain of identifying a few more problems per child, it may therefore be preferable to avoid screening children, a process that requires extra effort by children or their parents, who would need to complete surveys or undergo an additional question–answer activity. In most contexts, such a screening can be ethically questionable—for example, when testing at a school, it is not appropriate to exclude some children on the basis of certain personality characteristics. In other cases, it is simply impractical.

Analyzing Verbal Protocols

Depending on the purposes of the evaluation, different levels of detail and rigor may be needed to analyze verbal protocols. When conducting a formative evaluation as part of a tight iterative process, time may be at premium, so less effort may be spent on transcribing and analyzing the protocols. In other cases, a detailed record using logging equipment and software that allows annotation of the logs produced is necessary.

For example, if you are evaluating a concept prototype of a game and you want to find out the extent to which the game rules and some elements of a story line contribute to a fun experience, notes by an observer, or simply playing back and reviewing a tape of a test session, may be sufficient.

If you have specific choices that you wish to evaluate with your prototype and are therefore asking a set of closed questions from the evaluation (see Chapter 5 on setting the goals of the evaluation), it may be that you can create a coding sheet for the types of utterances that you are after—for example, requests for help, alternative interpretations of specific graphical elements, and so on. Again, depending on resources, you may simply use these as a "scoring sheet" while reviewing a video recording of a session; in a research project, you may need to rely on multiple coders scrutinizing the video and marking it with specialized software.

Although counting instances of specific utterances can lead to some quantitative analysis, verbal protocols are essentially qualitative data and require caution in their interpretation. In practical situations, simply reviewing and selecting utterances critically may be sufficient for guiding design decisions. In more research-oriented studies (e.g., Denzin and Lincoln, 2000; Bogdan and Biklen, 1998), the readers are referred to literature on qualitative data analysis.

Summary

Verbalization techniques are a valuable complement to observation during testing. They help in understanding why children behave the way they do, whether or not the system is clear to them, and whether or not it is fun or boring. Verbalization can be obtained from a structured monologue (think-aloud), through a structural dialogue with the tester (active intervention), or between children (constructive interaction and peer tutoring). For children over age 9, it seems that all techniques will work to some extent. Getting verbal data from younger children, especially preschoolers, is more difficult.

Exercises

1. Develop your own example for teaching think-aloud to a child of age 13 or 14. How would you change it to address a child of 7?

2. Make a 15-minute video recording of yourself learning how to use a new system, application, or website. Try to run a retrospective think-aloud of this session. What difficulties did you encounter?

3. Suppose you want to run an evaluation based on the post-task interview technique. What are the pros and cons of asking questions that correspond to the picture cards in Figure 11.2?

4. Consider an evaluation you have recently conducted or one you plan to run. Suggest your own picture cards that are appropriate for the issues you wish to obtain verbalization about and appropriate to the age of the children you are working with.

Further Reading

Readers who would like to learn more about the think-aloud method as a data collection procedure and its origins as a way to analyze thinking processes are referred to the book by Ericsson and Simon (1980).

Those who would like to find out more about analyzing qualitative data can consult the extensive literature on the topic. A good "handbook" for this type of work is the book by Miles and Huberman (1994).

CHAPTER 12

THE WIZARD OF OZ METHOD

In most interactive technology evaluations, the evaluation is carried out using functional or partially functional products. Where technology is particularly novel, and where the cost of producing the technology is high, it is sometimes necessary to carry out evaluations *before* any large investment of money and time. One well-used method for evaluating novel or incomplete products is *simulation*. Simulation is where a user engages with a product that "looks like," "behaves like," or "feels like" the eventual product but is in one way or another incomplete. The benefits of using simulations are that certain features of products can be evaluated before a fully functional version is available.

In human–computer interaction, evaluation using simulation has become synonymous with the term *Wizard of Oz*. A Wizard of Oz evaluation is one in which some or all of the interactivity that would normally be controlled by computer technology is imitated, or "wizarded," by a human being.

This chapter presents an overview of Wizard of Oz (WOz) as a method and then focuses on its use with children. The first section introduces Wizard of Oz methods with a short historical overview augmented with references from early studies that used the method. The second section presents the literature on the use of WOz with children before concluding with a taxonomy that describes the variability of WOz studies. The last section focuses on the process of carrying out a WOz study with children.

Wizard of Oz Studies

A traditional Wizard of Oz study (shown in Figure 12.1) has three components: a human wizard, an interface, and a subject (user). During the study, the human wizard manipulates the interface in such a way that the subject (user) is unaware (to varying extents) of the existence and impact of the wizard. There is some debate about the origins of the method because the concept was being used well before it was given a name. As a method, it can be traced back to an IBM technical report by Thomas (1976), but it is more often attributed to Gould, Conti, and Hovanyecz (1983), whose study of a listening typewriter (an early simulation of a

Figure 12.1

*The Wizard of
Oz setup.*

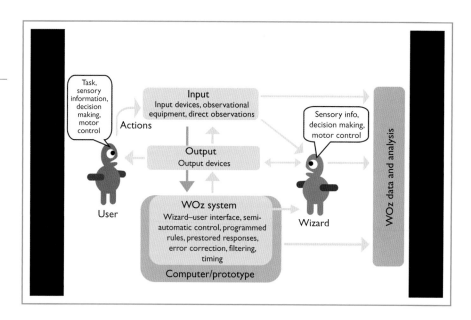

speech recognition system) is well cited. In the Gould et al. study, a skilled typist was employed to enter what the participants said to the computer and therefore to act as a wizard by mimicking the potential behavior of a speech recognition engine.

The term *Wizard of Oz* comes from the book *The Wonderful Wizard of Oz* by L. Frank Baum (1900). Central to this book is the character known as the Wizard of Oz, whom the other characters in the story believe to be the only one who can solve their problems. Unseen for most of the book, Oz is reluctant to meet the travelers and constantly appears in disguise—as a giant head, a beautiful fairy, a ball of fire, and a horrible monster. As the story progresses, it becomes apparent that Oz is actually none of these things but is in fact just an ordinary man who has been using elaborate magic tricks and props to make himself seem "great and powerful."

In a work that described a natural language interface to an office information system, Kelley (1984) was probably the first to associate a simulation interface with the wizard of Oz. He described his study as follows:

> [This is] an experimental simulation which I call the OZ paradigm, in which experimental participants are given the impression that they are interacting with a program that understands English as well as another human would. In fact, at least in the earlier stages of development, the program is limping along, only partly implemented.

Variability in Studies

Carrying out a WOz study includes the design of the evaluation, the design of the interfaces, the selection and training of wizards and participants, and the collection, analysis, and interpretation of the data. The following are some of the ways studies can vary:

The functionality of the technology: Some studies use fully functional prototypes, whereas others use low-tech or even nontech prototypes. The functionality of the prototype is in part determined by the stage in the lifecycle at which the WOz study is being done.

The discretion of the wizard: In some studies, the wizard is allowed to do whatever (s)he pleases, but in others the wizard is constrained to a set of options and in extreme cases can be replaced with a robotlike preprogrammed response.

The amount of wizard control: The wizard may be the sole provider of functionality in the system or may be only "wizarding" some of the interactions, with the interface providing some automatic control.

The visibility of the wizard: As shown in Figure 12.2, the wizard may be seen or unseen. In a study by Read, Mazzone, and Höysniemi (2005), it was shown that wizarding could easily be effected with the wizard in the same room as the users.

Figure 12.2
A Wizard of Oz evaluation with the wizard seen.

Figure 12.3

Setting up a Wizard of Oz study.

The number of wizards: In some studies, multiple wizards carry out different activities in a single study. In others, wizards are exchanged during the study (which will cause an effect, most obvious where the wizard has a high degree of autonomy). More commonly, there is one wizard who performs all the action.

Wizard knowledge: The wizard brings knowledge of the domain to the study. Some wizards are the system developers or designers; others are brought in for the experiment on an ad hoc basis and could be either experienced or inexperienced wizards. In WOz studies with children, it is important to consider the knowledge of the wizard in relation to the behavior of the children.

User knowledge: This is related to the amount that the user knows about the setup. Levels of deception vary across Wizard of Oz experiments, from the user believing that all is being done by a functional interface to the user knowing that the wizard is doing all the manipulation. It is common to give the user knowledge that lies between these two extremes. Users may alter their behavior when they know that a wizard is running the process.

Evaluation design: As with all evaluation studies, Wizard of Oz studies vary in many ways. There might be tightly controlled tasks or free exploration. With free exploration, the wizard either must be highly trained or must mimick a natural-language interface and have a high degree of autonomy. It is very difficult to

Figure 12.4

In this study, the wizard was in the background, but the interface was so engaging that the child did not see him.

allow free exploration in most Wizard of Oz studies. One method is to have a wizard action that embraces variable and unknown commands.

Studies with Children

Since 2000, an increasing number of studies have used the Wizard of Oz method with children. In light of this growing interest, guidelines and ethical discussion are needed to safeguard the participating children from any potential harmful effects of the method and to ensure that the experimental setups are properly designed. For example, one concern that is of increased relevance when designing a Wizard of Oz study with children is whether or not the wizard should be visible to the children. A visible wizard (as shown in Figure 12.4) requires less deception and is easier to set up practically.

Tip

Where the wizard is seen, try to provide an environment that will distract the children from noticing what the wizard is doing.

A study reported in Read et al. (2005) was designed to compare how children experience Wizard of Oz events when the wizard is hidden and when the wizard is seen. In this study, it was found that the majority of children remained unaware of the wizard activity throughout, with discovery taking place in the wizard-visible instance only with a speech recognition activity. This was due to the children listening to the sounds of the keyboard while they were doing the speech activity. Some children heard the typing but were unaware that it related to the speech recognition activity! At the end of this study, the children were told that because they had been deceived, they could withdraw their consent and have their data removed. No child took this option, which indicates that deception was less important than we believed. From this study, it appears that in many instances, especially where there is not a great deal of keyboard input or, more generally, where the operation of the wizard can be done inconspicuously, the wizard can safely be placed in the same room as the activity without a high risk of discovery.

When to Use a WOz Study

As specified earlier, a Wizard of Oz study requires an interface (to a system), a wizard, and a user (often referred to in the literature as a "subject"). It is not possible to use Wizard of Oz studies for all systems. This section of the chapter discusses where it is appropriate to use WOz methods and what precautions must be taken, and presents a case study that illustrates some of these points.

In some cases, the use of Wizard of Oz is limited by restrictions imposed by the system. Systems with analogue outputs (for example, pointing-based drawing applications), systems that require rapid responses (like some computer games or control systems) and systems that are difficult to observe (thought-based computing, for instance) are all problematic. Fraser and Gilbert (1991) specified that for a Wizard of Oz, it must be possible to (1) simulate the future system, (2) specify the future system behavior, and (3) make the simulation convincing.

The first of these constraints is largely concerned with the technology. The other two are much more concerned with the people in the system. People in Wizard of Oz studies pose several limitations, but these limitations have also supplied the field with opportunities for innovative solutions.

The wizard, for instance, must be able to mimic the behavior of the system and therefore must understand what the system would do. This means the system should not be too complex and, for convincing simulation, the wizard must not have too much to do. Several "assistants" for wizards have been developed to make the task easier and to reduce wizard error. For dialogue (question and answer) systems, a wizard would have to remember computer responses. For example, Dahlback, Jonsson, and Ahrenberg (1993) created ARNE-3, a simple menu-based tool that assists the wizard in this sort of application.

Besides having assistive tools and instructions, the wizard needs to understand the context in which he or she is doing the wizarding and is likely to need some associated training. Fraser and Gilbert (1991) identified three areas in which the wizard should be trained: the application area, the system capability, and the use of any assistive tools.

The user, or subject, in a wizard study is also a factor that should be taken into account. Users are known to be variable, so the same precautions that would be taken in any study apply equally to a Wizard of Oz study. Additional dimensions, however, would be subject gullibility and knowledge of the setup. When considering if a WOz study can be carried out with users without the users knowing the wizard is there, the engagement of the users can be taken into account. As shown in Figure 12.5, if the activity is very engaging the wizard may not be noticed at all. Children are generally quite engaged with the tasks they are asked to perform.

Figure 12.5
In this study, the child was distracted by the observer, so he did not notice the wizard.

Overall, it can be said that Wizard of Oz studies are more suitable in cases where the simulated functionality falls into the category of everyday human skills (so it is not too difficult for the wizard) but where that functionality is relatively hard to implement in an interactive product. Examples include the understanding of spoken language, perceiving user gestures, perceiving activity in rooms or tracking the location of objects, judging social situations, and so on. Wizard of Oz studies should be avoided when the inevitable variability in the behavior that might result from the human involvement could compromise the goals of the evaluation.

A Walkthrough of a WOz Evaluation

This is an account of the planning and operation of a WOz evaluation with children. The requirement was to evaluate a novel interface that read out children's stories, inserting the word *Jabberwocky* whenever there was an unrecognizable word. The concept was simple, but the implementation of the interface was known to be problematic. The evaluation planned to discover the immediate reaction of the children, whether they noticed if a spelling was missed, and what happened with a word that was spelled correctly but was not the word the child intended. Thus, if the child wrote the following:

> *The bog jumped high over the mownten and fond himself on the moon. There was a cow with a spoon and a pot of hony.*

the system would read:

> *The bog jumped high over the Jabberwocky and found himself on the moon. There was a cow with a spoon and a pot of Jabberwocky.*

A WOz study was chosen because the eventual product would use text-to-speech, which is ideally suited to WOz since it is relatively complex to implement but relatively easy to wizard.

The Wizard Interface

The children wrote their stories on digital paper, and this was uploaded into a laptop using a digital pen. The writing was displayed on the class white board (see Figure 12.6). A speaker icon on the display was clicked, and the text was "read" by the system. This reading was recorded so it could be replayed.

The reading was done by a wizard in another room. His interface (see Figure 12.7) showed the child's writing at the top of the screen. The wizard had to read all the

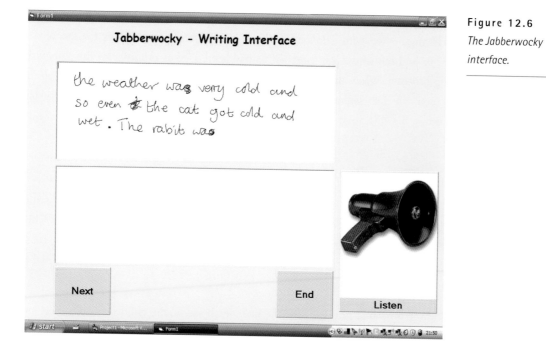

Figure 12.6
The Jabberwocky interface.

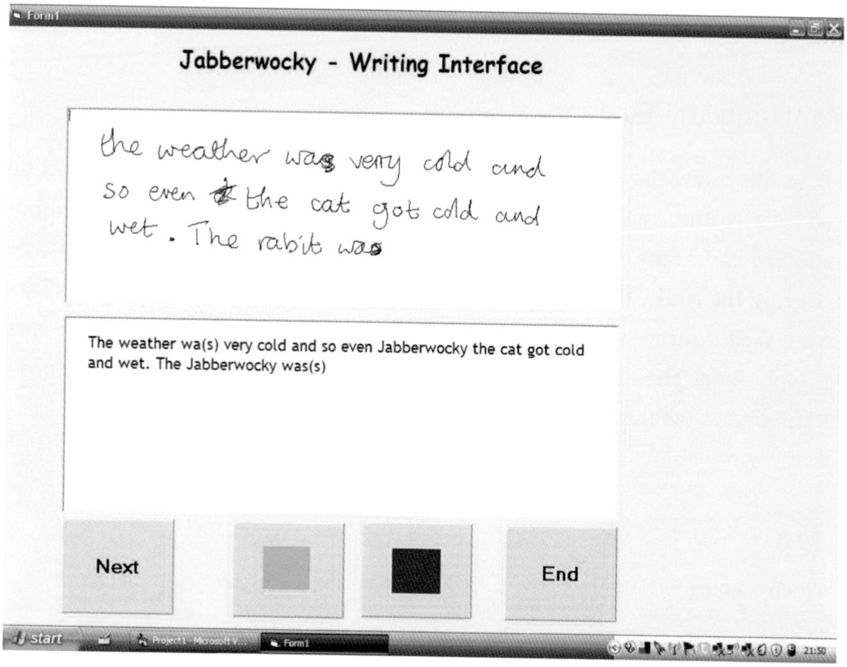

Figure 12.7
The wizard interface.

correctly spelled words but say "Jabberwocky" for the incorrect words. The interface was augmented with a *Jabberwocky* preset word and preset words for *the, a, dog, moon,* and *cow* (these last three words had been used as prompts for the story-writing process). When the teacher in the classroom pressed the speaker icon on the screen, she also sent a text message to the wizard, and this was his signal to start reading the writing.

Overcoming Problems

A pilot study was arranged with three children and a seen wizard. The wizard struggled to read the text accurately and had to correct the children's spellings while reading and so inevitably made mistakes. Thus, the spelling "huried" was read as "hurried" when it should have been "Jabberwocky." In addition, because he had to think as he read, the reading was rather slow.

To overcome this problem, for the later (real) study, the children wrote their stories before lunch, and the wizard used the lunch break to download them and prepare a script for each child. In the classroom, after the event, the children assumed they were downloading their stories for the first time, and in this instance, being prepared, the wizard had no difficulty with reading back.

Managing the Evaluation Study

Before the study, the children were told they were trying out a new program that read their writing back to them. They were told that the designers of the program wanted to know how easy it was to use and whether or not they (the children) liked it. During the study, which took place in the school classroom, children took turns having their writing read back to them and completed a small survey sheet about the application. The classroom was video-recorded, and in this way the reactions of the children to Jabberwocky were captured.

Tip

When training wizards, have them work the interface themselves to see how they behave.

After the study, the wizard revealed himself and admitted to the children what had been happening. The children were then given a chance to be wizards. At the end of the day, the evaluator spoke to the children about consent and deception, and the children had an informed debate about whether or not they had been unfairly treated in the evaluation. After the evaluation, all the children submitted their comments, and all were willing for their reactions to the program to be used.

Stages in Planning a Study

Planning a Wizard of Oz study has several stages:

Decide what will be wizarded. When deciding, consideration must be given to the "spy" method. For instance, if location tracking is being wizarded, methods must be devised to implement this. For simple mock-ups in the lab, the choice of features for wizarding will be easier.

Decide how many wizards will be used. If the study is lengthy, wizards get tired, so you may need more than one wizard. If you are observing many different things at a time, you may need more than one wizard at the same time. If wizards are being swapped, ensure consistency by training and preparation.

Design a WOz interface for the user (if needed). Sometimes the original interface can be used, but in many instances, depending on the "spy" methods, the interface used by the tester may have to be modified.

Determine the "spy" systems (the methods by which the wizard will know what the user is doing). If cameras are being used, their position and their visibility need to be considered. If the wizard is being shown a capture of the screen (as is common in interface wizarding), the means to carry this from one room to another also must be resolved.

Determine the wizard behaviors. For the intended system, the full set of user behaviors and user actions and a corresponding set of wizard behaviors and actions must be mapped out. If only a handful of behaviors are observed and the corresponding actions are simple, these can be presented in a tabular form for the wizard to refer to during training with the assumption that she will easily learn them once they have been practiced. For more complex situations, either multiple user behaviors or complex wizard actions, the wizard will need assistance—either the recruitment of another wizard or the implementation of a wizard interface.

Design a wizard interface (if needed). Consideration should be given as to whether one of the ready-made WOz interfaces can be used. If not, time must be allotted to design a robust WOz interface, and this will need user testing with the wizard. If visual information is being transmitted to the wizard, this may need to be incorporated into, or presented separately from, the wizard interface.

Train the wizards. As indicated by Gould et al. (1983), even expert wizards need training. The more complex the system, the more training the wizard will need. Aside from this training, the wizard may need instruction in the context and some information about the technical aspects of the simulated technology.

Pilot the study. With a selection of users, pilot the study to ensure that all that must be captured is captured, that all the responses needed are in place, and that the wizard is able to manage the study.

Carry out the study. Make sure you take variable factors into account.

Even with such detailed planning, it is still possible for things to go wrong, especially when the participants are children!

Problems

The problems with this method relate to the use of children, the possibilities for deception, and the fallibility of the wizard. These drawbacks are briefly expanded on in the next three sections.

Children as Users of Technology

Wizard of Oz experiments often use fragile technology, and there are several pitfalls associated with the use of it with children:

- Is the child able to understand the setup; understand the implications of any deception; or, especially in seen wizard evaluations, enter into the spirit of the role-play.

- Because children are often imaginative users of technology, the WOz system may not have the correct responses ready for their actions and the wizard might need to improvise.

- Diversity in the user population may result in erratic input; some children might be slower or faster than the wizard or might use unusual methods to make selections.

- When children are participating in WOz studies there are ethical concerns with the method.

Children are a vulnerable user group and need to be protected from harm during experimental work. Their ability to consent, especially to give informed consent, is questionable, and therefore the experimenter or researcher should take special care

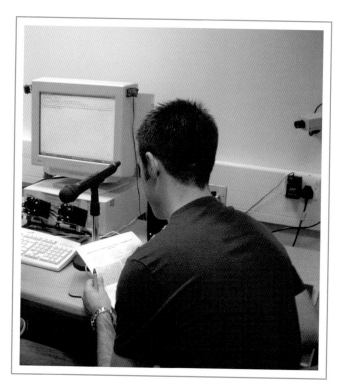

Figure 12.8
The wizard is a human being!

to ensure that the children know what they have participated in, at least after the event has finished.

The Wizard Is a Human Being

Most of the practical problems and concerns with the validity of the research in WOz setups are related to the fact that the wizard is a human being (see Figure 12.8). The wizarding process puts the wizard under high cognitive and physical load because the person must observe the user's input, make decisions on what response is appropriate for the input, and deliver system output using the available user interface. In addition to coping fluently with all "normal" user input, the wizard must be able to manage conflicting rules, interpret boundary values, deal with state transitions, and adapt to users' errors and sometimes their extraordinary behavior. Using a wizard increases latency, provides inconsistent responses, and causes errors from which the wizard must recover.

Several factors influence the wizard's reaction time and decision making. One of the key issues is the usability and natural controls of the WOz system. The number of input–output alternatives and their intuitive compatibility are crucial when the wizard has to act fast, especially in systems where a continuous interaction—for example, in computer games—is required. The wizard's motor abilities, including reaction time, response orientation, speed of movement, and manual dexterity, all affect the performance of the setup. This is why the wizard needs to practice and master the interaction before any participant is brought in. The practicing aims at faster reaction times, correct anticipation of user's actions, and recovery from errors without a long delay. The heavy cognitive and physical load causes stress that leads to perceptual narrowing and reduces the attention span of the wizard. This is why test session lengths and breaks should be carefully designed into a WOz study.

Summary

Wizard of Oz studies give evaluators the chance to test situations and technologies that might otherwise not be tested. This is a very good reason for considering a Wizard of Oz study. However, the study requires careful planning. With children, for the safest use of Wizard of Oz studies, deception should be minimized or eliminated altogether. After the study, tell the children exactly what happened, and ask for their consent again. If possible, use open setups where the wizard's roles and actions are explained to children before testing. Try to record the wizard so the wizard's errors can be distinguished from the child's. Multiple wizards should be used to minimize any one wizard's effect on test data. It is a good idea to let each child take a turn at being the wizard, especially once the deceptive nature of the evaluation has been disclosed!

Further Reading

Research literature on applications of the Wizard of Oz method with children extends to various contexts. For eliciting user requirements and evaluating design concepts for children's user interfaces, see Andersson et al. (2002), Buisine and Martin (2005), Hendersson et al. (2005), Montemayor et al. (2002), Hammerton and Luckin (2001), and Robertson and Wiemar-Hastings (2002).

For modeling children's performance and behavior during system use, see Robins, Dautenhahn, and Dubowski (2004) and Read, MacFarlane, and Casey

(2003). For collecting language and video for further design and evaluation purposes, see Ibrahim, Dimitrova, and Boyle (2004), and Höysniemi, Hämäläinen, and Turkki (2004).

For testing the applicability of the method in novel contexts, see Höysniemi, Hämäläinen, and Turkki (2004), Read, Mazzone, and Höysniemi (2005), and Robins, Dautenhahn, and Dubowski (2004).

CHAPTER 13

SURVEY METHODS

The method of eliciting information by question and answer is commonly referred to as a survey method. There are many such methods, and the term *survey* has many meanings. For the purposes of this chapter, however, *survey methods* are defined as questionnaires, rating scales, and structured interviews (Greig and Taylor, 1999).

Surveys are an established instrument for data gathering, and they have been reported as being used with children as early as the 1890s (Bogdan and Biklen, 1998). However, research and knowledge about the effectiveness of different child survey methods are scarce. In particular, when children are asked to contribute opinions, as with self-reported data, studies that examine the validity and reliability of the children's responses are rare.

This chapter considers the different purposes of surveys and introduces the reader to styles of questionnaires that are specifically for children. At the end of the chapter, a method for eliciting children's opinions, the Fun Toolkit, is described and explained.

What Is a Survey?

Surveys involve questions and answers, and they typically fall into one of two categories: questionnaires or interviews. The former is written, and the latter is spoken. In general, questionnaires are used for large groups and often administered at one time, whereas interviews are usually done in sequence with one respondent at a time (the person doing the survey).

Three people are involved in surveys: the designer, the administrator (the one who carries out the survey and may also be the designer), and the respondent (the one who takes part in the survey and, in our instances, is a child). In interviewing surveys, the latter two roles are sometimes referred to as the interviewer and the interviewee.

It is common to find reports of design projects that mention the use of survey methods with children. In some design projects and relevant research papers, children are asked to contribute ideas and suggestions for future or partially completed designs. Here are some that the authors have used:

- Eliciting children's mental models (Read, MacFarlane, and Casey, 2003)
- Gathering requirements for interfaces (Read, MacFarlane, and Gregory, 2004)
- Discovering the appeal of a product (Read, MacFarlane, and Casey, 2001)

Of specific interest in this chapter is the use of surveys in the evaluation of designs or products, where children are typically asked to comment on the appeal or usefulness of a product or supply some sort of product rating.

The Purpose of Surveys in Evaluation

A survey is generally administered for a purpose. This purpose may be to find background information about the children doing an evaluation study, to gather the children's opinions about the technology they are using, or to determine the answers to certain questions about the product being tested. Sometimes a survey is used to test a hypothesis—for example, if children prefer product A or product B.

To gather background information, a pretest questionnaire or interview is often used. This sort of survey will typically gather understanding of the prior knowledge of the children, as well as general preferences and habits relating to the purposes of the evaluation. This survey, as shown in Figure 13.1), is sometimes called a *user*

Figure 13.1

An image of a child's user profile survey.

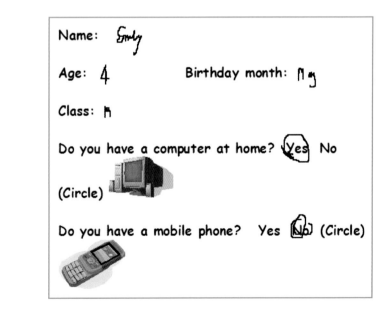

profile survey, and it discovers user experience or user data that are essentially independent of the evaluation.

A second type of survey is one that gathers children's opinions about a product—this would be termed an *opinion* survey. A survey that seeks to discover answers to questions about a product will, of course, be also opinion based, but because it concentrates on a different aspect, it is more accurately called a *product* survey.

Tip

Try to combine user profile data and product or opinion data in a single survey. This makes it easier for children, saves time, and keeps the data in one place.

Often a single survey gathers opinion- and product-specific information, so in the rest of this chapter we use *survey* in a general way that includes both these purposes.

Why Use a Survey Method?

Asking children for their opinions of interactive products can be very revealing. Adults and children perceive the world around them in different ways, so adults may have trouble figuring out what children want. According to Borgers and Hox (2001), "Survey researchers are realizing that information on children's opinions, attitudes, and behavior should be collected directly from the children; proxy-reporting is no longer considered good enough." There is also currently a move to include children in decisions about their own environments. This is a result of a greater awareness that children are actors and participants rather than only onlookers in society.

Borgers, Leeuw, and Hox (2000) said, "In most of the Western world, it is now recognized that children have a voice that should be heard and there is a new demand for research that focuses on children as actors in their own right." Another good reason to talk to children about their interactive technologies, and perhaps the one considered the most motivating, is that involving children in the design and evaluation of their own artifacts is fun and rewarding for researchers, developers, and, most important, children (Read, 2005).

Designing a Survey

If you have decided to use a survey as part of an evaluation study, you must determine (1) who will be surveyed, (2) what kind of survey you will use, and (3) how the

Figure 13.2

Children completing questionnaires.

survey will be administered. The first point concerns the selection of respondents. In a survey with children, it is easy to select only those respondents who will be able to complete the survey. This isn't the best practice, but is still very tempting. It is always preferable to decide who will be surveyed before choosing a method because it gives you the chance to create custom survey techniques and avoids bias. The survey may be intended for a large sample of children across many age groups, in which case it must be accessible to the youngest, or it may be intended for a sample from a large population, in which case decisions must be made about the selection of participants. (See Chapter 6 for a fuller description of sampling.)

Depending on the ages and the number of the children involved, the second decision is about the type of survey. Should it be an interview or a questionnaire (as seen in Figure 13.2.)? Interviews are best suited to confident children and a small number of respondents. They have the advantage that a lot of detail can be obtained (if the child isn't too frightened to respond!). Interviews do not require children to read and write, which makes them essential for surveying preschool-age children. Because the interviewer is present to clarify unclear responses or ask follow-up questions to interesting responses, the information gleaned can be more informative. With skill, the interviewer can also evaluate directly whether the child understands a question and can also determine the degree of comfort the child has with her answers.

Interviews are often one to one, which can make the child uncomfortable, but they can also be done in pairs or with small groups of children. In a classroom context, a larger group of children can be interviewed using what has been called a classroom discussion forum (Hall et al., 2004). This discussion forum is a structured question-and-answer session that involves a lot of brief questions and rapid responses from the children (Hall, 2004).

Classroom Discussion Forums: Interviewing in a Classroom Format

During the design of Fear-Not, a virtual learning environment where synthetic characters act out bullying scenarios, the children participating in a classroom discussion forum suggested that all the scenarios should have happy endings. The teachers agreed. The researchers who conducted the forum considered this a good example of pertinent information that would have been missed had the team relied exclusively on observations and questionnaires (Hall et al., 2004).

Interviews take time to conduct and, if recorded, to transcribe, and several ethical problems associated with the use of recording technology can arise. In addition, an interview can be very daunting. In one interview session carried out by the authors, one child came to the room so scared that she was unable to say anything and finally began to cry! (She was, of course, quickly returned to the safe confines of the shared classroom.)

Questionnaires are less threatening than interviews and are better suited to large cohorts because they can save time. The information that is gathered, however, is often restricted. One advantage of questionnaires is that it is possible to have a large group of children complete them together, maybe after they have seen the technology they are evaluating. Completing questionnaires in one group is time efficient, but, as demonstrated in Figure 13.3, children sometimes copy from one another. This may be because they are either unsure how to answer or they want to make completion easier.

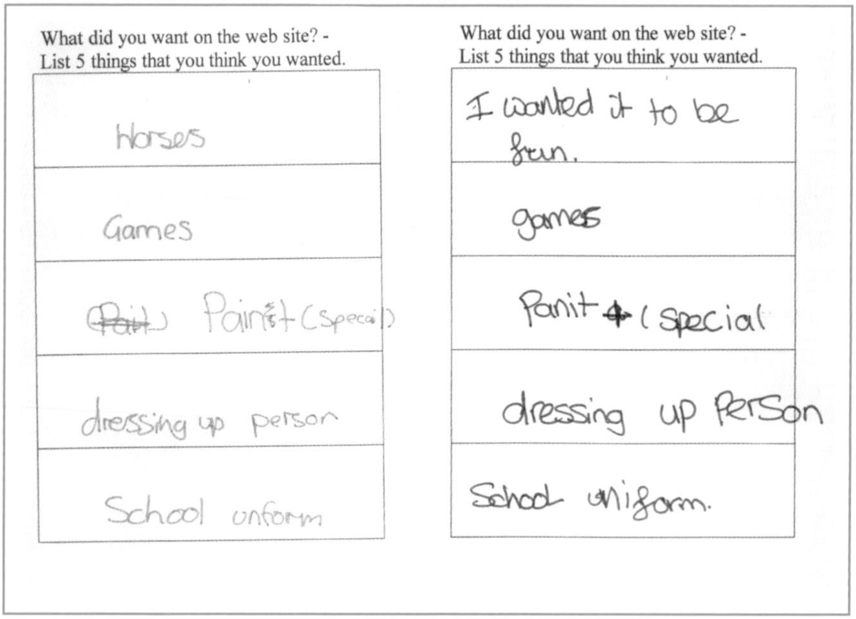
What did you want on the web site? - List 5 things that you think you wanted.

Horses
Games
~~Paint~~ Paint (special)
dressing up person
School unform

What did you want on the web site? - List 5 things that you think you wanted.

I wanted it to be fun.
games
Panit + (special
dressing up Person
School uniform.

Figure 13.3
Two questionnaires showing evidence of copying.

When questionnaires are completed singly, perhaps immediately before or after a child has seen the interactive product, the possibility of copying is removed but it takes longer. This single completion is preferred where children might need help filling out the survey.

Designing the Questions

Having settled on a method and a survey design, attention now must turn to the design of the questions. The best way to learn how to design good questions is to practice. At the very least, the questions must be easy for the children to understand, and the only way you can be sure of this is to try them out on a pilot sample of children.

Tip

If you want your survey to make sense, pilot-test it with a group of similar children.

Another good plan is to show the questions to a teacher. If questions are to be read by the children, the words must be clear and the font used should match the fonts children see in class. For spoken questions, the interviewers must be very careful not to overembellish the questions. A good learning experience for the interviewer is to sit in a classroom for an hour and listen to the kinds of questions the teacher asks.

What Can Go Wrong?

Survey methods rely on a question-and-answer process. Understanding this process is essential for both the interviewer and the person designing the questions. A question-and-answer process has three stages:

1. Understanding and interpreting the question being asked
2. Retrieving the relevant information from memory
3. Integrating this information into a summarized conclusion

If an answer must be coded, there is a fourth step:

4. Reporting the results by translating them into the format of the presented response scale

Tip

Try to avoid offering a long list of multiple-choice answers. Children may forget items that appear early in the list and pick more items from the bottom of the list.

Researchers often discuss the importance of the question-and-answer process in determining the reliability of responses provided by children in surveys (Borgers, Hox, and Sikkel, 2004). Factors that influence question answering include developmental effects (unable to understand); language (unable to find the words needed), reading age (unable to read the question), and motor abilities (unable to write neatly enough), as well as temperamental effects, including confidence, self-belief, and the desire to please.

Research into the completion of surveys has revealed four major issues that are particularly important in understanding how children deal with surveys:

- Satisficing and optimizing
- Suggestibility

- Specific question formats
- Language effects

The first two issues are phenomena that are partly temperamental and partly cognitive in nature; these will have an impact on the general design of survey studies. The last two have more to do with language and age, and are rather more concerned with the detailed design of the question-and-answer processes. In the example shown in the box that follows, Frankie is behaving in a typical way. He has difficulties with the language of the questions, and he is slightly worried about the impact of his answers. Given that these are important phenomena to understand when using surveys with children, they are covered in some detail in the next section.

Frankie Being Frank

Consider the following scenario:

> Frankie, age 7, has been shown three different word-processing interfaces. He saw the first two a week ago in his classroom. The third one has been shown to him today on a laptop. He wrote three stories on the three occasions that he saw the packages— one on ghosts, one on monkeys, and one on space travel.

As soon as Frankie has finished on the laptop, the evaluator asks him these questions:

1. Did you like this better than the last word processor you used?
2. Which of the three did you like best?

Then he shows Frankie pictures of the three interfaces and asks him to give each a score from 1 to 5, where 5 is best. What does Frankie do?

In question 1, Frankie is not sure what a word processor is, so he takes a guess and assumes it is the machine. He likes this one better, so he says, "Yes." In question 2, given that there were only two different machines, he assumes that this one must be about the activity. His favorite activity was writing about ghosts. This was the second one he did, but then he has a problem because he said 1 was better. He takes a chance and says he liked both 1 and 2 the same. In question 3, he gives all the pictures 5 out of 5.

Satisficing and Optimizing

Satisficing theory identifies two processes—satisficing and optimizing—that explain some of the differences in the reliability of survey responses. These processes are especially evident in surveys where respondents are asked to pass attitudinal judgments (Krosnick, 1991), so are less of an issue in a user profile survey.

For validity in the evaluation, optimizing is the preferred process. Optimizing occurs when a survey respondent goes thoughtfully and carefully through all three or four stages of the question-and-answer sequence. Thus, the respondent ensures that he understands the question, will attempt to give an appropriate answer, will think about how the response should be articulated so its meaning is clear to the surveyor, and, if there is a rating system, will carefully consider where on the rating scale the answer should be placed.

Satisficing is a middle approach that occurs when a respondent gives more or less superficial responses that generally appear reasonable or acceptable but without going through all the steps involved in the question-and-answer process. Satisficing has nothing to do with guessing at answers or choosing random responses, but is about picking a suitable answer. The degree or level of satisficing is known to be related to the motivation of the respondent, the difficulties of the task, and the cognitive abilities of the respondent (Borgers and Hox, 2001).

It is, therefore, the case that children are prone to satisficing as they find survey participation difficult and often lack the abilities to articulate answers or to fully understand the questions. In the story of Frankie, it is reasonable to suppose that Frankie's response to the third question may have been a result of satisficing. Satisficing is reduced and optimizing is increased by paying careful attention to the design of the questions and the answers.

Specific Question Formats

As demonstrated in the preceding example, the way in which children are asked questions in surveys has an impact on the reliability of the response. Breakwell et al. (1995) report that children have a tendency to say yes (acquiescence bias) irrespective of the question. This tendency means that questions with yes/no answers tend to be poorly suited to children. This is especially the case where the question is phrased in such a way that the yes answer may appear to be the correct one to the child. The younger the child, the bigger the problem. In one study with

Figure 13.4

A Wong-Baker pain rating scale.

5-year-old children, there were several inaccuracies in questions that relied on the yes/no format (Bruck, Ceci, and Melnyk, 1997).

Free-recall questions have been shown to be useful with children, especially in spoken surveys. One study involved several children who had the experience of being treated for an injury in an emergency room. A few days later, the children were interviewed with free-recall question formats such as "Tell me what happened" and specific questions like "Where did you hurt yourself?" It was shown that as the questions became more specific (i.e., "Did you hurt your knee?"), the response reliability decreased (Peterson and Bell, 1996).

One widely used question format is the Visual Analogue Scale (VAS). A VAS uses pictorial representations through which respondents identify their answers, feelings, or opinions. This approach has been adopted as an alternative to the traditional open-ended and closed-question formats, although some researchers suggest that VAS can only be used with children around age 7 and over (Shields et al., 2003). Studies by the authors and others have shown that visual analogue scales are useful for considerably younger children, but when these scales are used to elicit opinions about software or hardware products, younger children are inclined to almost always indicate the highest score on the scale (Read et al., 2002). Figure 13.4 shows an example of a VAS developed for children.

Language Effects

Children have varying abilities in spoken and written language, and this makes the design of questions for surveys problematic. As in the example of Frankie being frank, it is common for evaluators to use language without realizing that children may not fully understand the meaning of the words. What happened with Frankie is quite common. The child makes a guess that results in a plausible answer, and the evaluator has no way of knowing whether the language was understood. Besides avoiding words that children may not understand, vague and ambiguous words should not be used either. This does not mean that words should not be used at all. For instance, in visual analogue scales, or with multiple-choice responses, the response options should be clearly labeled to help children give reliable answers. That said, descriptors like "satisfying," "fairly satisfying," and "very satisfying" have little meaning for young children, so the words must be understandable.

Children tend to take things literally. In one study by the authors, it was noted that when a group of children were asked if they had ever been on a "school field trip," they answered "no" because they didn't call it a "school field trip." In a more recent study, when children were asked how "good" they thought a writing activity had been, some children gave an opinion of their writing as a product, thus interpreting the question in a completely unexpected way (Read et al., 2004).

In addition to concerns about the phrasing of questions, the choice of language in interview studies influences the rapport between the adult interviewer and the child interviewee. Children's vocabulary may be very limited at younger ages, and when it comes to adolescents the vocabulary may be a mysterious slang. Interviewers experienced with talking to children of the age in question find it easier to adapt their language. In general, however, it is not a good idea to talk down to children or, at the other extreme, to try to imitate the slang used in their own subculture (Keats, 2000).

Exercise

Consider the scenario in which you have been asked to interview children about their use of Microsoft Paint to determine which are the most loved and most disliked features of this application. Choose a target age group, and devise seven questions that you would ask them. Then, if possible, try out your questions on a child.

Carrying out the Survey

Having designed the perfect survey, now you must carry it out. Preparation is vitally important at this stage because you will not get the chance to do it over if it all goes wrong. Questionnaires must be copied well ahead of time, and where possible the children's names should be inserted on them ahead of the event (for removal afterward, of course!). In a group questionnaire session, ensure that all the children have writing instruments or, if they cannot write, pictures and glue sticks (if that is a method being used).

During questionnaire completion, it may be necessary to read the questions (and answers) to the children before they start, to be sure they understand the words. It is often necessary to have helpers in the room to assist the children during completion. With questionnaires that are taking place immediately after an evaluation activity (or even before the activity has begun), it is possible to make some additional notes during questionnaire completion, which can be useful if, for instance, the child has written something badly that cannot easily be deciphered.

In an interview, the main consideration for the interviewer is to have a script that details what needs to be said. The script might start with some operational information like the following:

> Hi! My name is Joe, and I'm from the university in the town. You can call me Joe if you like. I'm going to ask you some questions about what we did last Monday, but if you don't want to answer them, just say so. If you get tired and want to go back to your class, just tell me. I'm not a teacher, so you don't have to be here. Is that okay? Good! Now I want to record you. First, let's see if the recorder works. Good! Okay, do you remember . . . ?

Using a script will ensure that all the children are told they don't have to participate (consent) and that they are all aware they are being recorded. If the interviewer is making notes on a notepad, this should also be explained to the children.

One of the greatest threats to an interview or a one-to-one questionnaire is the influence of the interviewer or researcher. The fact that the children are younger than the interviewer, that the session is taking place in school, and even the gender of the researcher could have an effect. This effect is known as suggestibility.

Minimizing Suggestibility

Suggestibility is particularly important in surveys with children because it "concerns the degree to which children's encoding, storage, retrieval, and reporting of events can be influenced by a range of social and psychological factors" (Scullin and Ceci, 2001). In any survey, the interviewer or evaluator has an influence, even when trying very hard not to impact the question-and-answer process. When the respondents are children, however, it is sometimes impossible not to intervene. In one study, it was reported that "there were many silences that needed some input if only to make the children less uncomfortable" (Read et al., 2004).

Even when intervention is not deliberate, the interviewer still has an effect. In one study it was shown that children gave different responses depending on the status of the interviewer. This was illustrated when a research assistant who was pretending to be a police office asked the children questions about their experience with a baby-sitter. The children then assumed that the nature of the experience of being inter-viewed was bad, so the interviews yielded inaccurate and misleading results (Tobey and Goodman, 1992). It seems that authority figures may inevitably yield different results, as the child may want to please the person who is administering the survey.

Tip

Make notes *while* the survey is being completed. You will be surprised by the interesting things that happen that you might otherwise miss!

The gender and age of the interviewer or person conducting the survey can also have an effect on the reliability or detail of the children's responses. Borgers et al. (2004) suggested that teenagers in Germany were more open to older, female interviewers, but it cannot be assumed that this would be the case elsewhere!

All adults may appear large and intimidating to younger children. One way to reduce the impact of this physical difference is to have the adults sit in low seats, such as a child's chair, during the interview (Keats, 2000). This can be easily arranged in a classroom or inside an installation like the KidsLab described in Chapter 5.

In surveys in schools, children are especially likely to assume that the adult evalua-tor already knows the answers to the questions. Therefore, it is very important that the experimenter conveys convincingly that the child is not the one being evaluated and that there are no right or wrong answers.

Exercise

When nothing means something. In a survey study, it is very possible that a child will not answer questions. Drawing on the work presented in this chapter, and reflecting on your own experience, discuss what a null answer might mean if the respondent is (1) a 6-year-old boy or (2) a 13-year-old girl.

Reliability of Findings

It is inevitable that satisficing and optimizing, suggestibility, specific question formats, and language will all affect response quality and reliability when using surveys with children. Some of these effects will be more pronounced with younger children than with teenagers.

The younger the children, the less stable their responses tend to be over time. Thus, if Frankie was asked the same questions a week later, the odds are very high that he would give different answers. In addition, it has been noted that because children's responses are not very stable over time, it may be that all that can be elicited from a survey is a general feel for a product or a concept with a particular group of children at a particular time (Vaillancourt, 1973). In most evaluation studies, the stability and the reliability of responses are generally not critical (as can be the case where a child is being interviewed as part of a criminal investigation). Given this, there are several helpful approaches you can use to make the surveying process valuable and satisfactory for all parties.

Guidelines for Survey Design

Keep it short. Whatever the children are asked to do, make it fit their time span. This will reduce the effect of satisficing by keeping their motivation high. For young children, five minutes spent in a written survey is generally long enough; more time can be given as the children get older. For example, 30 websites are way too many for a 6-year-old to consider in one session.

Pilot the language. In a survey using written language, children will take shortcuts if they cannot read the questions. Teachers can be helpful in checking if the words used in the survey make sense. They can point out where words might have a different meaning to children. Avoid ambiguity by piloting with just a few children.

Provide assistance for nonreaders and poor readers. Even with the language checked, there will still be children who understand the words but not the questions. Try to read aloud written questions if possible. Do this for all the children (since some will not admit they do not understand what is written).

Limit the writing. Children often do not write what they want to say because they cannot spell the words, cannot find the words for what they want to say, or cannot form the letters for the words they have in mind. If an interview is not a good choice, children can be helped by being encouraged to draw pictures, using images and by being provided with essential words to copy.

Use appropriate tools and methods. Reduce the effects of suggestibility and satisficing by using special methods. The Fun Toolkit that is presented in the next section of this chapter provides tools to assist children in discriminating between rival products (Read et al., 2002). In interviews, use visual props to help articulate ideas, and consider taping the discussion so that the amount of "suggesting" can be examined later.

Make it fun! Introduce glue, scissors, sticky tape, and colored pencils to make the experience fun for the children. If at all possible, print the questions in color, and supply Thank You certificates when the children have finished participating. In the case study interview that's available on the Web, pictures were used as icons representing categories of questions making up the interview. The children could then have a view of the progress throughout the interview, and they enjoyed picking the next question they would answer.

Expect the unexpected. Always have a backup plan. If an entire project depends on the results of a survey with children, it may very well fail! Triangulate where possible by gathering self-reported data, observational data, and some post hoc thoughts from researchers and participants.

Don't take it too seriously. One of the greatest pitfalls in research and development work is reading too much into the data. The information gained from a single group of children in a single place is not likely to be especially generalizable.

Be nice! As outlined earlier, interviewer effects are significant. To get the most from children, interviewers and researchers must earn the right to talk to them. This may require several visits and an investment of time to learn about their culture and their concerns.

There is no doubt that designing and carrying out good surveys take practice and patience, but following these guidelines may avoid many of the common errors and minimize harmful effects.

Figure 13.5

The Funometer before and after completion.

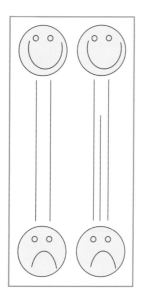

The Fun Toolkit

The Fun Toolkit is a selection of tools that were designed with these guidelines in mind. They use only essential language, lend themselves well to the use of pictures and gluing and sticking for input, are fun and attractive, and reduce some of the effects of satisficing and optimizing. The Fun Toolkit consists of four tools: a Funometer, a Smileyometer, a Fun Sorter, and an Again-Again table. In this section, the four tools are described and some suggestions are made for how they can be used.

The Funometer is a variation of a tool by Risden, Hanna, and Kanerva (1997). It has a vertical scale like a thermometer, on which the child draws a vertical bar that represents the amount of fun. Figure 13.5 shows two Funometers, one that is awaiting completion and one that has been completed.

Funometers require the evaluator to measure the height of the bar that has been drawn by the child and give it a score. It is easy to complete and can be used by very young children (ages 3 and 4), especially because it needs no words.

The Smileyometer is a discrete variation of the Funometer that was originally designed with the help of children (see Figure 13.6). Children are asked to make a checkmark on one face to indicate what they think of a product. This is a very easy tool for children, and it includes textual information to improve the validity. The Smileyometer can be easily coded, and it is common to apportion scores of 1 to 5 for the different faces. When used this way, the evaluator must be aware that the scale is

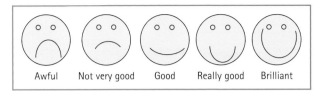

Figure 13.6

The Smileyometer.

only a rank ordering, since the difference between, say, 3 and 4 may not be the same as the distance between 4 and 5. These two tools can be used independently of each other. The child looks at a product or carries out a task and gives a rating using either the Funometer or the Smileyometer (but not both).

In many evaluation studies, the purpose is not to carry out an isolated evaluation but to rank a series of connected or competing activities or technologies. These comparative evaluations can help the evaluator determine which may be more appealing or which may be the least fun. Repeated instances of the Funometer or the Smileyometer can be used, but the Fun Sorter, a variation on a repertory grid test (Fransella and Bannister, 1977), can also be useful in this context.

The Fun Sorter has one or more constructs and a divided line (or table) that has as many spaces as there are activities to be compared. The children write the activities in the spaces; for younger children, picture cards can be made and placed on the empty grid (see Figure 13.7).

The Fun Sorter has the advantage of requiring the children to rank the items or activities in order instead of just using the Smileyometer over and over. Whereas the Smileyometer has been used for comparative studies, the tendency of children to give maximum ratings to products inevitably makes it difficult to figure out which item, from a set of four, is the least fun. The Fun Sorter can be used to measure things other than fun. It can measure how difficult a game was or how nice the interface looked. These are examples of different evaluation constructs. It was envisaged that children would find it difficult to discriminate between the constructs. This is indeed the case with younger children, but as they move into the stages of concrete thought, they seem to be able to deal with relatively similar constructs like fun and ease of use.

The Again-Again table can also be used to compare activities or events. This table lists some activities or instances on the left side and has three columns titled Yes, Maybe, and No. (See Figure 13.8). The child ticks either Yes, Maybe, or No for each activity, having in each case considered the question "Would you like to do it again?" The idea is that, for most children, a fun activity is one they want to repeat!

Figure 13.7

A completed Fun Sorter showing three constructs: "fun," "educational value," and "usability"; it also includes two extra questions. The children filled this in by sticking images of the software applications on a printed sheet. Each construct was completed independently of the other by folding the paper along the serrated lines. This reduced the effect of copying from one construct to another.

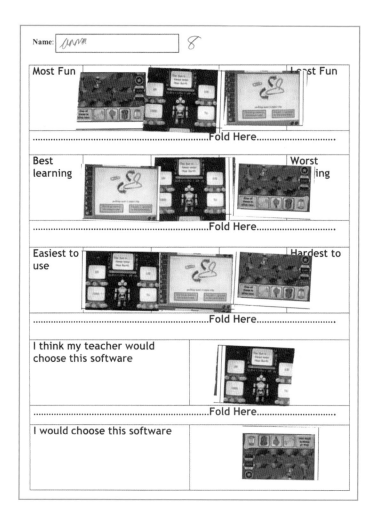

Figure 13.8

Part of an Again-Again table.

Would you like to do it Again?			
	Yes	Maybe	No
Visit U Boat	✓		
Puppet show		✓	

Smiley Mailboxes

An interesting Wizard of Oz study with children was carried out in 2006 by Benjamin Voss, a student from TU/e, who did the project for the Dutch Association of Public Libraries. The simulation was of an intelligent self-service children's book return corner. When returning a borrowed book to the library, a child would be able to express his or her opinion about that book by delivering it to one of three "smiley mailboxes." For example, delivering it to the far right "grinning" mailbox would mean the child really loved the book, while delivering it to the far left "frowning" mailbox would mean the child did not like the book. The installation is shown in Figure 13.9.

The choices for smileys (emoticons) as a representation of an opinion as well as of the number of mailboxes (three) were made on the basis of interviews and tests with children in the public library in Eindhoven. Emoticon cards were used during the interviews to investigate children's familiarity with each of them. In the tests, a cardboard mock-up of the concept replaced the existing self-service book return corner. Some children had difficulties understanding more than the eventually chosen three emoticons, and almost every child found it difficult to rate a book on a scale larger greater than 3. Virtually every child understood and was able to use the mock-up without help, apart from their parents' hints.

Figure 13.9

Using smiley mailboxes in a library.

Guidelines for Using the Fun Toolkit

Research has identified guidelines for the best use of the Fun Toolkit tools. As noted, young children who use the Funometer and the Smileyometer often report events as "Brilliant." In such cases, these tools are of limited value when used in isolation. Indeed, Smileyometers have been used before and after activities to measure expectations, and in most cases children almost exclusively report having had the experience (e.g., brilliant!) they expected to get (Read et al., 2002)! This suggests that fun measures might even be carried out before an evaluation takes place! It is highly possible that the child's perception of the fun she experiences during an evaluation session is governed by her expectations.

This problem is a special case of the "halo effect," known from testing products with adults for cases where the promotional campaign or the branding of the product may lead to positive or negative expectations. With adults, this can be addressed by careful selection of testers or by establishing a longer-term cooperation with testers so they learn what is expected from them and learn the type of feedback that a design team expects from them. In a recent design project where children were involved as testers at various phases of the design lifecycle, the children who had participated from early phases were found to be much more capable as testers than the children who only participated at the final stages of the game development (Metaxas et al., 2005). This approach is one of the motivations for long-term involvement of children in participatory design approaches (e.g., Druin, 1998).

Both the Fun Sorter and the Again-Again table can help in discrimination. It has been noted that children sometimes change their responses on the Fun Sorter, especially when they are young. Anecdotal evidence suggests that they do not like to give one feature or one product the worst score in everything (Read et al., 2001). This behavior, called fair play, has not been seen when using the Again-Again table, so it may be a better tool.

Summary

This chapter provided an overview of the general pitfalls and difficulties associated with the use of survey methods with children, and it provided design pointers for questionnaires and interviews. Many areas remain unexplored in the use of surveys for children. One concerns the possibilities for standard satisfaction questionnaires, such as the Questionnaire for User Interaction Satisfaction (QUIS), with children. Another concern is the contentious area of discovering user experience, as in a user profile survey, when the respondents are children. Although the construction of surveys is an area reasonably well studied in psychology and education, there is still much work to be done!

Further Reading

As background reading for this chapter, the reader would gain a lot from some of the educational research texts that cover interviewing and survey design. Two highly recommended books are *Doing Psychology Experiments* by D. W. Martin (2005), which is a general text not related to children, and *Research with Children: Perspectives and Practices* by P. Christensen and A. James (1999).

CHAPTER 14

DIARIES

Much of the discussion so far has been about tests that are conducted in the presence of a test administrator, are of relatively short duration (an hour or two at most), and are carried out in an environment that can be easily controlled. As discussed in Chapter 5, such settings can be unrepresentative of actual use. When realism (ecological validity) of the test is important, the best choice is often to deploy and test over time, in the field, and without a test administrator present.

Evaluation in the field requires methods for instructing participants regarding their test tasks and ways for collecting information from them so both the accuracy and the completeness of this information are protected. This chapter discusses some of the requirements for field evaluations and long-term evaluations, and it introduces the diary method and the parent evaluator method, which was developed as a way to evaluate at home products for children who cannot yet read and write.

Field Evaluation

Field evaluation is particularly useful when the evaluation goals concern longer-term use rather than first exposure to the tested artifact. Whereas short-term evaluations are helpful for discovering how a new product is used, many aspects of interaction become important only *after* the child has mastered some basic aspects of the system. For example, a longer-term evaluation could examine whether the child wishes to use a product again (an indication of fun) and might discover the negative or positive experiences resulting from longer-term use.

The methods discussed in this chapter are also useful when the evaluation team simply cannot be present where children use the product or prototype. In recent years, interest in these methods has grown as interaction design for children extends beyond educational software for the classroom or the home computer and considers the everyday use of computer and communication applications in a growing range of contexts.

Using Diaries to Evaluate Interactive Products with Children

Diary methods are used for longitudinal studies that take place in a location where the evaluator is not present. A diary can be described as a form of survey in which a diarist, the participant in such studies, independently answers questions set by the evaluator over a sustained period of time. Usually diarists are expected to write their answers in a diary (sometimes called a journal), which is a booklet prepared by the evaluator.

Diary methods share many of the characteristics of survey techniques, so they are well suited for discovering thoughts, feelings, and generally subjective experiences. They are also useful for those situations where it is practically difficult for an observer or test administrator to be present when the product is used—for example, because the evaluator cannot be at the child's home or school for the duration of the study. In these cases, keeping the diary is also an indirect method of observation, where the diarist self-monitors himself or herself.

Compared to other methods, diaries are particularly appropriate for collecting the opinions and thoughts of testers in context, close to the time of the event or experience studied. The diary helps the evaluator understand contextual factors that influence how a product is used and avoids the problems associated with recollection that would arise with traditional surveying of participants at the end of a long period of use.

Figure 14.1

Writing notes in a diary can help a child record opinions and impressions over a period of time.

When using a diary, participants report opinions and attitudes repeatedly over time, and this allows the evaluator to put together a picture of longer-term usage patterns or to discover how problems are encountered and addressed by the diarists/testers over time. A diary evaluation study consists of the following steps:

1. Design the study.
2. Prepare the diary questions and materials.
3. Dispatch diaries and brief diarists for their tasks.
4. Monitor and encourage diary keeping.
5. Conduct the debriefing interview.

Design the Study

Depending on the goals of the evaluation, a diary study can take many forms. Some important parameters that must be established are discussed in the following sections.

Diarists (Informants)

The diarists could be the children who are using the product that is being evaluated, or they could be adults who are observing the children. For example, you may have the parents or the teachers who are in close contact with the children fill in the diaries. Sometimes a combination of the two is required (see Figure 14.2).

Any diary must be designed to meet the capabilities of the diarist. Where diary entries are to be entered in writing, children should be old enough to write and capable of writing text that has meaning. Questions for the children need to match their intellectual abilities and cognitive development. The ability to describe and reason about abstract concepts and to self-reflect is not sufficiently developed in children under about the age of 12, who typically can record only more factual information. In cases where another person, such as a parent or teacher, must record the information, the evaluator should consider carefully whether the diarist can observe correctly and record the required information at the same time.

Structure of the Diary

Like questionnaires, diaries can be highly structured or very open. The structure of the diary is determined partly by the sampling it is intended to support and partly by the kind of questions you choose to ask.

Figure 14.2 *This diary was completed together by a father and son, and it concerned the emotions of the child during a troubling period. It applied time-based sampling, asking the child to record his feelings every few hours. The child could not read or write, so he placed a sticker in the diary, and the father then spoke to his son and wrote corresponding entries in the diary. Source: Johanna Riekhoff, Eindhoven University of Technology.*

Sampling

The diarists may be asked to report at regular intervals (time-based sampling) or to report the occurrence of specific events (event-based sampling). An example of event-based sampling would be making an entry every time a game is played or each time the child engages in a chat session over the Internet. When choosing which mode of sampling to use, the choice will determine where the diarists spend the most effort. Time-based sampling can help portray patterns of use over time, which is not so reliably done with event-based sampling. In event-based sampling, it is difficult to distinguish whether irregular diary entries are due to irregular use of the product or irregular diary keeping. An event-based sampling may be more appropriate when the product is used sporadically and you want to maximize the number of instances captured in the diary of specific types of incidents.

Media Use

Diarists typically capture information in writing (on paper or electronically) or by using cameras or even audio- and video-recording equipment.

Prepare the Diary Questions and Materials

A diary study may wish to address the following questions:

- Do users find solutions to problems they encounter at first contact with the product?
- What patterns of use emerge?
- How is the product appreciated after longer-term use?
- Are specific features used?

Depending on the nature of the questions asked, the diary can be designed to invite open and extensive answers or brief, easy-to-write answers from a closed set of options. A structured diary might look like a questionnaire repeated over consecutive pages of a booklet. Participants can also record the exact time or event that the diary entry describes. For guidance in creating such questionnaires, the general advice in Chapter 13 on survey methods is helpful.

An unstructured diary may include simply an empty space in which information can be written regarding the event or experience described. If necessary, the page can provide, in illustrations or margins, reminders of the topics of interest or of aspects of the product that are being evaluated (see Figure 14.3).

Choosing the right structure and level of prompting for the diary is a decision that requires some deliberation and is one for which pilot-testing is necessary. Repeatedly asking a set of closed questions can help get focused and precise data that may uncover trends and usage patterns. Conversely, less structure and open-ended questions can help the evaluator find unexpected benefits or problems experienced during use.

These are the typical contents of a diary:

- A cover that includes a reminder about how the diarist should record all the information.
- A set of instructions for filling in the diary, on either first page or inner cover.
- An example of a diary page completed by the evaluator. This should be designed carefully because diarists may imitate the writing style, size, and structure of this example or adjust the tone and content of their report accordingly.

Figure 14.3

Examples of a structured diary and an open diary. (a) The structured diary was aimed at understanding whom children choose to communicate with and for what purpose. (b) The open diary focused on their motivations; instead of questions, it included cues printed in the margins regarding what the children could fill — reasons, emotions, contacts, experience, and so on.

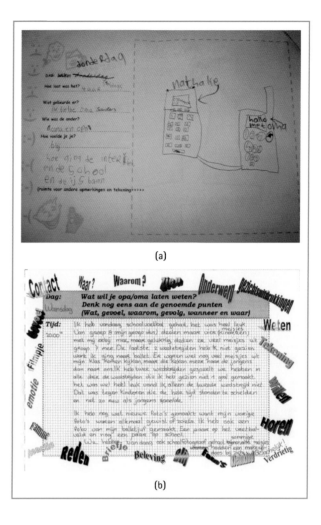

(a)

(b)

Monitor and Encourage Diary Keeping

It is very important to the success of a diary study to convey to diarists how crucial it is to keep their diaries accurately and punctually. It helps if the evaluator speaks to each participant during the period of study to remind him and encourage him to maintain his diary and check if the instructions are being followed correctly. This can be done by phone or e-mail, but it has more impact if direct contact is made. The unexpected should be expected, and a follow-up meeting early in the study period can help improve significantly the quality of diary keeping.

Perform the Debriefing Interview

Typically diaries are associated with a briefing interview at the start, where informed consent can be obtained and the participants can be instructed and encouraged to keep the diary. At the end of the study period, a debriefing interview will allow the evaluator to do the following:

- Examine the contents of the diary and check that everything is legible and understandable.
- Use the contents of the diary as a basis for a semistructured interview, where more data can be obtained regarding the experience studied.
- Cross-check the completeness and accuracy of the diary keeping—for example, by comparing records to the diarists' recollection or comparing records by different individuals about the same event.

One of the major challenges in diary studies is keeping participants motivated. Children can enjoy diary keeping initially, but eventually the compliance required can make it feel more like a chore or (worse!) homework. For this reason, it is important that the materials are designed to be attractive, fun, and playful. For example, in a recent study by one of the authors of the use of communication technologies for cross-generational communication, different materials were designed for children and for their grandparents. The materials for the children were funny and jovial though not childish, such as a funny edited image of an adult on the cover. For the grandparents, a simple and appealing image of happy children's faces was used. It was interesting to compare the information recorded by grandparents and grandchildren, the former being deeply reflective and revelatory and the latter being brief, to the point, and recording very dry and unrevealing facts.

With the advent of digital photography and the decreasing costs of hardware, it is quite common to enhance or even replace diary keeping with the use of audio or photographic records. These can then be used as a basis for a debriefing interview, discussing them with the diarist. Which media are best for your evaluation will be very much specific to your product and your evaluation goals.

The debriefing interview can be structured, or it can be an informal discussion about the diary. In this context, the interviewer can do the following:

- Make sure she can read and understand what is captured in the diaries.
- Ask for clarifications or impressions of the participants not captured in the diaries.

- Ask follow-up questions on the basis of what is recorded in the diaries in written or other form.

In general, you should expect the diary to produce incomplete data that is sometimes illegible and sometimes presented outside the context in which it is meaningful. The debriefing interview is an essential step for obtaining high-quality information and for filling in gaps in the written records created by your informants.

The Parent Evaluator Method

The parent evaluator method is a diary method for evaluating interactive products in the home. In this method the children's parents are required to keep a diary regarding the use of the product. The method requires a fully working prototype and was initially designed specifically for children around age 4 to 6, who are too young to read and too young to execute written instructions for a usability test. This method has several purposes:

- Young children may be uncomfortable or unable to respond to interview questions from an adult test administrator they do not know.
- Children may be uncomfortable or unable to participate in a test at the evaluator's location. On the contrary, their home should be a familiar and comfortable environment where children often engage with technology, such as personal computers, consumer electronics, or video games.
- Parents of young children are often involved anyway in evaluations involving their children, even if only to provide transportation, comfort, or consent.
- Parents are knowledgeable about the habits and behaviors of their children and should be able to judge when they are truly appreciative of and enjoying an interactive product.
- The testing situation in this method emulates situations where a parent introduces the child to an interactive artifact.

Procedure

The core of the parent evaluator method is that a parent acts as a test administrator, an observer, a technical troubleshooter, and a diarist during test sessions executed at home. Several of these test sessions could be spread over the testing period. It is not essential that a test session accompany every instance of product use. In this method, the child has no specific task other than to use the product on a few occasions during the study period. The intention is that usage should be pleasant and that the child should need little or no encouragement to use the product.

The parent is expected to do the following:

- Learn how to use a product so he can act as an administrator and instructor during test sessions.

- Follow some simple instructions regarding how to interact with the child during test sessions: (1) let the child try to solve problems alone and offer help only if necessary; (2) don't let the child struggle for too long before offering help; she may become discouraged, and the situation is not likely to reflect realistic usage; (3) when you do offer help, do not do the task yourself but verbalize and explain to the child what she must do.

- Assist with capturing data in two forms: *verbalization data* in the form of records of the conversations between parent and child and *observation data* recorded in the diaries during or shortly after a test session.

- Answer questions by the evaluator at various points in the study. Questions can be issued as an interview or a questionnaire. They may cover the profile of the child as a user but also retrospective accounts of the whole period of testing or explanations of particular entries in the diary.

Parents are not expected to act as testers themselves while they are getting familiar with a product, since this could lead them to focus only on those problems.

Apart from capturing data during interaction with the product, the parent can be asked to record in the diary interesting incidents and any obvious usage defects (whether concerning usability, fun, or learning) they become aware of—for example, from conversations with the child. Even when the diary is very structured, there should be some room left for open comment inviting the parent to report what he finds important. This provides the parent with the opportunity for a more retro-spective and reflective analysis plus the ability to provide a longer-term view of product use.

Structuring Diaries

Having parents assume the roles of observer and diary keeper creates many challenges. Some of these are discussed here. The importance of a good diary design cannot be overstated. Apart from good question design (that is needed to obtain written data anyway), the diary should be structured in such a way that even someone who isn't an expert (not trained in evaluation or interaction design) will be guided to provide useful observations.

An important consideration is to minimize the diarists' workload. For example, where interaction involves navigating and progressing through different screens, diaries can be adorned with screen shots. These can be repeated for every required sampling period (e.g., thumbnails could be printed on each page corresponding to a separate sampled period or event). Alternatively, the whole diary can be structured around screens, letting diarists record the time and date that correspond to the comments they make. This allows diarists to annotate printed illustrations and point to their elements rather than having to describe them in diaries.

Here are some diary questions that may help parents focus their observation:

- Is your child surprised or even annoyed by the outcome of one of her actions on this screen? Please explain.
- Please describe aspects of this screen that your child needed help with (if any).
- Please describe aspects of this screen that made your child impatient (if any).

Tip

Train parents carefully for their role as evaluators. Also, some will need reassurance regarding their own performance.

How Good Is the Method?

The parent evaluator method is a new and still unproven method that has potential but also poses several challenges. In the first experiences with the method (see Markopoulos et al., 2005), parents found it hard to stop treating the session as a test for their children. This was reflected in their comments and in the fact that some of them pressured their children to execute the test tasks. This had not been anticipated, and it is something that better instructions to the parents could have prevented.

Another problem was that diary entries they provided tended to be very abstract and unspecific—for example, "This was too difficult." The first runs of this method show that more effort should be spent on training the parents for their role. As in all surveys, careful preparation and piloting can help prevent some of the most obvious problems, and the method should be combined with interviews or other evaluation techniques to help understand, cross-check, and make better use of the data recorded in the diaries themselves.

More Guidelines for Diary Studies

If you do not have graphic design skills, use imagery from age-appropriate magazines or websites to decorate diaries. Note that all such artwork (or its absence) sets the tone of communication with the diarists and will influence the type of data you get. Pilot the diaries, and use some of the pilot entries as a basis for an edited personal example on which the participants can model their own entries.

Summary

This chapter has outlined some of the key aspects of the diary method for evaluation. It has described how to design diaries, how to organize diary studies, and how to engage parents in the evaluation of interactive products. Diary methods appear to have considerable potential, especially when an evaluation needs to be carried out over an extended period of time, or when the evaluation is better carried out in a home situation. More research needs to be done to determine guidelines for the best design of diaries for various purposes. The parent evaluator method seems to be a good choice for evaluations with preschool children and may also be useful with babies and toddlers.

Exercise

Pick an application or product you have evaluated already or one that is popular with children. Choose an age group of children that you are interested in and design a diary to support evaluating the product. If possible, ask a child of that age group to try it out.

Further Reading

For a specialized and in-depth discussion of diaries as a tool for social research, readers are referred to Alaszewski (2006).

A practical guide for using diaries as a way to analyze user experiences and for usability testing can be found in Kuniavsky (2003), where issues such as compensation of participants, analyzing data, and different ways to structure diaries are discussed.

Some good discussions for the use of voice mail and other media in diary studies can be found in Palen and Salzman (2002) and Carter and Mankoff (2005).

CHAPTER 15

INSPECTION METHODS

This chapter covers methods where an expert or, better still, a team of experts analyzes the designed interaction with the goal of creating a list of design improvements. An *expert* in this context is someone who is trained in the use of the evaluation method, is not a user, and preferably is not a designer of the product being evaluated.

Inspection methods have been quite well studied in the literature, where they are referred to by a variety of names, such as *expert evaluations, reviews,* and *analytical evaluation methods.* These terms are not exactly synonymous and are not used consistently in different texts. Here, the term *inspection* implies that (1) the evaluation is not empirical, so it does not require that children use a product or prototype, and (2) the evaluation requires the judgment of an expert rather than calculating quality metrics or running simulations.

Inspection methods are a good option when it is difficult to involve children in the evaluation process directly. Relying exclusively on the judgment of experts, rather than watching or asking children, carries some risks; these are discussed at the end of this chapter.

The nature of inspection methods is such that some detailed decisions must be in place regarding the interaction design, and the evaluation requires some level of detail in the prototypes to be evaluated. In some cases, a paper prototype might be a sufficient basis for an inspection, but inspections can generate more substantive results from a relatively detailed and functional prototype that allows relevant parts of the interaction to be tried out. In the case of products for children, the analyst can be a usability expert, a designer with experience in the domain, or even a teacher in the case of educational products.

We will first examine *heuristic evaluation,* a very popular and influential inspection method originally developed for evaluating products intended for adults. Often inspection techniques are called walkthrough methods because they involve a step-by-step examination of how the interaction unfolds. Walkthrough methods exist in many variants. One of them is the SEEM method, which is a structured method for evaluating games for children that has been shown to work for products targeting children ages 5 to 11, although its application to a broader age group and range of products should not be excluded. Evaluation using personas is also introduced. This is followed by a discussion of the merits and pitfalls of inspection methods.

Heuristic Evaluation

Heuristics are generic design guidelines—that is, rules of thumb for good interaction design. The essence of heuristic evaluation is to apply an appropriate set of heuristics and to examine the product or prototype to see whether, how, and how severely it violates them. Each of the problems found in this way is likely to be a problem for the actual users as well, so the evaluator can suggest a corresponding design improvement.

Traditionally, the term *heuristic evaluation* as it was introduced by Nielsen and Molich (1990) refers to usability evaluation using either their set of usability heuristics or the improved set of heuristics that Nielsen proposed in his later research (Nielsen, 1994a). Compared with typical design guidelines, like those found in company style guides, standards, and design guideline documents, heuristics tend to be fewer, more robust, and less specific. This means that they can be applied to a broader range of products, contexts, and interactions, though they do require skill and training to be interpreted and applied correctly during the evaluation.

The Process

Like any evaluation method, a heuristic evaluation requires careful preparation. The first step is recruiting the evaluators. Although it is often the case that a single expert who is reviewing a particular interactive product or a prototype will claim to be using heuristic evaluation, the advice by Nielsen (1994b) and other researchers is to involve more than one expert evaluator. Nielsen (1994b) suggests that a team of 3 to 5 experts is quite sufficient for uncovering about 80 percent of the usability problems that could potentially be uncovered through this method. Recent research has shown that this is a rather optimistic estimate and that the actual number required is case-dependent. For more on this, see How Good Are Inspection Methods? (page 291) later in this chapter.

Evaluators usually work individually; however, they may need to be assisted by a domain expert or a member of the development team. For example, in evaluating a computer game, it may be impossible for the evaluator to know how to overcome game obstacles and reach all parts of the game that should undergo testing.

Someone familiar with the game may then help the evaluator progress through the game play to make good use of the evaluator's time.

Heuristic evaluation sessions are usually no longer than a couple of hours; if necessary, they should be split up to keep sessions to about one hour each. The session should start with a familiarization with the whole product or application before the detailed analysis can be carried out. This gives a feeling for the logical organization of the whole system.

Depending on the time available and the size and complexity of the product evaluated, it may be necessary to restrict the evaluation to only certain parts of the product. For example, the evaluator (or the client) may choose to examine how some common tasks are performed or may simply explore the application, trying to interface with as many of its parts as possible. Focusing the evaluation around representative user tasks—for example, playing some parts of a game, trying to edit and print a small document on a text processor, and so forth—can help make efficient use of the evaluator's efforts. On the other hand, such a focused evaluation may miss serious problems that are related to uncommon tasks or that are not strictly necessary for the performance of the selected task.

Where the evaluator has to go through a particular task scenario, a written step-by-step description of the scenario should be provided. This should describe the intermediate goals that the child must achieve with the product in a language that is appropriate for the child rather than the evaluator. Using child-appropriate goal descriptions reminds the evaluator of the child's perspective and clarifies the nature of the child's tasks and knowledge. In turn, this helps the evaluator to judge the appropriateness of the wording and organization of the interactive product or application.

Evaluators must identify the flaws with the interaction design without forgetting to accompany them with an explanation of which heuristics are violated and in what way. If a particular element of a design violates more than one heuristic, then the explanation should include all the heuristics it violates.

The final step of this process is a group session where the evaluators are debriefed regarding fixes to design problems and where problems and relevant design improvements can be prioritized. To help with this, Nielsen (1994b) suggests that evaluators rate the severity of each problem. This can be done during the group session, but it is usually done individually during the inspection. Nielsen proposed five levels of severity: a *non-problem*, a *cosmetic* problem, a *minor* problem of low priority, a *major* problem of high priority, and a *usability catastrophe* that is imperative to fix before releasing the product.

Different factors can affect the severity rating. It may refer to how frequently the problem is encountered during actual use, its *impact* (meaning how difficult it is to overcome), and finally its *persistence* (meaning whether users will be able to find a way around it once they learn about it).

Nielsen (1994b) and others found that severity ratings are unreliable, and there is much disagreement among evaluators regarding the severity of the problems they find. The reliability improves dramatically if severity ratings are averaged among several evaluators, and this is an important reason to obtain them from each analyst during the group session after a complete list of usability problems has been compiled.

The process of combining severity ratings as a part of heuristic evaluation is one of the "hidden costs" of this method (Cockton and Woolrych, 2002). In setting up a heuristic evaluation, it is worth planning this from the start, taking project-specific factors into account: Are absolute values for severity ratings needed? What would be the consequences of an incorrect prioritization? Is it only necessary to know which problems to fix first within a given time allowed for the design iteration?

Nielsen's Usability Heuristics

Nielsen's (1994a) set of heuristics is not specific to products made for children. Although the flexibility of these heuristics makes them easy to apply to children's products, questions about whether they are appropriate remain. These are Nielsen's ten usability heuristics (adapted from his 1994a publication):

1. *Visibility of system status:* The system should always keep users informed about what is going on through appropriate feedback within a reasonable time.
2. *Match between system and the real world:* The system should speak the users' language, with words, phrases, and concepts familiar to the user rather than system-oriented terms. Follow real-world conventions, presenting the information in a natural and logical order.
3. *User control and freedom:* Users often choose system functions by mistake and will need a clearly marked "emergency exit" to leave the unwanted state without having to go through an extended dialogue. Support Undo and Redo.
4. *Consistency and standards:* Users should not have to wonder whether different words, situations, or actions mean the same thing. Follow platform conventions.
5. *Error prevention:* Even better than good error messages is a careful design that prevents a problem from occurring in the first place.

6. *Recognition rather than recall:* Make objects, actions, and options visible. The user should not have to remember information from one part of the dialogue to another. Instructions for use of the system should be visible or easily retrievable whenever appropriate.

7. *Flexibility and efficiency of use:* Accelerators (unseen by the novice user) may often speed up the interaction for the expert user such that the system can cater to both inexperienced and experienced users. Allow users to tailor frequent actions.

8. *Aesthetic and minimalist design:* Dialogues should not contain information that is irrelevant or rarely needed. Every extra unit of information in a dialogue competes with the relevant units of information and diminishes their relative visibility.

9. *Help for users to recognize, diagnose, and recover from errors:* Error messages should be expressed in plain language, precisely indicate the problem, and constructively suggest a solution.

10. *Help and documentation:* Even though it is better if the system can be used without documentation, it may be necessary to provide help and documentation. Any such information should be easy to search, focus on the user's task, list concrete steps to be carried out, and be as brief as possible.

Tip

Choose a set of heuristics that has been validated for use with heuristic evaluation.

Problem Reporting

The set of defects and fixes that the inspection will produce must be documented in some more or less structured format. The following should be described:

- The affected part of the product, such as the screen, menu, game level, and so forth
- Which heuristic is violated
- Justification of how the evaluator thinks this heuristic is violated
- The severity of the problem
- A possible fix for the problem

For screen-based applications, it helps if prior to the evaluation session the evaluators are equipped with printouts of all screens with enough space for keeping notes regarding the problems they find. Alternatively, screens may be described by short names or numbers for reference purposes, and problems can be noted directly in a form.

Proper problem reporting is not just a "ceremony" added to the evaluation process or simply a matter of thorough documentation. It has been shown that proper documentation of each problem found, the suggested improvements, and even the reasoning leading to its discovery can have a great impact on the effectiveness of the method and the quality of the recommendations that result (Cockton, Woolrych, and Hindmarch, 2004).

Problems with Heuristic Evaluation of Children's Products

The heuristic evaluation method assumes the existence of a set of heuristics that instill good design practice for the domain of interest. Where the users are adults, this is a reasonable assumption for a wide range of situations, and heuristic evaluation is largely considered a cost-effective and useful method, even if few people would suggest that it provides sufficient safeguards for usability on its own. Where the users are children and the evaluation focus extends beyond usability, there is much less established "theory" or established design knowledge on which to rely. This raises doubts about how well the method will work and how reliable an evaluation instrument it is. There has been very little research done on this topic, so it is a good idea to be cautious and aware that this method has limitations. If possible, you should double-check (triangulate) your conclusions using other methods.

Heuristic evaluation requires the expert to identify breaches of guidelines that are anticipated to cause problems for children. This requires that they have some insight into how children would behave in particular circumstances. This may not be easy for evaluators without extensive experience in working with children. Often, children turn out to be surprisingly resilient to issues that adults perceive as potential problems. For example, in a study by MacFarlane, Sim, and Horton (2005), expert evaluators consistently pointed out a problem with the wording of instructions in a product for young children and rated it as quite severe. However, in observation studies of the product being used by children, none of the children showed any evidence of a problem with these instructions, nor did they ask questions about them. It was likely that most of them could not have understood the wording, so they simply guessed at what the instructions meant.

The main benefits of the method are that it is quick and cheap. It also appears relatively easy for evaluators to learn and execute. In many contexts, it is difficult to recruit children for empirical tests, so heuristic evaluation can provide a practical alternative.

Using the Heuristic Evaluation Method with Other Heuristics

This section discusses alternative sets of heuristics that can be used to evaluate children's products. Not all heuristic or guideline sets that codify good design practice within a particular domain will work equally well as analytical criteria. It is advisable to use sets that have been validated for their utility as evaluation tools. Nielsen's heuristics have been through several iterations, reflect considerable experience in designing for usability, and have been designed specifically for use with this method. By now, a considerable amount of research has been invested in assessing and improving them. For alternative sets of heuristics available in the literature, there is hardly any published information regarding how well they can be used for heuristic evaluation.

Tip

Before running a heuristic evaluation with an alternative set of heuristics or guidelines, it is a good idea to first pilot your study to spot practical problems that may arise during an inspection session.

Heuristics for Evaluating Fun

A seminal work in game design is the set of design guidelines for enjoyable interfaces, constructed from an analysis of instructional games by T. W. Malone (1980) in his doctoral thesis. The world of computer games (and instructional games for that matter) has changed a lot since, but this set of heuristics remains very useful today. Malone proposed the heuristics mostly as a design aid, and there is still limited experience with their use as evaluation tools. The following box contains these heuristics in epigrammatic form, adapted from Malone (1981) and Malone and Lepper (1987).

Molone's Game Design Heuristics

Intrinsically Enjoyable Interaction

Challenge: The interaction should have a clear goal. Clear performance feedback should be provided about how close the user is to achieving the goal. The outcome should be uncertain. There should be multiple goal levels and multilayers of challenge so the user will feel initial success and continue to see improvements (sense of accomplishment). Also, goals associated with fantasy elements are preferable.

Curiosity: This is the motivation to learn independently of any goal seeking or fantasy fulfillment. It breaks down to sensory curiosity and cognitive curiosity.

Sensory curiosity: This refers to the use of sound and graphical effects to hold the attention of the player and that can act as a decoration to enhance fantasy, as a reward, or, even better, to present information essential to game play and the learning activity.

Cognitive curiosity: This involves showing players how their knowledge or skills are incomplete or inconsistent and making them want to strive to solidify them.

Fantasy: The system should embody emotionally appealing fantasies that evoke mental images and situations that appeal to the user. Malone distinguishes between extrinsic and intrinsic fantasies for computer games; he considers the latter more interesting and instructional. With extrinsic fantasy, playing the game allows for presenting the fantasy elements, but these are not essential components of the game play itself. With intrinsic fantasy, the game goals cannot be described independently of the fantasy world—for example, solving a riddle. Identifying with a character in the game is useful for intrinsic fantasy.

Control: The players should feel that the outcomes are determined by their own actions.

Appropriate feedback should help players monitor their progress in the game; feedback should be constructive and (if appropriate) surprising.

Extrinsically Motivating Factors

Cooperation: The interface should allow the user the opportunity to work with others (system or other users) to promote interactive learning in a social environment.

Recognition: The interface should allow the user to recognize the purpose of the interface elements presented to her.

Competition: The interface should provide the user with some method of comparing his skills to other users' or to benchmarks set within the system.

Data from MacFarlane and Pasiali (2005) indicate that expert evaluators found the usability heuristics by Nielsen easier to use when compared to a set of heuristics for fun adapted from Malone and Lepper (1987). This may be because they found it harder to relate to children's conceptions of, for example, fantasy, whereas the concepts involved in the usability heuristics were felt to be more universally applicable.

Heuristics for Evaluating Games

Unlike generic products and applications that help a user achieve a task, games created for entertainment are not designed to help users to be efficient and effective. Some games are designed to keep players engaged for as long as possible, and they are enjoyable exactly because they provide challenges and obstacles before players can reach the game goal. Usability appears to work against the aim of making the game fun to play. On the other hand, poor usability of the game interface can actually keep the user from playing and enjoying the game. This apparent conflict between two design goals is easier to resolve when discussing a specific game, where the evaluator decides whether an aspect of the interface constitutes a gaming challenge or a usability hindrance that keeps the player from the actual play.

Korhonen and Koivisto (2006) propose a set of heuristics for evaluating mobile games. These build on several earlier works that combined the heuristics of Nielsen and Malone. These heuristics are split into three categories that address, respectively, the playability of the game, the usability of the game, and mobile issues. The three categories can be used independently to evaluate these different aspects of the game. There is not much known about how well these heuristics support the evaluation of games, let alone games for children, but given the current state of the art on this topic, this set of heuristics is a good place to begin.

Playability Heuristics for Mobile Games

Game Usability

- Audiovisual representation supports the game.
- Screen layout is efficient and visually pleasing.
- Device interface and game interface are used for their own purposes.
- Indicators are visible.
- The player understands the terminology.
- Navigation is consistent, logical, and minimalist.
- Control keys are consistent and follow standard conventions.
- Game controls are convenient and flexible.
- The game gives feedback on the player's actions.
- The player cannot make irreversible errors.
- The player does not have to memorize things unnecessarily.
- The game contains help.

Mobility Aspects

- The game and play sessions can be started quickly.
- The game accommodates the surroundings.
- Interruptions are handled reasonably.

Game Play

- The game provides clear goals or supports player-created goals.
- The player sees the progress in the game and can compare the results.
- The players are rewarded, and the rewards are meaningful.
- The player is in control.
- Challenge, strategy, and pace are in balance.
- The first-time experience is encouraging.
- The game story supports the game play and is meaningful.
- There are no repetitive or boring tasks.
- The players can express themselves.
- The game supports different playing styles.
- The game does not stagnate.
- Units in the game are designed so they are functionally different.
- The player does not lose any hard-won possessions.

Source: From Korhonen and Koivisto (2006).

Heuristics for Evaluating Websites

Currently there is no special set of heuristics that can guide the design and evaluation of websites for children. A report published by the Nielsen and Norman group (Gilutz and Nielsen, 2002) proposes a set of 70 guidelines that may help the design and evaluation of children's websites. Given such a large set of guidelines, there is less scope for walking through scenarios as in a heuristic evaluation. When checking compliance to a large set of guidelines, the evaluator must inspect all parts of the product, such as screens, subgames, or in this case web pages in the website, looking for cases where the product fails to comply with the guideline set.

The relevant web design guidelines for children by Gilutz and Nielsen (2002) are discussed here briefly to orient the reader regarding the evaluation of websites. For a more extensive discussion and examples, readers are referred to the original report. Many of these guidelines are consistent with standard web design practices for adult websites. The following summary highlights those guidelines that are more specific to children:

General interaction: Guidelines in this category refer to child-specific issues of interacting with the Web, like purchasing misspellings of a domain name that could lead to sites that are inappropriate for children, fitting information within one screen because children do not like to scroll for more page content, avoiding "members-only" sections or features because children are usually not allowed to become members, and not asking for personal information that could identify them. Quick rewards should be preferred over long interaction sequences or long downloading processes.

Text: Large text fonts should be used. Avoid text on background images or animated text. Text should be used parsimoniously, since too much of it can put children off.

Navigation: Standard navigation aids should be used instead of inventing special "child-friendly" navigation schemes that are inconsistent with standard and familiar conventions for the Internet. There should be a constantly accessible search feature and a clear indication of the location within the website structure ("You are here.")

Graphical user interface: Purely graphical icons can be ambiguous; labels with icons and text buttons are preferable.

Advertisements and banners: Guidelines in this category mainly advise some parsimony in advertising practices, clear separation from content that is not promotional, and marking exits from the site clearly.

System errors and help: Apart from general advice that is also relevant to adults (see Nielsen's general heuristics on page 272), guidelines in this category advise against pop-ups or dialogue boxes that offer to change browser settings.

Content: Avoid oversimplifying content and indicate clearly the age group for which a site is intended. Include characters in the site, especially if they can be interactive.

Using Children as Evaluators

It is possible to use heuristic evaluation where the evaluators are not interaction design experts but are children of or above the age range for which the product is intended. The rationale for this is that these children might be better able to relate to the intended users of the product and can make better judgments regarding the compliance to heuristics. For example, they might have a better idea of aesthetics or appropriate language. This has been tried in a small study (MacFarlane and Pasiali, 2005) that used both usability and fun heuristics. Results indicated that the children spotted fewer usability problems than did the adult experts, but they did better than the adults (in terms of the number of potential problems noted) with the fun heuristics.

Asking children to carry out a heuristic evaluation brings about new difficulties: The children do not necessarily understand correctly the meaning of the heuristics and cannot predict the implications of problems in the interface.

The SEEM Method

SEEM is a recently introduced inspection method for evaluating usability and fun for educational computer games for children. SEEM stands for Structured Expert Evaluation Method, and it was developed by Baauw, Bekker, and Barendregt (2005). The SEEM process is very similar to Kahn and Prail's (1994) formal usability inspection method, but it goes beyond traditional usability inspection techniques in that it helps evaluate fun aspects of the interaction.

SEEM was developed for evaluating screen-based games where the story line is organized in subgames that correspond to different "screens" or "locations" of the game. This means that each subgame has its own goal constrained within one screen, and the player can navigate to and from that screen. Many computer games follow this general organization. Indeed, many other applications do as well. The difference in comparison with general applications like drawing programs or websites is that each of the subgames is associated with its own game goal that the child acquires and pursues as part of playing the game. A simplified and operational description of SEEM follows. A more extensive discussion can be found in Bekker, Baauw, and Barendregt (2007).

In SEEM, the evaluator proceeds step by step through the game, trying to track the reasoning of players as they discover how the game is played. The evaluator tries to answer a fixed set of questions for every step concerning the reasoning players are expected to perform. As this reasoning unfolds, it exposes problems the players might face, which the inspector can record on a problem report sheet. The granularity of this analysis is deliberately high to avoid becoming tedious. The questions are asked only for each subgame/screen as a whole, rather than each action sequence the user might want to perform while playing the game. The evaluator must ask two types of questions: (1) questions that refer to how the child discovers how to play the game, which assume that this discovery is like a problem-solving process, and (2) questions that refer to what makes a game fun, inspired by the conception of fun by Malone as discussed earlier in this chapter. For each "screen" of the game, the evaluator must ask the following questions:

1. Can children perceive and understand the goal of the (sub)game?
2. Do children think achieving this goal is fun?
3. Can children perceive and understand the actions they have to execute to reach the goal?
4. Do children think the actions they have to execute to reach the goal are fun?
5. Are children able to perform the physical actions easily?
6. Are the navigation possibilities from this (sub)game clear?
7. Are the exits from the (sub)game clear?
8. Is the goal getting closer fast enough?
9. Is the reward in line with the effort children must expend to reach the goal?
10. Can children perceive and understand the feedback (if any)?
11. Is the feedback (positive or negative) motivating?

SEEM is an example of a method that is theoretically motivated and has been validated with a formal experimental comparison. Bekker et al. (2007) provide experimental evidence that suggests that SEEM is more effective than heuristic evaluation for identifying usability and fun-related design defects. Experiences with SEEM are limited to three research studies that involved children ages 5 to 11 and only a specific genre of computer games. It is, however, very plausible that the method is applicable for children of other ages or for different kinds of products.

Practical Tips for Setting up a Predictive Evaluation or Training

Matthilde M. Bekker, Eindhoven University of Technology

When developing SEEM, we determined that it is very important to have an integrated set of questions or heuristics. In an initial study, where experts had a separate set of usability and fun heuristics, evaluators frequently had trouble choosing an appropriate heuristic for the problem they described. One of the main contributions of SEEM is that it provides a way to examine both usability and fun by integrating fun concepts into the various phases of the action cycle.

When we train people who are new to the method, they first get a tutorial on the concepts of usability and fun, such as having to do with hindrances in the interaction and with providing an appropriate and appealing challenge and interesting feedback, respectively. This is extended with an explanation, according to Norman's action cycle, of how users often follow a goal-oriented strategy when interacting with products. Subsequently, they receive a training session in predicting usability and fun problems of a different game than the one that really needs to be evaluated. They receive a manual, including a question checklist and a description of the game with a flowchart of the various screens in the game. Finally, they receive a problem report template to help them describe the various aspects of the problem as accurately as possible. After the training session, they get specific feedback about what problems they missed, which problems they predicted that were not found in user tests, how they can improve the quality of the problem descriptions, and how they have misinterpreted the SEEM questions.

Here are some examples of the things that can go wrong with less experienced evaluators. Because sometimes many things happen at the same time in the interaction, experts forget to write down some problems. They have to practice switching between taking notes and actually playing the game. Another important aspect of uncovering problems is to imagine both first-time and later use of a game. What will children do differently, and how does the game behave? In a similar way, experts have to explore both correct and incorrect actions to uncover possible problems. Finally, it is very important to practice how to fill in a problem report template. Inexperienced experts often forget to be specific enough or forget to fill in a part of the template. For example, they may only state as a problem "Children will have a problem here," without saying to which part of the screen the problem is related—for example, that the spoken introduction by the main character is unclear or the information provided on the screen is unclear. Or they might forget to mention possible causes of the problem, such as children not being able to find the right information, not being able to understand the information that is provided, or finding the provided challenge boring. A good exercise is to have experts try to interpret each other's problem reports and afterward discuss their differences in interpretation.

At first, experts often have trouble distinguishing between problems related to a goal of a subgame and to the actions required to reach a goal. For example, for a particular subgame (see Figure 15.1) in which the main character has to catch flies, one problem may be that it is unclear to children that the *goal* is to bring the flies to the toad, while another problem may be that it is unclear to them *how* to get the flies to the toad. The flies can be brought to the toad by clicking on the flowers. If you click on a flower above or below a fly, the fly gets sucked up by the flower and comes out of the other flower of the same type. Thus, by planning well the flies can be moved until they are near the toad on the right side of the screen. Experts also sometimes have trouble distinguishing between problems related to the planning of actions and actually performing the actions. For example, it may be clear to children playing a subgame that they have to catch a ball with the right answer to a question by using the cursor keys (*planning*), but they are unable to quickly enough position the character to catch the ball using the cursor keys (*action*).

While we have had people with very different backgrounds trying out SEEM, it has become clear that good designers are not necessarily good evaluators and that training is often crucial for a good result.

SEEM, like the other inspection methods discussed so far, requires the evaluator to make judgments regarding the comprehension of the child or what she will experience as fun. Further, to specify the process for doing so, SEEM does not provide help in answering these questions. The characteristics of the children concerned, their interests, prior expertise, and so forth, are all left implicit, as is the case with heuristic evaluation. A practical extension to all the methods considered so far is to make the assumptions about the intended user explicit through the use of personas. Personas and their use in evaluation are discussed in the next section.

Figure 15.1

A screen shot of the game Milo and the Magical Stones, in which the mouse Milo (on the left) must bring flies to the toad (on the right) before he and his friends can continue with the game.

Persona-Based Evaluation

Personas were introduced by Alan Cooper (1999, 2003) as a technique to encapsulate, represent, and use information about intended users during the design of an interactive product. The main idea behind personas is that they describe an archetypal user in a compelling and succinct way, making it possible for members of the design team to rely on a shared understanding of the needs and goals of this persona. The argument is that when designing for a specific persona rather than for an abstract and unclear "average" user, it is easier to make deliberate and coherent design choices.

Tip

Combine personas with heuristics and walkthrough methods.

The reader is referred to Cooper (2003) and Pruitt and Adlin (2005) for extended descriptions of how to use personas. Related methodological discussions will not be repeated here apart from two important issues for personas:

- The persona describes coherent narrative information about the targeted user segment. This information should be based on user research rather than being assembled arbitrarily. Such narratives should aim to accurately reflect the user research rather than resorting to stereotypes of users.

- The persona is associated with goal-driven scenarios that explain how the persona is driven by its needs and motivations to achieve a goal.

It is interesting to see how personas can be used for evaluating a product. Pruitt and Adlin (2005) describe an informal inspection technique supported by personas. They suggest that a persona can be used in a relatively informal "walkthrough" of the interaction by one or more team members. Evaluators act out how the personas achieve their goal with the system by walking through the interaction and reasoning about the reactions and thoughts of the persona. The inspector must examine what sense the persona can make of the interface at each interaction sequence step. Team members can ask each other questions throughout. Compared to SEEM, the question-asking protocol is relatively loose and resembles more a role-play in which actors think aloud about the interaction. The next box shows an example of how a persona can be useful.

Claire Acts out Cristina

Cristina is one of the main personas used by a web design project that is making a children's section for the website of a mainstream television broadcaster. Claire and Henry are the two designers for the project. Claire has constructed the persona of Cristina, a 9-year-old girl who is interested in pop music, celebrities, and drama classes. Cristina uses the Internet regularly to download music and to browse sites intended for girls. Cristina likes to browse with friends or her sister.

Claire acts out a scenario where Cristina enters the website to read news and play games. Claire has the information assembled about Cristina in front of her and tries to follow her intuition in guessing how Cristina will react to the website.

> *Claire:* I go to the website by typing in the address. There are lots of things here. . . . The tiger must be for younger children.

> This stuff is for painting on the screen. Here is something with music in the middle. I'll click on the "Listen to radio" link.
>
> *Henry:* What do you expect to happen if you click on this one?
>
> *Claire:* Well, this other one is about making music. I want to find new pop hits, and there seems to be nothing else like that. Here I get lots of TV programs listed. They all have songs and tunes, but they are all for children. I have to go back and find pop hits on the first page.

Claire acts out Cristina and makes several assumptions about just how Cristina would interact. These reflect the recognition of prompts in the interface and preferences, real-world experiences, and deciding what is childish and what is appropriate for Cristina's age. In these judgments, Claire is supported by the persona. Her conclusions will depend on the quality of the research supporting the construction of the persona and on her ability to empathize with it and bring elements of the persona into the walkthrough performed.

In this imaginary vignette, the team finds that the design is too childish for this persona and that the content she is looking for is not easy to find. Henry prompts Claire very much like an experimenter would in a think-aloud session (see Chapter 11) to get her to verbalize her thoughts. Since Claire and Henry are working together, Henry has to jot down the conclusions and track Claire's reasoning based on his own understanding of the persona of Cristina.

This type of inspection can help uncover learnability problems, but it can also allow for broader discussions relating to appeal, preferences, and even the broader context of the interaction: where the product is used, who else is present, and so on. It is essential that the team member who is role-playing the persona strive to make plausible inferences about likes, dislikes, and motivations based on what is known about the persona. Clearly, there is little rigor in this process, which carries the danger that arbitrary conclusions may be made.

Using Child Personas in Evaluation

Alissa N. Antle, SIAT, SFU, Canada

Introduction

The CBC4Kids.ca redevelopment was an experimental web development project completed in 2002 for the Canadian Broadcasting Corporation (CBC), Canada's largest cultural institution. CBC4Kids.ca is predominantly targeted to a Canadian 8- to 12-year-old audience. The goal for the experimental CBC4Kids.ca pilot was to make the site reflect children's voices, their concerns, their energy, and their opinions. The project involved the design of a new brand, a home site, and three online activities: storytelling, mentoring, and current news. The core team consisted of an executive director, a project manager, a user advocate, an interface designer, an information architect, an art director, a developer, and a database programmer. Contractors were involved as required to augment the core group (e.g., writer, technical programmer, Flash developer). The development project lasted four months, followed by a four-month pilot.

Following a user-centered approach requires methods that include information about children in the design process in ways that are engaging for the team and represent children in a complex and realistic manner. Early in the project, access to children was extremely limited due to policy and liability issues at CBC. Children were not permitted on-site. It was difficult to obtain clearance from the local school board or community centers to work with children on short notice. In addition, the team had limited experience working on new media products for children.

A solution to this dilemma was to create and use child personas. However, the approach implemented differed in several ways from Cooper's original method (see [3] for details). First, since CBC4Kids.ca is a home edutainment product, the creation of the personas was driven by children's developmental needs and abilities in everyday life rather than by adult-oriented goals related to productivity tools. Second, the personas reflected goals for the kinds of experiences that were envisioned for children using the site. Partway through the development process, off-site access to children was granted through a local private school. This led to the third difference: The CBC4Kids.ca personas were validated and used during interviews with children where early design concepts were evaluated.

Creating Child Personas

Based on the team's detailed market research, psychological literature review, field exercises, intergenerational interviews, day-in-the-life time line, home visits, and expert interviews, each team member created one or two personas, resulting in 15 candidate personas. They were created using a template that contained questions and age-specific guidelines related to children's childhood needs, developmental abilities (e.g., motor, social, intellectual), and the experiential goals for each online activity.

Excerpts from the two primary persona profiles are given below.

Rachel, age 10, almost 11, lives in Toronto, Ontario. Rachel is in grade 6 at an elementary school north of Yonge and Bloor streets. She skipped grade 2 and is one of the youngest kids in her class. She is the oldest daughter of a rabbi and his wife, a teacher. Rachel has three siblings: Becky, age 9, Samuel, age 7, and Sally, age 2.

For Rachel, the theme of love, security, and independence is paramount. Rachel is torn between trying to meet adults' expectations (and the security their positive feedback gives her) and her desire to find out who she really is. Rachel can't wait to leave home and have her own life. She needs the courage to cope with these dueling desires and often finds this in her choice of books. She reads Lemony Snicket books the way other kids eat potato chips.

Rachel is an experienced and capable Windows and Internet user. She knows how to find files with Windows Explorer and how to connect her computer to the Internet. However, she has less patience with things not explained up front.

Dodge, age 10, lives in rural Saskatchewan, Manitoba. Dodge is in grade 4 at Waschicho Elementary School in a mixed class of grade 4 and 5 students. He is quite bright (although he doesn't like to admit it) and excels in science, math, and art. Easily bored, he often listens in on the grade 5 classes, only to drift and be abruptly accused of daydreaming. He can watch the colors in the sky change for hours and not get bored. He eats Spaghetti-Os one at a time. He holds the record for tacoed bike wheels. His stories reveal his sensitivity juxtaposed with his attempts to deal with issues of poverty and isolation.

Compared to Rachel, Dodge is less familiar with computers (including common interface conventions and terminology) but much more willing to explore and experiment with unfamiliar sites and features.

Using the Personas

Persona Use during Design Generation

Review of meeting documentation revealed that Rachel and Dodge were instrumental in the development of brand, concepts, content, functionality, user interface, and usability (as discussed in [1]). The practice of thinking and talking about Rachel and Dodge was instilled in design meetings and informal discussions. As a result, the personas quickly became the core focus of most requirements and early design sessions.

One of the primary benefits of using the personas as a design tool was that they prevented us from speaking about children in nonspecific ways. As the team continued to work with the personas, its changing understanding of children and their ability to incorporate this information in design trade-offs became evident. For example, in a discussion of interface labeling for the mentoring application, one team member said to another, "I don't think that Rachel would understand what that meant." From here, they referred to her profile to examine this point in more detail instead of looking for empirical evidence to support a general statement such as "I don't think *children* will understand that." The personas were more frequently referenced during early generative stages of design than later testing phases. However, while the frequency of direct reference to the personas tapered off, their impact did not. The information contained in the personas was assimilated by the team. This was evident in the progression of design discussions and design rationale from intuitive (and often assumptive) to rational (and referenced) explanations of end users. The team learned basic concepts from developmental psychology, learned to apply that information to children they observed and worked with, and dug deeply into needs-based design as the project proceeded. The ability to see the direct relevance in design for the ongoing persona work was cited by team members as a factor promoting engagement. The personas were also educational for new members joining the team, and served as a record for future projects targeted at this market segment [2].

Using Personas in Informant-Based Sessions

Using personas during concept evaluation sessions with children enhanced the value of these sessions for several reasons [1]. First, it provided content for the sessions. The team came to the sessions with design ideas created "on behalf of" the personas that could be shown to the children. Second, by positioning questions relative to the personas, the power imbalance between adults and children was reduced. Children were comfortable criticizing designs the personas had "suggested" (i.e., the personas were seen as peers) where they might not have had been comfortable challenging an adult. Third, the personas gave the child informants users other than themselves to relate to and to design for. For example, a 10-year-old girl asked, "Do you think Rachel would like this?" This helped her peers to abstract the user beyond themselves.

Using Personas in Cognitive Walkthroughs

The Rachel and Dodge personas were used in a series of five cognitive walkthroughs. The reviewers were other employees in the local news media group at CBC. The walkthroughs were done on the earliest working version of the home site and the three activities. Critical tasks were selected (e.g., register as a new user, create a story page, make a movie clip, submit a news commentary). For each task, the set of steps required to complete it was compiled. Reviewers conducted the walkthrough for each task from the perspective of either Rachel or Dodge. Each reviewer was given one persona profile for the user description. The profile provided details of what kinds of knowledge, abilities, and experiences the reviewer could assume about the persona. For example, the aspects of the child personas that dealt with intellectual ability (e.g., reasoning, reading level), computer experience, motivation, and related personality attributes were provided to the reviewers.

The focus of the walkthroughs was on how easy it would be for the persona to accomplish a task for the first time using an exploratory approach (rather than following instructions or using help). The result of each walkthrough was a series of problems that were described and prioritized. One of the benefits of persona walkthroughs is that they allowed us to quickly and easily get early feedback on implemented designs. A large component of the feedback concerned how the reviewer thought the persona would deal with problems encountered, based on their interpretation of the persona's personality and experience. While the reviewer's reasoning was very subjective, this approach allowed us to identify common problem areas where the task flow might be suboptimal. The main problems from this stage were fixed before the prototypes were tested with real children—a process that is much more time intensive.

Using Personas to Brief an External Quality Assurance Team

At the beta stage of the development cycle, a quality assurance (QA) firm was hired to test the entire website's functionality and performance to ensure that the site worked as expected across different browsers, operating systems, and system configurations. They were provided with a detailed document outlining the testing requirements. One section of the requirements included a review of graphics and content. For example, they were asked to check for error message consistency in appearance, wording, and flow across the site. The QA team leader requested descriptions of the target users. All six persona profiles were provided. The QA team later reported that this helped them understand the user in the context of the test requirements. They provided comments on content above and beyond the requirements, based on their understanding of the user group as expressed by the personas. In addition, as their error lists were sorted, the personas were used along with the results from in-house child usability tests to determine the priority for fixing problems. For example, if an error was surmountable based on the experience, ability, and attitudes of two or more personas, its severity rating was downgraded.

Summary

Child personas were instrumental in both the design and the evaluation of the CBC4Kids.ca project. They were used in various forms of evaluation, both formative and summative, to help identify areas where the designs fell short of goals. Analysis of server data indicated that the CBC4Kids.ca website received over a million visits, with an average session time of 20 minutes, during the first three months of its pilot phase. Part of this success may be attributed to the creation and use of child personas that enabled a small team with a short time line to practice user-centered design.

References

[1] Antle, A. N. (2006a). Child-Personas: Fact or fiction? *Proceedings of Designing Interactive Systems*, Pennsylvania State, PA, 22–30.

[2] Antle, A. N. (2006b). Child-user abstractions. *Extended Abstracts of Conference on Human Factors in Computing Systems*, Montreal, 478–483.

[3] Antle, A. N. (2007). Child-based personas: Need, ability, and experience. *Cognition, Technology, & Work, Special Issue Child Computer Interaction: Methodological Research*, London: Springer-Verlag.

How Good Are Inspection Methods?

A typical argument for using inspection methods is that they are cheaper to run than tests. You don't have to recruit children, use special labs, or obtain specialist technology. All you need is a few experts trained in the method. Indeed, the process can even be executed by a single person; this is often what is done in practice.

Unfortunately, the truth is not so rosy for inspection methods. Evaluating with just one or a few inspectors can be misleading. It has been shown that one evaluator alone will uncover only a small proportion of problems and will not be able to reliably assess the severity of problems identified (Nielsen, 1994b). Recent studies raise to 12 the number of evaluators required for a reasonably complex system (Bekker et al., 2007; Hertzum and Jacobsen, 2001).

It is useful to remember that inspection methods are essentially ways to make predictions regarding how users will experience a product. It is hard to get such predictions right, and experts will vary in their ability to do so and in how well they apply a method. When the intended users are children, this prediction becomes especially hard, requiring insight into children's changing abilities, interests, and knowledge, at different ages, and the ability to empathize with them and have an educated opinion regarding what will be appealing in terms of aesthetics, fantasy, and so forth.

A conservative approach is to combine inspection methods with empirical tests (triangulation). One could even go further and ask inspectors to observe a test session or examine survey-based evaluations. Besides cross-checking their predictions, it could inform and improve their own analysis.

The quality of the predictions made by inspections can be described numerically. Predictions of problems are called *positives*; assessing that no problem is expected is a *negative*. Actual problems predicted by the method (true positives) are counted as *hits*; actual problems the method fails to predict (false negatives) are counted as *misses*. When children do not experience the predicted problem, the method produces a *false positive*, or a false alarm (see Hartson et al., 2003). (See Figure 15.2.)

Two numeric criteria for describing the performance of different inspection methods are their *validity* and *thoroughness*. Sears (1997) introduced the following

Figure 15.2 *Hits, misses, negatives, and positives—a vocabulary to describe validity and thoroughness of inspection methods. In reality, actual problems are not known, so methods must be devised to approximate this diagram's sets.*

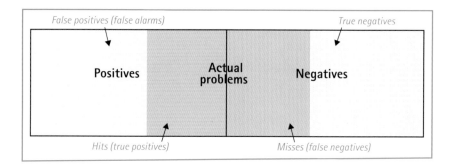

definitions of these metrics, which are still used today by researchers. *Validity* describes the confidence in the prediction made by an inspection method and is defined as follows:

$$\text{Validity} = \frac{\text{Number of hits}}{\text{Number of positives}}$$

Thoroughness describes the proportion of existing problems that are identified through inspection. It is described as follows:

$$\text{Thoroughness} = \frac{\text{Number of hits}}{\text{Actual problems}}$$

The set of actual problems is in practice not known. Researchers approximate it with the set of problems that extensive empirical testing can find. More interesting than the actual numbers arising from calculations is that validity and thoroughness present an interesting trade-off with regard to the number of inspectors. Adding more inspectors should increase the number of positives and eventually the number of hits. The thoroughness of the method will increase correspondingly. On the other hand, more evaluators will also identify more false positives. This reduces the validity metric unless there is a procedure for eliminating false positives.

The conclusion from this discussion is that it is important not only to have a sufficient number of evaluators but to pay attention to the correct application of the method, perform the proper documentation of its results, and base the application of the method on good user research to sensitize evaluators to information about users and context. An assessment of heuristic evaluation practices showed that embellishing commonsense reasoning with reference to heuristics is something evaluators often do (Cockton and Woolrych, 2001). In such a case, the method is only a smokescreen for an informal inspection and becomes counterproductive by obscuring the actual reasoning followed by the inspector.

Summary

By their very nature, inspection methods limit the aspects of the design evaluated to a narrow set of issues that are captured by the heuristics, guidelines, or questions asked during the walkthrough. Context, user preferences, knowledge, and habits are largely neglected or, in any case, are limited to what the design team already knows before the evaluation. During actual use, contextual factors, user abilities, and motivation may mean that expected problems are overcome, are found irrelevant, or are much more severe than anticipated.

Exercises

1. Select an application or interactive product that interests you, like a website, an educational computer game for a PC, or a new portable game platform, and construct the personas for two different children, a boy age 5 and a girl age 8. Make sure your personas have enough substantiated detail regarding the children's experience with computers and the type of application or product you are studying. Examine what types of predictions you can make based on the personas. If doing this exercise as a pair, each of you can role-play the personas.

2. Perform a heuristic evaluation for the chosen application, using an appropriate set of heuristics from this chapter. If you are working in a group or in pairs, try to rate the severity of the problems you identify individually, and compare your notes with others.

Further Reading

Nielsen and Mack's (1994) book is relatively dated but is still the most definitive reading on usability inspection methods. It includes the most complete tutorial descriptions of heuristic evaluation around. An up-to-date overview of usability inspection methods is available in Cockton, Lavery, and Woolrych (2002).

A succinct version of the critique leveled against inspection methods can also be found in Cockton and Woolrych (2002). More detailed arguments and some remedies have been proposed in some of the other papers by Cockton and colleagues cited in this chapter.

PART 4

CASE STUDIES

CHAPTER 16

CASE STUDY 1: GAME-CONTROLLING GESTURES IN INTERACTIVE GAMES

This case study describes how the Wizard of Oz (WOz) method was employed in the design of computer vision–based action games that are controlled with body movements. The QuiQui's Giant Bounce game is aimed at 4- to 9-year-old children and uses simple movements that vary according to the game task. The game does not require keyboards or traditional game controllers, and it uses a web camera and a microphone to "see and hear" the player.

The main challenge in the interaction design of perceptual action games is to ensure the usability and playability of the game controls. These qualities are, on the other hand, highly dependent on the intuitiveness and physical appropriateness of the movements used to control the game character. The Wizard of Oz study was carried out with 34 children ages 7 to 9 to determine what movements and gesture patterns emerge when children control the game prototypes without any instructions given (by the researchers), relying only on the visual cues in the game. This case study also illustrates how the selection of the evaluation method is bound to the features of the interactive product, context of use, and target user groups.

We first describe how the evaluation method was chosen and continue with descriptions of the main features of the study (reported in full in Höysniemi et al., 2004). This is followed by an overview of the issues the case study brings up from the point of view of carrying out evaluations with children.

Finding a Suitable Evaluation Method

After some preliminary evaluations of the game tasks, we discovered that the major issue in ensuring a usable and enjoyable play experience was finding intuitive and appropriate control mappings between the children's movements and the game events. However, due to the novel gaming context, there are no established playing movements for game controls or any evaluation methods to collect those movements. Thus, the first phase of the study was to decide which evaluation strategy we could use to find answers to our research questions without excessive effort.

To find a suitable evaluation method, we began by studying the evaluation goals, the interaction model, the features of the product, the vision-based game design process, the main user groups, and the context of use to set requirements for the methodology. The main characteristics and associated evaluation requirements are shown in Table 16.1.

Table 16.1

Characteristics of the Evaluation Context and Requirements for the Methodology

Characteristics	Evaluation Requirement
Evaluation goal: What are the *intuitive* and *appropriate* game-controlling gestures in specific action game contexts?	Children should be comfortable showing and using the play movements, and those movements should emerge without any guidance External validity over internal validity (generalizability) A child must not have played the game before (background questionnaire) Free exploration to find intuitive movements (game itself provides "tasks" instead of predefined tasks) Interviews for getting information about the appropriateness of the movements
Interaction model: Game controlling with body movements	Difficult to "low-tech prototype" the game movements without animated feedback Functional prototype is needed because action games require immediate feedback from the system
Context of use: Game is aimed at homes and schools	Field testing
Contents of the data: Collected data should contain children's movements in relation to game events	Observation method Video recordings that show both the children's movements and the game screen
User group: Children between 4 and 9 years of age	Participants should fit into that age group Older children within the age group are more capable of providing feedback on the physical appropriateness of the game gestures (aiming for 7- to 9-year-old testers)
Social play context: Physical game play is social, and movements are often invented together with friends	Pair or group testing Children tend to be more relaxed with a friend in the test space Children can choose with whom they want to play (real social context)
Data that must be collected: Versatility of the game movements between children	Number of participants should be high enough to reveal movement patterns
Spatial requirements: Physical game play requires space	Test space with video cameras: 5×5 m required
Resources: Iterative design of computer vision algorithms is highly time consuming	As little redesign of vision algorithms as possible during testing Game design is easy using commercial authoring tools Design of vision algorithms should be based on children's intuitive movements, not vice versa
Data analysis: Limited set of tools and methods to analyze captured movements	Requires piloting the analysis of the collected data with different movement analysis methods

The main characteristics and evaluation requirements helped us to narrow down candidate evaluation methods. To sum up, we needed an observation method that enabled pair testing in a school environment to gather data on children's movements but that did not require putting extensive effort into building functional computer vision–based prototypes. The latter part of the requirement implied that simulation of the actual interactive system could be employed.

Being inspired by the wide usage of the Wizard of Oz method to design and collect language corpora in speech-based systems (Dahlbäck, Jönsson, and Ahrenberg, 1993; Gould et al., 1983; Kelley, 1984), we decided to experiment with the WOz approach. We replaced the computer vision technology with a human wizard who observed the users and controlled the prototypes with a mouse and a keyboard. Unfortunately, we soon found out that there were no guidelines for how to apply the method in this new domain with children. This highlights the fact that practitioners often need to adjust existing methods so they can be used for evaluating children's products.

There was no formal hypothesis for the study because it was impossible to fully anticipate beforehand which movements would emerge in certain gaming contexts. Therefore, we were interested in gathering as wide a range of data on the movements as possible. The study aim was also to simulate a real-world play situation where learned movements in one game affect the movements in another game. So we decided to run the evaluation as a within-subjects study with a "large" number of participants. Also, the number of participants had to be big enough to be able to discern any distinctive patterns in the data. Additionally, two children were present in the test space. This balanced the ratio between adults and children and also provided a more natural social context in which the play movements were imitated and modified between children. Note that it is well justified to say that this kind of evaluation is exploratory; there was no clear hypothesis, and the evaluation aimed to answer open questions and discover usage patterns of a novel interactive system.

The Study

After selecting the WOz method, the actual evaluation study needed to be designed so that it fulfilled the evaluation requirements. The following sections describe the study in more detail.

Preparations

Before the evaluation began, the researchers prepared background questionnaires, implemented and tested the game prototypes, piloted the test setup, and made certificates for the children to thank them for taking part in the study. The head-master of the school was approached, and he provided contacts with teachers who wanted to take part in the study. Two meetings were arranged with teachers to agree on the selection criteria for the participants and on an appropriate schedule so that schoolwork would be disturbed as little as possible. The teachers delivered the background questionnaires and participation forms to homes and ensured that all were signed.

Interactive Prototypes

The study concerned gathering game movements for four different game proto-types: a spider game, a jumping game, a swimming game, and a running game (Figure 16.1). The animations and game controls were designed so that they provided the wizard with flexible control over the game events and enabled consistent behavior among the participants. The prototypes were programmed using the Macromedia Flash multimedia authoring tool. The view of the webcam connected to the computer was placed in the bottom left corner, as shown in the figure. However, the prototypes were controlled entirely by mouse and keyboard.

Figure 16.1

The four game prototypes: spider game, jumping game, swimming game, and running game.

Test Setup

The tests were held in a local primary school during four days in the 2003 spring term. The test space was an ordinary large classroom reserved for the testing, and the wizard was located in the same space to facilitate the test arrangements, as shown in Figure 16.2.

Our WOz approach involved a wizard, a pair of children, and an adult researcher called the experimenter, who introduced the test setup, guided the testing, and interviewed the children between the tests. The wizard controlled the games, operated the video cameras, and took notes during the interviews. As outlined earlier, the test was carried out as pair testing to reduce shyness and to balance the ratio

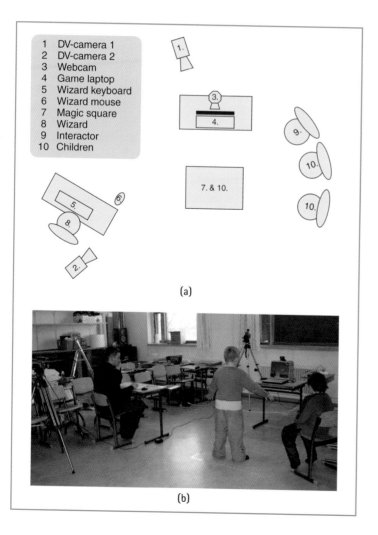

Figure 16.2

The layout of the test setup.

between adults and children. According to our previous experience, young children are more relaxed and more able to communicate with adults when there is another child in the test space. We had two wizards, one with extensive computer gaming experience and another who was a novice computer game player. Before the tests, the wizards agreed on common rules for controlling the games.

Participants

The participants were 34 children ages 7 to 9. Fourteen boys and 20 girls participated in the study. Children who had played QuiQui's Giant Bounce before were not selected to participate in the testing. Both the children and their parents were asked permission for participation in the tests. The parents also filled in a questionnaire with their children to provide us with background information. The testing was carried out as a pair testing in 17 pairs (11 pairs of first-grade students, age 7 to 8, and six pairs of second-grade students, age 8 to 9). The experiment was designed to balance the order of the games introduced to the children and the games played in pairs.

The nature of participants's relationships affects the results and the test setup. Thus, the children were asked to name two or three classmates with whom they wanted to test the prototypes. The pairs were formed according to the children's wishes. The test sessions for each pair lasted between 15 and 30 minutes, depending on how much the children wanted to comment on the game.

Test Space Design

The layout of the test space is shown in Figure 16.2. The test setup consisted of two DV cameras, a laptop computer, a mouse and a cordless keyboard, and a web camera. The DV camera marked as number 1 in the figure was placed so that the recorded material could be used in the design and evaluation of the computer vision algorithms. Camera 2 recorded material for the purposes of movement analysis and matching movements with game events. The furniture in the classroom was moved so that the wizard could easily see both the computer screen and the players' movements. Since the game allows free movement in the gaming space, we used a "magic square" marked on the floor to show the children the optimal playing area in front of the screen in plain view of the video cameras.

Procedure

Before the actual testing commenced, the experimenter introduced herself and the project and explained the overall testing procedure to the children. When the children entered the test space, the video recording was started. The actual test session was divided into three phases: the introduction of the test setup, the play session, and the interview.

The wizard was introduced briefly, and the test setup was presented to the children by the experimenter; however, the real role of the wizard was not described. The wizard then started the actual WOz procedure with a randomized selection of game prototypes. The first child stepped into the magic square, and the other child sat in a chair until they changed turns. At the beginning of each game prototype, there was a spoken introduction that briefly explained the idea of the selected game but did not give any information about the movements expected.

When the game began, the wizard started to control it, attempting to match the child's movements. Once the first child had completed a game task, it was the other child's turn to play the next game. This procedure continued until both children had played all four game prototypes. After the play session, the children were interviewed about their preferences for game events as well as the appropriateness of the movements they used to play.

Children's Movement Analysis

Our evaluation had several aims: to collect video data of children's movements, to analyze the resulting movement patterns in certain game contexts within the video data, and to study children's perceptions about the appropriateness of the movements. The remainder of this chapter discusses the issues in video analysis and in studying children's movements in the design of computer vision–based games.

Preliminary Video Analysis

Human movements can be represented in digital form in various ways: Some examples are videotapes, notation systems, and movement databases. The difficulty in analyzing and representing human motion is often caused by the large size of the collected time-based data and a very specialized application area. Because the main challenge of the study was to find the appropriate movements for a large number of players, the categorization of and comparison between children's movements were crucial. Even though inexpensive annotation tools such as Anvil (Kipp, 2001) exist, we also needed tools that allow the presentation of each child's movement sequences simultaneously and the grouping and maneuvering of these sequences.

The movements appearing in the videos could be divided into two categories—*obvious* and *nonobvious*—according to how easily most participants adopted the movement style and whether it could have been anticipated beforehand. For example, because of the game character animations, running is an example of an obvious movement. Most of the children ran when the game character was running. However, in the swimming game children adopted various swimming styles, such as the dog paddle or crawl, which both belong to the "swimming" category but are very different movements from the perspective of computer vision design.

The analysis is different for obvious and nonobvious movements. The main emphasis in the definition of obvious movements is to find accurate descriptions that define, for example, how participants run when they control the game character and then to collect a set of video sequences that illustrate how most of the children performed that type of movement. The analysis of the nonobvious movements focused on categorizing the children's movements and finding underlying patterns that could further be used to define guidelines for computer vision and animation design. The video libraries based on the nonobvious movements are more versatile. Even one child can change his or her movement from one style to another during game play.

Another characteristic of movement description is *accuracy/ambiguity*. These qualities are closely related to the specific needs of computer vision design. The level of accuracy depends on input device technology—for example, whether the final system is based on one or two cameras—and what body parts are influencing the visual input. It is also important to define what parts of the data can be described in a less unambiguous manner to save time—for example, in cases where the computer vision design is still open to big changes and alternative options are available.

The videos of the 34 children playing the games contained a substantial amount of data. One means to simplify the description process is *sampling*—that is, only selected sequences of a child's movements are described. This is especially useful in situations where a child's movement pattern remains similar for longer periods of time. The sampling method was defined to cover all variations in the children's movements (see Figure 16.3).

Figure 16.3

A jump sample.

Experimenting with Movement Description Methods

After the preliminary data analysis, two approaches that allow visual comparisons between children's movements were tried out: (1) using Laban notation to describe the movements and (2) describing the movements using simplified logging techniques and visualizations.

Laban Notation

Developed by Rudolf Laban (1975), Laban notation is a symbolic system for representing movement of the human body in space and time. Similar to music notation, which uses a staff, Laban notation consists of columns for indicating the body part that is moving. The duration of a gesture is represented by the length of the symbol. The benefits of Laban notation are evident: It allows visual comparisons between the participants' movements and the symmetry and asymmetry of the movements, as well as the rhythm and length of the motion. However, the Laban notation staffs were too detailed for the design needs of the system being developed.

The biggest drawback of Laban notation is not its laborious nature but that to master the notation system, a lot of practice is needed. It is also difficult to use the staffs as a communication tool in the design process if not all team members fully understand the notation. Nevertheless, it is worth noting that Loke, Larssen, and Robertson (2005) have been studying the advantages and disadvantages of Laban notation as an analysis tool for movement-based interaction in the context of two EyeToy games.

Low-Level Description Techniques

Because Laban notation requires so much effort, we decided to experiment with less complicated description and visualization methods. The tools used were image and video editors, spreadsheets, and pen and paper. First, all the events appearing in the videos were listed, and then the appropriate movement sequences were sampled (such as a child's running movements in the beginning, middle, and/or end of the game, as well as in places where there were distinctive variations in the running pattern). In addition, each nonobvious movement type was analyzed based on its popularity—for example, if it was the first movement type a child tried, if it was the main movement type for that child, and how many children actually used the style in question.

The coding schemes were further defined according to the requirements of the computer vision design. It was important to describe the movement on a 2D plane and focus on its speed and extent, with particular focus on the movement of the upper body (since children varied their distance from the display and webcam, which partially hid their legs). The computer vision algorithms that, for example, detect a child's running can be based mainly on physical cues appearing above the waist level. Additionally, all anomalous happenings needed to be reported, such as rapidly moving braids of hair and clothing or knees raised high.

The challenges for defining the coding schemes were to define the codes for each different movement and to measure, and often estimate, numeric values such as the angles of the joints and the child's vertical movement during the movement cycle. For example, we used the proportions of the head as a measuring unit for comparing vertical movement along the running cycle. Fortunately, precise values were not necessary from the point of view of computer vision design, which in the end mainly relied on the video sequences produced during the description process.

The detailed analysis of the movements was based mainly on image sequences of the videos, which are typically only 5 to 25 PAL video frames (200 to 1,000 milliseconds) in length (such as one running or jump cycle). The sequences are usually easier to analyze with all the frames visible side by side, compared to the frame-by-frame manipulation of video editors or annotation tools. Another benefit of having the movement cycle visible in its entirety was that the frequency of steps, different phases in the movement cycle, and the phrase durations were relatively easy to measure. Additionally, the sequences could be used more easily than the Laban notation staffs to inform the game character design later on, as it did not require learning any particular notification system.

Results from the Study

The full results are reported in Höysniemi et al., 2004, and Höysniemi et al., 2005. In summary, the study showed that WOz prototyping of perceptive action games is feasible despite the delay caused by the wizard. The results also show that distinctive movement categories and gesture patterns can be found by observing children playing games that are controlled by a human wizard. The approach minimizes the need for fully functional prototypes in the early stages of the design and provides video material for testing and developing computer vision algorithms, as well as guidelines for animating the game character. The next section briefly describes the set of results obtained while studying one particular movement style: swimming.

Intuitive Movements for the Swimming Game

The analysis of the swimming game revealed four main swimming stroke categories: (1) the dog paddle (a child moves his hands exactly as a dog does when swimming; the arms stay in front of the body and move in a circular pattern, alternately thrusting forward and back); (2) the breaststroke (a stroke in which a child extends the arms in front of the chest and then sweeps them both back laterally); (3) the crawl (i.e., freestyle); and (4) the "mole" stroke (similar to the dog paddle, but both hands move together). As shown in Figure 16.4, the dog paddle (which children in

Figure 16.4

*Four different ways
to swim: (a) the mole
stroke, (b) the crawl,
(c) the dog paddle, and
(d) the breaststroke.*

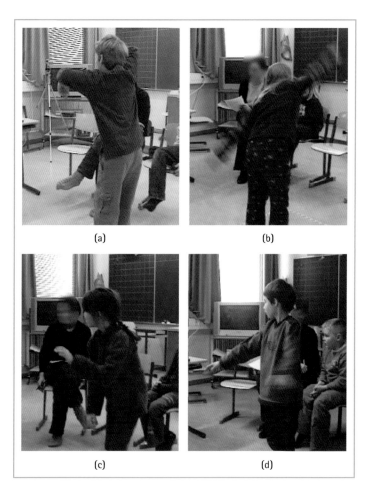

Finland often learn as their first swimming stroke) and the breaststroke were the most prominent.

The popularity of the breaststroke surprised us because the children who participated in our study were first and second graders, and Finnish children usually learn this swimming style in third or fourth grade. It was also interesting to see that so many children used the breaststroke even though the avatar animations would have suggested to them to try only the crawl. Thus, the Wizard of Oz study revealed swimming styles that were not anticipated by us. The results also show that finding intuitive movements is not restricted to the avatar responses, since children were not afraid to try out other movements than those proposed by the avatar animations (see Figure 16.5).

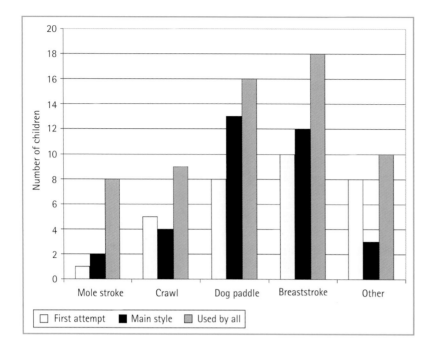

Figure 16.5
Swimming styles.

Commentary on the Study

This case study dealt with how selection of an evaluation method is based on the characteristics of the particular research domain and the evaluation aims. It also illustrates a situation where the aim is to collect a large set of behavioral data for design purposes instead of an experimental setup where variables are strictly controlled. Although there are many points for discussion in this case study, we focus here on a few of the most important issues that might help practitioners in carrying out a simulation study with children. Those issues are ethics, test setup arrangements, and pilot analysis of the test data.

Ethics

Simulation studies, such as WOz setups, pose challenges for ensuring ethical conduct during the evaluation, as discussed in Chapters 4 and 12. When applying an approach where either the responses of the system to be evaluated are "preprogrammed" or the functionality is simulated on the fly by a human being, it is essential that the rationale for doing so is well thought out. We had a lot of discussion about ethics and the ways in which we could minimize the potential risks, as described next.

Lack of existing data/research: The method provided us with invaluable information on the intuitiveness of the movements. It also allowed us to collect a "movement corpus" that we could not find in any previous research. There was no existing research on what movements children prefer in different game contexts.

Instability of the early computer vision prototypes: Using a wizard ensured that the experience was not unpleasant, frustrating, or discriminating for the children, since the wizard was more likely to be able to interpret their movements than a computer vision system developed with no prior usability tests.

Applicability of the results: Based on our earlier experience in developing perceptive games, we deemed that we would be able apply the results in practice, possibly benefiting children's physical health and activity.

Allowing freedom for children's physical expressions: We reasoned that although using a wizard would increase latency, the children would be able to adapt to it. The wizard, better than an actual implementation, would also be able to empathize with the children, guess what they were attempting to do, and try to control the game accordingly, which would not constrain the children's possible physical expressions.

Hiding the wizard's role: We assumed that children would have behaved differently if they had known the game was controlled by the wizard. However, we placed the wizard in the same room so that the whole setup was visible for the children. The wizard's presence also made it easier for the wizard to respond accurately due to the children's spontaneous comments during game play.

Emphasizing functionality defects: Children were told that the prototypes were not ready yet and that if they did not function properly, it was definitely not their fault. We felt that it was even more important to make sure that children did not feel they were being judged if the simulated system functioned a bit strangely.

Telling the truth: There are several approaches to when and how to tell children that they have been evaluating a simulated system. We decided to tell the children only if they asked whether a wizard was actually controlling the system.

Although we have had very positive experiences with a simulation study in terms of the results and the applicability of the method in evaluation studies with children, we advise that practitioners critically think through alternative options before using such a methodology in their work. However, sometimes an evaluation of a simulated system provides the most valuable data and may lead to future innovations.

Test Arrangements

It cannot be emphasized enough how crucial cooperation with teachers and parents is when carrying out tests in the field. When carrying out group testing, teachers can provide valuable information about group dynamics and participants' developmental stages. Additionally, parents informed us about the physical educational background and possible physical limitations that would affect their children's behavior and the versatility of the movements observed.

The tests showed that the wizard can be present in the same space with participants, which makes it easier to organize tests, especially in schools or day care centers. However, a few children were distracted by the wizard's actions, apparently because the mouse clicks were audible—for example, every time the child jumped, a clicking sound followed as the wizard reacted. We propose that control devices should be as inconspicuous as possible. The keyboard and mouse controls should also be designed so that the wizard's hand movements are slight and quick.

Pair testing proved to be a good choice, since the children were talkative and provided us with valuable information about their mental models of the games. For example, some children did not understand that in the swimming game the main character was under water in the beginning, so they tried to control the character in ways not anticipated by the "swimming character." As a result, the story leading to the swimming game and the audiovisual cues in it had to be redesigned and evaluated with children.

Pilot Analysis of the Test Data

The successful design of an evaluation very often contains a pilot-testing phase where the key practicalities are tried out and refined. However, the pilot analysis of the test data is often a forgotten practice because researchers feel they can utilize the data and data analysis tools immediately after the evaluation. Unfortunately, this is not always the case; sometimes the data are not even gathered during the pilot testing.

One of the key lessons of this case study was that by piloting more with the data obtained from pilot tests, we could have facilitated some measurements (such as jump height) more easily—for example, by adding a measuring rod in the background of the test space. Instead, we needed to use video editors to add a grid over the videos, which was a significant effort compared to the alternative "low-tech" solution. Additionally, we could have studied the available human movement analysis tools further to understand that none of the existing inexpensive tools supported the type of analysis we were aiming for. This finding led to a more time-consuming analysis process than we anticipated because we needed to experiment with multiple solutions to analyze the movements.

Summary

The main lesson learned from the study is that the design phase (Chapter 6) is the most critical step of a successful evaluation. Even though we had put considerable effort into studying the requirements and designing and pilot testing the setup, we found that the phase after the evaluation required more attention. This post-test phase is crucial, especially when gathering data that require immense treatment before they can be presented in numbers and words, or when using analysis tools in which the feature set does not absolutely suit the purpose. Thus, to avoid surprises, it is advisable to spend time designing, playing with, and actually employing data analysis tools during the test design phase.

CHAPTER 17

CASE STUDY 2: EMBEDDING EVALUATION IN THE DESIGN OF A PERVASIVE GAME CONCEPT

This chapter illustrates how evaluation with children can be embedded in the interaction design process. It is largely based on an earlier publication coauthoured by Jannek Verhaegh, Iris Soute, Angelique Kessels, and P. Markopoulos (Verhaegh et al., 2006). It describes a series of evaluations that informed the design of Camelot, a mobile outdoor game intended to encourage social interaction among children ages 7 to 10. Reflections on the methodological choices made are discussed.

The Design Project Context

The project was executed by a team of three postgraduate students who were studying interaction design. (From now on, we refer to them as the "designers.") The educational objective for this project was to learn how to embed evaluation methods in the interaction design process. The designers had varying levels of experience and a mix of educational backgrounds (mechanical engineering, psychology, computer science). The team possessed some skill in putting together simple electronics and software, and they all had considerable affinity with, and experience in, user research methods. This is worth keeping in mind should other teams wish to follow similar practices. If such a mix of expertise is not available, slightly more time would be needed to obtain input from outside (e.g., programming support or technicians).

The project was conducted over a period of six months, during which the equivalent of three months of full-time work was allocated to it. The designers and all the children involved were Dutch, and all of the study's evaluations were conducted in Dutch.

Although this was a design project, it also had an exploratory nature. The designers were encouraged to apply innovative methods and to break new ground where possible in the methodology. The objective of the design process was to develop and evaluate a game concept rather than go all the way to developing a marketable product.

Children and the Design of Camelot

Eight girls who were 7 to 10 years old and two 8-year-old boys participated in the design of Camelot. They were all pupils of a small primary school in a rural area of

The Netherlands. The children were taught as a group in the school, and no child from this group was excluded from the study. The same children participated at all stages of the design where their involvement was judged useful and feasible.

After discussing and agreeing with the teachers regarding the nature of the activities that would be carried out at the school and with the children, parents were asked to complete consent forms that provided them with a description of the study that outlined the nature of the activities their children would participate in and the intended use of audio or video recordings. Designers could work with the children during afternoon hours dedicated to extracurricular activities. The teachers were consulted and involved throughout the study.

The Mission from Mars Method

At the opening and formative stages of the design project, it was decided to survey children about the outdoor games they play. This study was not evaluative in purpose, but it is described here because of its interest as a survey technique. Unstructured naturalistic observations had already been conducted in the playground, as well as some informal and unstructured interviews through which the designers became acquainted with the children and their playing habits. The challenge facing the team at this point was that children were asked to reflect on an activity very familiar to them (play). It seemed inevitable that children might assume that adults know enough about play already and that they were soliciting a specific "correct" set of answers.

The team chose to apply the Mission from Mars method, introduced by Dindler et al. (2005). Mission from Mars is an interview technique where children are questioned through an audio link by a supposed Martian whom they cannot see. Children are told that the Martian is completely ignorant about the topic discussed. During the interview a researcher acting as the Martian elicits explanations at a very basic level about this topic. Such simple questions may not seem natural to the children if they come directly from an adult interviewer.

The Interview

The preparation and the execution of the interview took two days. On the first day, the designers told the children that they had received a signal from space that after "translation by a supercomputer" turned out to be a request for help. The message said that Martians only knew how to work, which was boring to them, so they wanted to know more about games and how these are played by children on Earth. Children were asked to translate the second part of the message using "The Martian translator," a simple software application where children could paste in an unreadable text that would be translated into Dutch. The text further elaborated the scenario of the Martian and the Martian's interests.

Following the translation and discussion of the Martian letter, the designers asked children to take photographs as a preparation for the second day, when they would encounter the Martian. On the second day, the children divided themselves into four groups so that they could work with friends. The children took pictures of game play on the playground and created a collage with pictures of their favorite games.

For the encounter with the Martian, two adjacent rooms were used: the interview room for the children and the "Martian room" (see Figure 17.1). In the interview room, the children sat facing a video camera, through which they could be observed by the Martian, and faced a loudspeaker through which they could hear the Martian.

One of the designers took the part of the Martian. Her voice was distorted to disguise it and create a more convincing "Martian experience." Before the start of the

Figure 17.1
Setup of the two rooms for the Mission from Mars session.

interview, the children were told that they could only hear the Martian but that the Martian could both hear and see them by means of a camera, so they could show their collage and explain its content. The groups had 15 minutes to talk with the Martian. During this conversation, one of the designers sat with them in the room in case they needed reassurance or help. The interviewer acting as the Martian was assisted by a "prompt," who helped her choose the questions to ask.

The interview was semistructured, involving simple laddering—for example, asking children to elaborate on aspects of games they mentioned as fun and explain what made these enjoyable to them. After finishing the conversation, the children returned to their classroom. At the end of the day, a small debriefing was held, in which the children could ask questions about the toest. At this point it was revealed to them that the Martian was not real, and they were shown the interviewer's room and the camera setup through which they had been observed.

Interview Outcome

The interview yielded some conclusions about what the characteristics of the game to be designed should be.

- The game should involve rigorous physical activity, such as running and chasing.
- The game should have an element of suspense, such as hiding in hide and seek.
- The game should allow make believe and role playing.
- The children should be involved continuously, avoiding situations when, for example, someone is tagged or knocked out, albeit only temporarily.

Reflections on the Mission from Mars Interview

The procedures of this study followed those of the original application of the method by Dindler et al. (2005), with the addition of the collage activity. The abilities of our participants to read and write varied drastically. Some children were very fast and translated the Martian's letter within 30 minutes. Others were easily distracted and did not complete the task. The translation was stopped after 45 minutes, and the designers discussed the session with the children. The idea to make a collage came spontaneously from one of the children during a discussion about another planned activity. This project gave the children the opportunity to be active in shaping their participation in the design process, allowed them to have fun, and was simple to do.

Most of the children took pictures of games they liked, as instructed. A few took pictures of less relevant topics. A designer guided each group while they were making the collage. This was necessary because some children found it difficult to stay focused. Two groups of children (7–8 years) tended to include as many pictures as possible, regardless of their relevance. The oldest children in the study were very conscious about what to display, describing several games, the rules of the games, and the objects needed.

By this time, the children had become comfortable with the designers and were quite talkative during the collage making. Unexpectedly, the collage making turned out to be a good moment to ask questions about playing games in general. In a project that is more pressed for time and resources, it might be preferable to run the interviews purely during and after collage making, omitting the Martian setup.

Some children were intimidated at first by the Martian voice, but after a while they answered all of the Martian's questions, including the "stupid" ones like "What is a ball?" This was in line with the motivations of the method. Confirming the core rationale of this interview method, one girl mentioned, "You already know a lot about games, so I don't have to explain everything to you. But for the Martian it is different."

Questions like "Why is that game fun?" were too hard for the children to answer, requiring a level of reflection and abstract thinking that the children did not yet possess. Common answers to this question were "Just because" or "I don't know why. I think it just is." In retrospect it seems clear that such questions should have been avoided.

The success of the interview does not seem to have depended on whether the children believed the story about the Martian; this was also reported by Dindler and associates. A week after the session, the children were interviewed regarding the credibility of the Martian story. The children said they had enjoyed all the related activities and that they would like to talk to the Martian again, even after they were told there was no real Martian!

A major drawback of the Mission from Mars interview method is that it involves deceit, even though the children are told the truth afterward. As it turned out, one of the youngest children became slightly apprehensive during the interview, which indicates that this method should be avoided for younger children. For children around age 9, the interview method seemed to work well: It was fun and allowed the designers to get to the level of the children. A couple of children had guessed correctly the nature of the setup and played along happily. Our conclusion is that the deceit involved in Mission from Mars is enjoyable and harmless but probably not necessary and, on balance, should be avoided. A valuable element from this method is the dimension that appeals to the fantasy and playfulness of children.

The effort involved in setting up the Mission from Mars interview seems to be justified only when talking about daily activities and very familiar situations where answers to fundamental (even naive) questions are sought. When evaluating an application or experience that is new to children, this need does not arise. A practicable subset of the study reported is the collage activity and the related interview.

Paper Prototypes with Observations and Picture Card Interviews

Based on the interview study, three game concepts were developed (see, for example, Figure 17.2). The following evaluation was conducted to obtain some quick formative input from the children.

Paper Prototype Evaluations

Paper prototypes for the three game concepts were made. Each game was introduced to the children in the classroom, after which they played the game outside. For each game, one of the designers was the game leader who answered the children's questions during play and helped apply the game rules. The children were

Figure 17.2
Early nontechnology-based testing of one of the game concepts in the school gym.

observed during play and were interviewed after each game in groups of two or three. All three games were tested on the same day.

To help the children stay focused on interview questions, picture cards were made to be used as prompts during the interview (see Figure 17.3). Questions were divided into five categories: *My Input, Playing Together, Collecting, End,* and *Other,* and each category was represented by a card. The cards were placed facedown on the table, and the children were asked to turn a card over. Depending on which icon was revealed, the designer would ask the questions of the corresponding category, thus helping the children understand the structure of the interview (around the themes), to observe the progress through the interview (how many questions were still remaining), and to some (limited) extent give a sense of shaping the interview process, since the order of the questions depended on the card the child turned over.

Outcome of the Evaluations

The observations showed that the children enjoyed the running and tagging involved in one of the game concepts. As they often do in normal play, they were observed adapting game rules; children would switch the ranks given to them as part of the game rules, giving the highest rank to the team member who could run the fastest. Concerning our interest in supporting social interactions, we found that during the game there was no time for the children to discuss game tactics; this was mainly done before the start of the game. Also, observations showed how children would "cheat"— for example, holding more cards in their hands than was allowed by the game rules.

The interviews revealed difficulties the children had with playing the game. For example, one of the game concepts involved collecting cards and carrying them

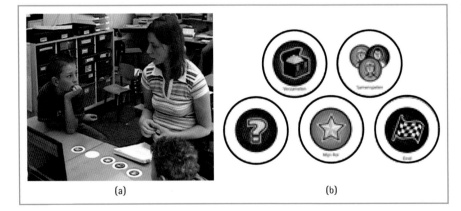

(a) (b)

Figure 17.3

(a) Interview with picture cards and (b) images on the picture cards.

between set locations. Children mentioned that they had trouble remembering these locations. Interviews also showed the preference of children for playing as a team rather than individually.

Reflections on Concept Testing

The evaluation concerned paper artifacts and focused on game mechanics. Observing game play proved invaluable for understanding how children experienced the play, and it would not have been feasible if they had just been asked to comment on a game description and visualization. Especially for designing games, it is good practice to move on early during the design process to play-testing game concepts.

Making interviews semistructured and using category cards turned out to be good decisions. After the first interview, children started to anticipate the questions associated with each category. The cards helped in drawing the children's attention back to the questions when they were distracted. Interviewing in groups of two or three children proved effective; in larger groups, children tend to distract each other.

Evaluating Interaction Styles with Peer Tutoring

A single game concept named Camelot was formed as a synthesis and adaptation of the earlier game concepts. The Camelot game concept is described briefly next.

The Camelot Game

The aim of Camelot is to construct a toy castle before the opposing team constructs theirs. To build a castle, teams need to collect virtual resources spread around a large playing area, which could be the size of a playground. They need to bring the right amount of appropriate materials to their castle construction site and also earn parts of the castle and thus construct it little by little.

Players can use special "collector" devices to collect virtual resources from zones that are spread throughout in the playing field. To acquire a resource—say, water—players must remain in a zone where this resource is available for a predefined period (10 seconds). Once they have acquired a resource, the players can take it back to the construction site or trade it with other players. A player can carry a maximum of two resources at a time. Resources that are not immediately needed can be stored for later use at the castle construction site.

At random times in the game, a virtual ghost appears, who steals resources from the teams. To avoid this, players have to capture the ghost. The team that is the last to prevent the ghost from taking their resources loses, even if their completed construction phases are untouched.

Peer Tutoring Evaluations

Prototypes of the tangible collector devices were made using Phidgets (sensors and actuator devices that offer a very simple high-level programmable interface, allowing for prototyping of interactive devices using a nonstandard interaction technique). Two different interaction techniques were implemented for collecting resources: the *proximity* interaction and the *shake* interaction. The two techniques were compared using peer tutoring (see Chapter 11).

First, five children were given "tutor training," in which the test administrator explained the roles of tutor and tutee and demonstrated the tasks the tutors would have to explain to their peers, such as picking up a resource at a zone, transferring it to the castle, and so on. The tutor training was carried out in two sessions: one with two children and one with three children. Each trained tutor tutored one peer (see Figure 17.4). To prevent tutors from taking over from the tutee during the play sessions, the children were seated on opposite sides of the table. After the session,

Figure 17.4

Peer tutoring: a tutor training the tutee about the tangible interaction styles that were supported. One of the designers watches the procedure.

the children were allowed to play with the devices and were interviewed about the interaction techniques used.

The test showed that the children clearly understood the feedback given by the tangible devices. They found that the proximity-based interaction was the easiest to use, although the shake interaction was more fun.

Reflections on Peer Tutoring

The peer tutoring method worked well for most children, making it easy to find out whether they understood the interaction. Some children forgot the tasks they were supposed to tutor and needed help from the experimenter. It is worth noting how the conduct of the experimenter can strongly influence the process and the outcome of the test. In the first tutor-training session, the experimenter gave a shorter explanation of the test than during the second. This difference was reflected in the tutor sessions: The children who were trained in the first session explained less than the children trained in the second session. (See Figure 17.5.)

Surveying Form Preferences

Several different shapes for the collectors were considered: a stick, an egglike shape, and a wristband (set 1). Furthermore, three different ways of visualizing the type of resource (water, wood, and bricks) were created: icons, colored fabric, and colored paper (set 2). Nonfunctional mock-ups were created and tested with the children.

Figure 17.5

Paired comparisons of different form designs.

The Paired Comparison Test

The children were asked to do a paired comparison test individually. They were shown the two sets of shapes, and within each set they did repeated paired comparisons and chose the preferred interface. Analysis of the results revealed that most children preferred the wristband combined with an icon for information visualization.

Reflections on Paired Comparisons

It had been expected that this method would make it easier for children to choose and rationalize, since the items were presented two at a time. Indeed, it turned out that some children were better able to explain their choices, compared to previous interviews where multiple choices were discussed at once.

Evaluation Summary of the Camelot Design Concept

Three types of untethered devices were built: two devices that represented the castle construction sites for each team, six small portable "resource collector" devices, and the three zones where resources could be acquired. These devices were implemented using programmable microcontrollers. The ghost and the castle were acted out during user testing by members of the design team (see Figure 17.6).

The collector and zone devices in the prototype communicate with each other through infrared LEDs and IR detectors. To acquire a resource, the player must place her collector on top of the resource zone. Trading is also supported; by holding a full collector to an empty or half-full collector, the two units of the former collector are traded for a unit on the latter collector. Game rules such as

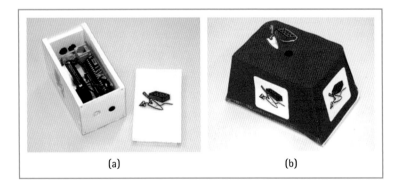

(a)　　　　　　　　(b)

Figure 17.6
(a) The resource collector and (b) the resource zone.

waiting in the zone for 10 seconds or the capacity of a collector are applied by the embedded software. Feedback is displayed through LED lights. The castle site for the evaluation was a cardboard construction containing several drawers. When a team assembled sufficient resources, they were allowed to take a part of the castle from one of the drawers. Players could use parts obtained in this manner to assemble the castle bit by bit.

Play Testing of the Camelot Prototype

The prototype was evaluated to answer questions that ranged from the suitability of the designed interaction elements to higher-level questions, such as whether the game is fun and whether the desired social interaction and physical activity take place as intended. Because of bad weather on the day and to facilitate setting up recording equipment, the evaluation was held in the school gymnasium.

The designers introduced Camelot to the children and demonstrated how the collectors worked. Then the children were split in small groups to familiarize themselves with the equipment. Next they were divided into teams of two for the test. The research team assembled teams of equal strength, based on the earlier experiences with these children. Every team participated in one session of about 20 minutes that consisted of two games. A test administrator stood next to each castle to keep track of the collected items and to help players when they did not know what to do.

All the games were recorded on video, with cameras placed at two corners of the room so the actions of each team would be captured for subsequent analysis. After each game session, both teams were interviewed separately. Interviews were semi-structured using cards, as was done during the earlier concept testing.

Interviews and observations showed that the children had no trouble interpreting the interactions with the collectors. Feedback was successfully obtained on a variety of issues. For example, the waiting time at a zone for collecting a resource was felt to be too long. Such a result was not obtained when evaluating the paper-based prototypes, where the children could cheat and wait for a shorter time at the zones. With the interaction between devices implemented, the act of collecting a resource was experienced as more challenging and more exciting thanks to the visual feedback. The children indicated that they liked running as a part of the game and thought that it balanced well with resting, such as during acquisition of the resources or building the castle (see Figure 17.7).

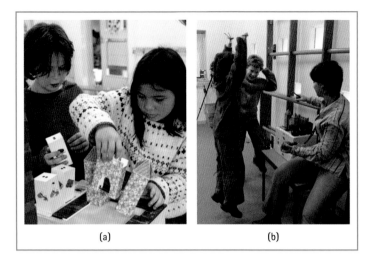

(a)   (b)

Figure 17.7

(a) Building a castle and (b) winning the game. One of the designers sits by the castle to ensure that the game rules relating to the (not yet implemented) castle are followed.

Cooperative social interaction could be observed in the form of talking or yelling, which occurred frequently between players on the same team. The players would encourage each other to hurry up or advise a teammate which resource should be collected next. The children also celebrated together when winning the game by jumping and cheering loudly. During the interviews, the children clearly indicated that the game with the ghost was the most fun and said they appreciated the suspense that the ghost brought to the game.

Reflections on the Play Testing of Camelot

The play-testing evaluation of Camelot had more of a summative role compared to the earlier evaluations discussed in this chapter. For this purpose, including children who had not participated in the earlier evaluations, and perhaps having a larger number of evaluators, would have led to results in which one could have more confidence.

A structured observation (as was originally planned) proved difficult to do well in practice. During the play test, several interactions between the players and with devices were taking place at once, in various locations in the room. Obtaining video recordings for post hoc analysis is much more challenging in this context than when evaluating desktop applications. During the session, the designers could also act only as observers in a very limited way because they were occupied with multiple tasks in administering the test session.

It is worth reflecting on how the approach to prototyping and evaluation may have influenced the findings. In this case, the ghost was simulated by one of the designers.

The fun that the children associated with the ghost could be attributed to interacting with her as opposed to the ghost (as a game element) adding fantasy and suspense to the game. Although the design project ended at this stage, it is clear how this series of design and evaluation activities could continue further to address such issues and to work out the details of the game further.

Summary

This chapter illustrated how some of the techniques discussed in earlier chapters of this book are recruited and combined throughout the design of an interactive game. Each of the evaluations was effective in informing and adjusting intermediate design decisions leading up to the eventual design concept. The case study also illustrates how working with a small number of children who participate in all evaluations can be an efficient and effective way of involving children, although, at the end, testing with a different group of children could have been beneficial.

Several ethics issues arose and were dealt with: choosing participants, obtaining consent, making choices regarding deception, explaining how to show the parts that were not implemented, as well as allowing children to participate in shaping both the design and the design process.

The entire study could not have been possible without the enthusiastic cooperation of the school staff, who ensured that the children's participation fit well with their activity program and became an enjoyable and rewarding activity for the children, too. This cooperation was possible to obtain for nonprofit purposes but may not be as easy to achieve in an industrial context.

Finally, it should be noted that many of the difficulties for the team arose out of the unconventional nature of the interaction design, including several children moving around, children interacting concurrently with each other, and children handling the designed artifacts. Such interaction challenges methodologies that originate in the evaluation of desktop computer applications with adults, and it is bound to become increasingly common. Compared to a decade ago, evaluators need to become increasingly inventive in adapting methods but at the same time need to be conscious of how evaluation outcomes can be affected by methodological limitations or necessary adaptations of the methods.

CHAPTER 18

CASE STUDY 3: USING SURVEY METHODS AND EFFICIENCY METRICS

This case study illustrates several issues, including the selection of participants, the selection of metrics, and the difficulties in gathering opinions from children, especially where novel technology is involved. The study that is described was intended to determine the relative usefulness of four different input technologies for children. It compared four input methods—a mouse, a keyboard, speech recognition, and handwriting recognition—and included children between ages 6 and 10.

This case study's most important characteristics were the organization of the study and the methods used to ensure that the findings had reasonable reliability. The reader should consider what the options were at different stages of the design of the study and what might have happened if other options had been chosen.

The chapter begins with a description of the salient features of the study (reported in full in Read, MacFarlane, and Casey, 2001), followed by an overview of the issues that the case study brings up and then some discussions and questions for reflection.

The Study

This study was conducted as part of a larger piece of work that evaluated the use of handwriting recognition technology with children. It was designed to compare four input devices so that future work could be benchmarked against the findings from this initial study. The hypothesis was that the four input methods would differ in speed of entry, accuracy of entry, and children's preferences. The design was a between-subjects study with a small number of participants.

Because of time constraints (the study had to be completed over three days), to balance out the order of the activities, a decision was made to run the keyboard and the mouse activities consecutively. This made it appear as if there were only three cases to consider instead of four. To minimize the effects of learning, as discussed in Chapter 6, a pseudo–Latin Square approach was taken (see Table 18.1). The table shows how the four input methods, speech (S), keyboard (K), mouse (M), and handwriting (H), were allocated to the children in turn.

Table 18.1

*The Order in Which
Children Met Each
Technology. Note how
the keyboard and
mouse were considered
as a single evaluation
in order to allow for a
design that minimized
learning effects and
improved validity.*

Child	1st	2nd	3rd
1	S	K/M	H
2	S	K/M	H
3	S	H	K/M
4	S	H	K/M
5	K/M	H	S
6	K/M	H	S
7	K/M	S	H
8	K/M	S	H
9	H	S	K/M
10	H	S	K/M
11	H	K/M	S
12	H	K/M	S

S, speech; K, keyboard; M, mouse; H, handwriting.

Before the evaluation began, the evaluator prepared questionnaires, created four different texts to work from, created interfaces, and made a set of certificates to thank the children for participating. The school was approached, the work explained, and contact made with the teachers of the children who were to take part.

The study was carried out in a small U.K. primary school on three days over a two-week period. The evaluation took place in the library, which was a reasonably quiet place, and the children came there one at a time and worked alongside a single evaluator.

The 12 children who took part in the study were selected in a systematic way by arranging all the children in the school (between 6 and 10) in order of age and selecting every tenth child; as a result of this method being used, there were unequal numbers of girls and boys (see Chapters 5 and 6 for a discussion of sampling methods). The parents of the selected children were contacted to obtain consent for their children both to take part in the work and to be videotaped. Each time the children came to the study, they were told that they did not have to take part and advised that they could leave if they wanted to; no child took this option.

Over the two-week period, each participating child used all four input methods. To avoid fatigue, the children did only one task per day (this took 15 to 25 minutes), and for individual children at least two days separated each task. For each input method were being studied, the children were required to carry out three activities: initial orientation and/or training, a copying task where they copied writing that was put in front of them, and a composition task where they added their own ideas to a story starter.

Training

Each task required different training to ensure that, on commencing the main activity, the child was comfortable with the hardware and the software interface. A training activity was therefore designed for each input method, and the children carried out this activity until it was seen that they were sufficiently competent. The training needs had been established in a pilot study with four children who did not take part in the final study (see Chapter 6 for a discussion on the use of pilot studies with children).

The keyboard was familiar to all the children, so for training they simply typed their name. If it was seen that they had problems—for example, dealing with capital letters or finding the space bar—then they were given instruction and the specifics of the keyboard were explained (principally the use of shift, caps lock, space bar, backspace, and delete). The mouse interface (shown in Figure 18.1) had a

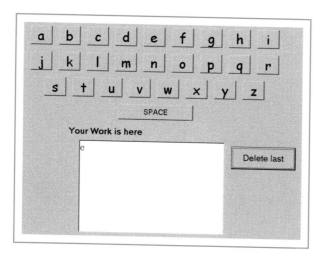

Figure 18.1

The mouse interface that the children used.

virtual alphabetic keyboard and a text display box. The children were shown how to select characters and were then asked to input their name. This activity highlighted those who were unsure about how to use the mouse, and these children were then shown how to proceed.

The speech recognition software used was IBM's ViaVoice Millennium, version 7, which had been previously customized (trained) by a young female with a local accent. The children used a headset microphone, and they tried out the software by reading some text, during which time they were given advice (speak clearly, talk naturally) on how to get good recognition. The handwriting was enabled with a Wacom tablet and pen, using Paragraph Pen Office software. Initially the children were encouraged to use the pen to trace over the letters that were on the screen, and then they wrote a few words of their own. They were given advice relating to the size and orientation of their script.

Test Task Design

Four different texts to copy and four different story starters were used to initiate the composition work. The text that the children copied in each instance was constructed using words from a reading list that was appropriate to the youngest children and was similar in structure to text that the children would have encountered in their school's reading scheme. An example is shown in Figure 18.2.

Each child worked on all four methods, and the text used in each input method was constant. Thus, it was the case that for the speech input, for example, each child copied the same text and used the same story starter. The Microsoft Word grammar-checking tool was used to ensure that readability and word length

Figure 18.2

Example of text children copied.

A5 (Handwriting)
Ben lived near the supermarket
One day he went to get food for the cat.
He saw a big green lion sitting on the cat food. It was called Matt.

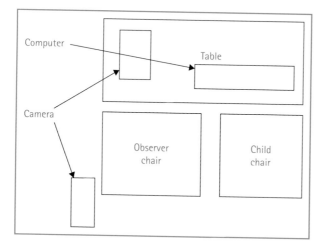

Figure 18.3
The setup of the study, showing the camera position and the layout of the room.

were consistent across all of the presented texts (see Chapter 6 on designing tasks for tests).

During the tasks, recordings of the children were made using a video camera that was positioned alongside the monitor of the PC and was set up to capture the children's expressions and to record, as audio, their verbalizations during the study. (See Figure 18.3.)

Constructs Being Evaluated

The evaluation assessed usability by considering the efficiency, satisfaction, and effectiveness of the four systems, following the ISO/IEC definitions of these criteria (1998). The measures of effectiveness centered on the error rates of the input method, so they were more about the technology than the child. (These are not discussed in this book; the reader is encouraged to see Read, MacFarlane, and Casey, 2001.) The remainder of this chapter discusses the measurement of efficiency and satisfaction, from which interesting lessons can be drawn regarding evaluations with children.

Measuring Efficiency

For text input systems, two common measures of efficiency are inputs per unit of time and keystrokes per character (MacKenzie and Soukoreff, 2002). The two usual "inputs per unit of time" measures are characters per second (CPS) and words per minute (WPM), where

$$CPS = \frac{\text{Characters input}}{\text{Time taken}}$$

$$WPM = \frac{\text{Words input}}{\text{Time taken}}$$

In this study, both of these measures were required because two of the input methods, the keyboard and the mouse, were essentially character based (words are entered one character at a time) and the voice input was word based. The handwriting input could have been calculated as either word based or character based; in this instance, the character-based metric was chosen because the children tended to write words using discrete characters rather than connected letters.

To calculate keystrokes per character, it is necessary to capture all the incorrect (mistakes) or erroneous (slips) keystrokes as well as the correct keystrokes. This is very easy in a keyboard application (several key-logging applications can be downloaded for free) and could be easily implemented in the mouse-driven application by recording the screen or the mouse clicks. For speech and handwriting, however, capturing keystrokes (and indeed identifying what makes up a keystroke) was more complex. For this reason, keystroke measures were not used (see Chapter 9 for a discussion of data logging).

To calculate CPS and WPM, the time taken was recorded from the start of each activity to the end. This was done by using the clock on the computer, which was set up to show hours, minutes, and seconds. Two separate times were recorded, one for the copying exercise and one for the composing exercise.

Measuring Satisfaction

To measure satisfaction, two methods were used. The first was to use the Fun Toolkit (as described in Chapter 13), and the second was to observe the children's expressions (as described in Chapter 10). Children were shown Smileyometers (see Figure 18.4) before and after each input method. These allowed the capture of both "expected" and "experienced" opinions.

Once these Smileyometers were collected, they were coded so that each child/method resulted in two scores: one for before and one for after. For example, for

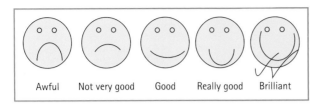

Figure 18.4

A completed Smileyometer.

Figure 18.5

A completed Fun Sorter.

"Child 7, Mouse B4, A5" would indicate that the child rated the technique as "Really good (4)" before using the mouse input and as "Brilliant (5)" after using it.

When all four tasks had been completed, the children were presented with a Fun Sorter (see Figure 18.5). They were given four identical sets of four small paper cards of 2 cm × 3 cm (1.5 × 2 inches) with icons representing the four input methods they had used, and they were asked to place these icons on the Fun Sorter. Once the icons were in place, they were stuck down with adhesive tape, and later the grid was scored, with a number being given to each method ranging from 1 (worst) to 4 (best) for each attribute (see Chapter 13 on using physical artifacts in evaluations).

Immediately after completing the Fun Sorter, the children were asked to rate each input method using a set of four vertical Funometers (Figure 18.6). The children

Figure 18.6

A set of completed vertical Funometers.

drew lines to the point that they considered appropriate, and then, because each column on the grid measured 10 cm, a score out of 10 was obtained for each method. The rationale for giving the children all these different methods was to see which methods worked the best and to establish, if possible, some consensus views—and gather reliable preference data.

During each task, video recordings were taken to capture facial expressions and verbalizations, and these were used to establish a measure for engagement. The videos were replayed, and a count was made of positive and negative instances. Positive instances included encouraging comments, smiling, laughing, and leaning forward. Negative instances included ear fiddling, frowning, leaning back, and sighing (see Chapter 9 for a discussion on interpreting video data). A score was given to the observed signs by summing the positive (scored positive) and negative (scored negative) instances and recording the balance.

Child	Copied	Composed
1	0.22	0.21
2	0.12	0.07
3	0.18	0.18
4	0.19	0.19
5	0.12	0.19
6	0.15	0.16
7	0.06	0.17
8	0.09	0.10
9	0.10	0.15
10	0.22	0.23
11	0.12	0.14
12	0.14	0.08
Mean	*0.143*	*0.156*
SD	*0.051*	*0.051*

Table 18.2

Characters per Second for the Two Instances of Mouse Use

Results from the Study

The full results from the study are reported in Read et al. (2001). In summary, the study showed that handwriting and keyboarding were reasonably comparable with respect to speed of input, that the mouse and the keyboard were the most accurate, and that speech input was the quickest to use but also the most erroneous. The satisfaction data showed that the children preferred speech and handwriting over the keyboard and the mouse. There was a lot of variability in the data from the children. Table 18.2 shows, for instance, a summary of the CPS for each child for the two mouse activities of copying and composing.

For most of the children, their performance in copying and composing was very similar, but for child 7 and child 12 performance on one activity was not a good indicator of performance on the other: Child 7 was considerably slower at copying than at composing, whereas child 12 was almost twice as fast at copying than at composing.

Commentary

Although many points of discussion came out of this case study, the focus here is on the evaluation measures that were used and on how they might have affected or influenced the results of the evaluation.

Efficiency

Efficiency was recorded by logging start and finish times. This is a rather crude method of recording time, but it has some validity because, generally, during the copying task the children were "on task" for the entire time. During composition activities, the children were inclined to stop and think or to ask for spellings. This time was included in the task time, but an interesting point can be made about whether these times should be deducted from the text input task, especially as they may vary across children and thus perhaps should be further explored. Certainly, it is likely that children will spend more time off the text input task than adults when the task requires more complex cognitive activities, such as those involved in spelling. Work by Beamish, Ali Bhatti, and MacKenzie (2006) modeled text input processes with regard to thinking time, and it would be interesting to see whether their model, which was intended for adults, can be applied to children.

Another interesting aspect of the efficiency evaluation centered on the use of the two metrics, CPS and WPM. In most of the work on text input, a standard five-characters-per-word average is used to convert between CPS and WPM, but in this study the words were from children's vocabularies, and an investigation of the words used revealed that on average the words had only three and one-third characters, which had an implication for the conversions between WPM and CPS.

In making conversions, the lower (more child-appropriate) rate of three and one-third was used, but this means that the reported results are harder to compare with those from other text input studies. This demonstrates that even well-used metrics might need to be modified for children.

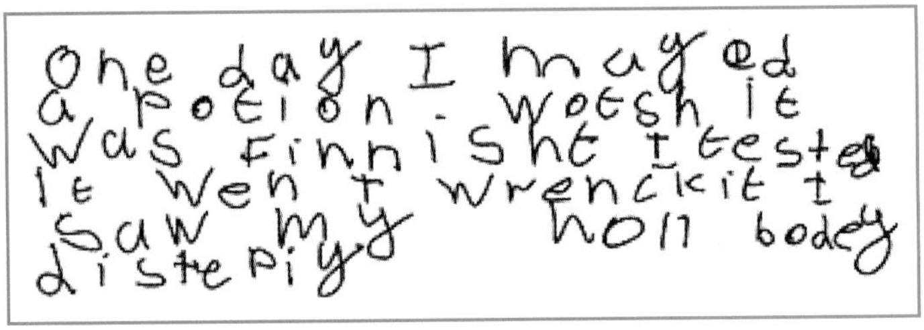

Figure 18.7

Children's writing can be difficult to interpret.

Satisfaction

The satisfaction measures in this study could be divided into two types: self-reported measures from the survey instruments and observations. Considerable problems arose with some of the children's self-reported satisfaction measures. When children were presented with the Smileyometer, they were generally "very kind" to the activity; they typically thought things were going to be "Brilliant". When converted into scores out of 10 (by measuring the height of the child's bar), the average score on the Funometer was 8.1, and the average on the Smileyometer was 8.2 (using ratings of 2, 4, 6, 8, and 10 for the Smiley faces). The study showed that the children seemed not to demonstrate the adult tendency to avoid the extreme values in a Likert scale (Read et al., 2001).

In the Fun Sorter, some of the younger children had difficulty understanding the differences between constructs like "Worked the best" and "Liked the most," so some of the ratings were probably not entirely valid. An interesting observation was made by the evaluator, who was sitting with the children, that points to the need to gather as much information as possible about the context in which evaluations take place. Children were seen shuffling the Fun Sorter icon cards after it appeared they had finished. One child moved a mouse picture toward the more positive side of the grid when it appeared that the mouse was getting a poor score (this motivation was established in the conversation that took part once the grid was completed).

The observation scores were based on negative and positive actions that were determined by the evaluator. These actions are largely beyond the child's control, and the children did not know in advance which actions were being observed. Several children were much less expressive than others, so as a single measure, the method would perhaps result only in a limited amount of data. During one input method (speech), the children were constrained with respect to their body movements and verbalizations, since they could not comment while talking into the microphone, and the microphone's physical presence on the head might have also limited movement.

Summary

This case study demonstrated some key aspects of using small groups of children in observational and behavioral studies. The use of survey methods was explored in the study, and interesting aspects about children's views of input technologies were gathered.

It is fair to say that the study was probably too small to allow generalizations regarding the input techniques or the methodologies used. The variability in the small sample was high, and the spread of children across a large age group made comments about age and behavior difficult to support.

The study took a considerable length of time. Because it was effectively a field-based usability study, the logistics were complex, and on three occasions during the study the work was interrupted by external activities, including band practice, a visit by a special needs teacher, and a classroom incident.

REFERENCES

ACM. (1992). ACM Code of Ethics and Professional Conduct. Retrieved January 2008 from *http://www.acm.org/about/code-of-ethics*.

Acuff, D. S., and Reiher, E. E. (1997). *What kids buy and why: The psychology of marketing to kids*. New York: The Free Press.

Agresti, A., and Finlay, B. (1999). *Statistical methods for the social sciences* (3rd ed.). Englewood Cliffs, NJ: Prentice Hall.

Alderson, P. (2004). Ethics. In S. Fraser, V. Lewis, S. Ding, M. Kellett, and C. Robinson (Eds.), *Doing research with children and young people* (pp. 97–112). London: Sage.

Allen, G. (2005). Research ethics in a culture of risk. In A. Farrell (Ed.), *Ethical research with children* (pp. 15–26). Maidenhead, UK: Open University Press.

Al Mahmud, A., Mubin, O., Octavia, J. R., Shahid, S., Yeo, L. C., Markopoulos, P., and Martens, J. B. (2007). aMAZEd: Designing an affective social game for children. *Proceedings of Conference on Interaction Design and Children*. Aalborg, Denmark, 53–56

Als, B. S., Jensen, J. J., and Skov, M. B. (2005). Comparison of think-aloud and constructive interaction in usability testing with children. *Proceedings of Conference on Interaction Design and Children*, Boulder, CO, 9–16.

Alaszewski, A. (2006). *Using diaries for social research*. London: Sage.

Andersson, G., Höök, K., Mourão, D., Paiva, A., and Costa, M. (2002). Using a Wizard of Oz study to inform the design of SenToy. *Proceedings of DIS*. London: ACM Press.

Antle, A. (2003). Case study: The design of CBC4Kids' StoryBuilder. *Proceedings of Conference on Interaction Design and Children*, Preston, UK, 59–68.

APA. (2002). Ethical principles of psychologists and code of conduct, APA. Retrieved January 2008, from *http://www.apa.org/ethics/code2002.html*

Baauw, E., and Markopoulos, P. (2004). A comparison of think-aloud and post-task interview. *Proceedings of Conference on Interaction Design and Children*, Baltimore, 115–117.

Baauw, E., Bekker, M. M., and Barendregt, W. (2005). A structured expert evaluation method for the evaluation of children's computer games. *Proceedings of Conference on Interaction Design and Children*, 457–469.

Badler, N. I., and Smoliar, S. W. (1979). Digital representations of human movement. *Computing Surveys*, 11(1), 19–38.

Barendregt, W. (2006). Evaluating fun and usability in computer games with children. PhD Thesis, University of Technology, Eindhoven, The Netherlands.

Barendreget, W., Bekker, M. M., and Baauw, E. (2008). Development and evaluation of the problem identification picture cards method. *Cognition, Technology and Work* (in press).

Barendregt, W., Bekker, M. M., and Speerstra, M. (2003). Empirical evaluation of usability and fun in computer games for children. *Proceedings of Conference on Interaction Design and Children*, Zurich, 705–708.

Barendregt, W., Bekker, M. M., Bouwhuis, D. G., and Baauw, E. (2006). Identifying usability and fun problems in a computer game during first use and after some practice. *International Journal of Human-Computer Studies*, 64, 830–846.

Baum, L. F. (1900). *The wonderful* Wizard of Oz. Chicago: George M Hill Co.

Beamish, D., Ali Bhatti, S., and MacKenzie, I. S. (2006). Fifty years later: A neuro-dynamic explanation of Fitts' law. *Journal of the Royal Society Interface*, 3, 649–654.

Bekker, M. M., Baauw, E., and Barendregt, W. (2007). A comparison of two analytical evaluation methods for educational computer games for young children. *Cognition, Technology and Work* (in press).

Bogdan, R. C., and Biklen, S. K. (1998). *Qualitative research for education: An introduction to theory and methods*. Boston: Allyn and Bacon.

Borgers, N., and Hox, J. (2001). Item nonresponse in questionnaire research with children. *Journal of Official Statistics*, 17(2), 321–335.

Borgers, N., Hox, J., and Sikkel, D. (2004). Response effects in surveys on children and adolescents: The effect of number of response options, negative wording, and neutral mid-point. *Quality and Quantity*, 38(1), 17–33.

Borgers, N., Leeuw, E. D., and Hox, J. (2000). Children as respondents in survey research: Cognitive development and response quality. *Bulletin de Methodologie Sociologique*, 66, 60–75.

Boren, M. T., and Ramey, J. (2000). Thinking aloud: Reconciling theory and practice. *IEEE Transactions on Professional Communication*, 43, 261–278.

Bowers, V. A., Snyder, H. I. (1990). Concurrent versus retrospective verbal protocol for comparing window usability. *Proceedings of Human Factors and Ergonomics Society, 46th Annual Meeting*, 1270–1274.

Breakwell, G. (1995). *Research methods in psychology*. London: Sage.

Brederode, B., Markopoulos, P., Gielen, M., Vermeeren, A., and de Ridder, H. (2005). pOwerball: The design of a novel mixed-reality game for children with mixed abilities. *Proceedings of Conference on Interaction Design and Children*, Boulder, CO.

Bruckman, A. S., and Bandlow, A. (2003). Human-computer interaction for kids. In J. A. Jacko and A. Sears (Eds.), *The human-computer interaction handbook* (pp. 428–440). Mahwah, NJ: Erlbaum.

Bruck, M., Ceci, S. J., and Melnyk, L. (1997). External and internal sources of variation in the creation of false reports in children. *Learning and Individual Differences*, 9(4), 269–316.

Buckleitner, W. (1999). The state of children's software evaluation—yesterday, today and in the 21st century. *Information Technology in Childhood Education*, 1, 211–220.

Burmeister, O. K. (2000). Usability testing: Revisiting informed consent procedures for testing Internet sites. *Proceedings 2nd Australian Institute of Computer Ethics Conference*, Canberra, Australia, 3–9.

Buisine, S., and Martin, J. C. (2005). Children's and adults' multimodal interaction with 2D conversational agents. *Proceedings of CHI*, Portland, OR.

Carroll, J. M. (2002). *Human-computer interaction in the new millennium*. New York: Addison-Wesley.

Carroll, J. M. (2004). Beyond fun. *Interactions*, 11(5), 38–40.

Carter, S., and Mankoff, J. (2005). When participants do the capturing: The role of media in diary studies. *Proceedings of CHI*, Portland, OR.

Cassell, J. (2002). Genderizing HCI. In J. Jacko and A. Sears (Eds.), *The handbook of human-computer interaction* (pp. 402–411). Mahwah, NJ: Erlbaum.

Christensen, P., and James, A. (Eds.) (1999). *Research with children: Perspectives and practices*. London: RoutledgeFalmer.

Clarke, A. (2005). *Guidelines for the design and deployment of ICT products and services used by children*. Sophia Antipolis, France: ETSI.

Cockton, G., Lavery, D., and Woolrych, A. (2002). Inspection-based evaluations. In J. A. Jacko and A. Sears (Eds.), *The human-computer interaction handbook* (pp. 1118–1138). Mahwah NJ: Erlbaum.

Cockton, G., and Woolrych, A. (2001). Understanding inspection methods: Lessons from an assessment of heuristic evaluation. In B. Blandford, J. Vanderdonckt, and P. Gray (Eds.), *People and computers XV* (pp. 171–192). London: Springer.

Cockton, G., and Woolrych, A. (2002). Sale must end: Should discount methods be cleared off HCI's shelves? *Interactions*, September–October, 13–18.

Cockton, G., Woolrych, A., and Hindmarch, M. (2004). Reconditioned merchandise: Extended structured report formats in usability inspection. *Proceedings of CHI, Extended Abstract*, 1433–1436.

Coolican, H. (2004). *Research methods and statistics in psychology* (4th ed.). Abingdon: Hodder and Stoughton.

Cooper, A. (1999). *The inmates are running the asylum*. New York: Macmillan.

Cooper, A. (2003). *About face 2.0: The essentials of interaction design*. Indianapolis: John Wiley.

Courage, C., and Baxter, K. (2005). *Understanding your users—a practical guide to user requirements, methods, tools, and techniques*. San Francisco: Morgan Kaufmann.

Crane, H. D., and Steele, C. M. (1985). Generation-V Dual-Purkinje-Image Eyetracker. *Applied Optics*, 24, 527–537.

Dahlback, N., Jonsson, A., and Ahrenberg, L. (1993). Wizard of Oz studies—why and how. *Knowledge-Based Systems*, 6(4), 258–266.

Damon, W., and Phelps, E. (1989). Strategic users of peer learning in children's education. In T. Berndt and G. Ladd (Eds.), *Peer relationships in child development* (pp. 135–157). New York: John Wiley.

Danby, S., and Farrell, A. (2005). Opening the research conversation. In A. Farrell (Ed.), *Ethical research with children* (pp. 49–67). Maidenhead, UK: Open University Press.

Davis, F. D. Perceived usefulness, perceived ease of use, and user acceptance of information technology. *MIS Quarterly*, 13(3), 319–340.

Denzin, N. K., and Lincoln, Y. S. (Eds). (2000). *Handbook of Qualitative Research*. Thousand Oaks, CA: Sage Publications.

Department for Education and Skills. (2005). *Harnessing technology*. Nottingham, DfES: 71.

Dindler, C., Eriksson, E., Sejer, O., Lykke-Oleson, A., and Ludvigsen, M. (2005). Mission from Mars—A method for exploring user requirements for children in narrative space. *Proceedings of Conference on Interaction Design and Children*, Boulder, CO.

Dix, A., Finlay, J., Abowd, G., and Beale, R. (2004). *Human-computer interaction* (3rd ed.). Harlow, UK: Pearson.

Donker, A., and Markopoulos, P. (2001). Assessing the effectiveness of usability evaluation methods for children. In N. Avouris and N. Fakotakis (Eds.), *Advances in human-computer interaction* (pp. 409–410). Patras, Greece: Typorama Publications.

Donker, A., and Markopoulos, P. (2002). A comparison of think-aloud, questionnaires and interviews for testing usability with children. People and computers XVI—memorable yet invisible. *Proceedings of HCI*, 305–316.

Donker, A., and Reitsma, P. (2004). Usability testing with young children. In A. Druin, J. P. Hourcade, and S. Kollet (Eds.), *Interaction design and children* (pp. 43–48). Baltimore: ACM Press.

Draper, S. W. (1999). Analysing fun as a candidate software requirement. *Personal Technology*, 3, 117–122.

Druin, A. (Ed.) (1999). *The design of children's technology*. San Francisco: Morgan Kaufmann.

Druin, A. (2002). The role of children in the design of new technology. *Behaviour and Information Technology*, 21(1), 1–25.

Duchowski, A. T. (2007). *Eye-tracking methodology: Theory and practice* (2nd ed.). London: Springer-Verlag.

Dumas, J., and Redish, J. (1993). *A practical guide to usability testing*. Norwood, NJ: Ablex.

Ericsson, K. A., and Simon, H. A. (1980). Verbal reports as data. *Psychological Review*, 87(3), 215–251.

Ericsson, K. A., and Simon, H. A. (1993). *Protocol analysis. Verbal reports as data* (revised ed.). Cambridge, MA: MIT Press.

Farrell, A. (Ed.) (2005a). *Ethical research with children*. Maidenhead, UK: Open University Press.

Farrell, A. (2005b). Ethics and research with children. In A. Farrell (Ed.), *Ethical research with children* (pp. 1–4). Maidenhead, UK: Open University Press.

Forlizzi, J., and Battarbee, K. (2004). Understanding experience in interactive systems. *Proceedings of Conference on Designing Interactive Systems: Processes, Practices, Methods, and Techniques*, 261–268.

Fransella, F., and Bannister, D. (1977). *A manual for repertory grid technique*. London: Academic Press.

Fraser, N., and Gilbert, N. S. (1991). Simulating speech systems. *Computer Speech and Language*, 5, 81–99.

Fraser, S., Lewis, V., Ding, S., Kellett, M., and Robinson, C. (Eds.) (2004). *Doing research with children and young people*. London: Sage.

Gaustad, J. (1993). Peer and cross-age tutoring. *ERIC Digest*, 79.

Gilutz, S., and Nielsen, J. (2002). *Usability of websites for children: 70 design guidelines*. Freemont, CA: Nielsen Norman Group.

Gould, J. D., Conti, J., and Hovanyecz, T. (1983). Composing letters with a simulated listening typewriter. *Communications of the ACM*, 26(4), 295–308.

Greig, A., and Taylor, A. (1999). *Doing research with children*. London: Sage.

Hall, L., Woods, S., Wolke, D., Dautenhahn, K., and Sobreperez, P. (2004). Using storyboards to guide virtual world design, *Proceedings of Conference on Interaction Design and Children*, Baltimore.

Hämäläinen, P., and Höysniemi, J. (2002). A computer vision and hearing based user interface for a computer game for children. *Proceedings of 7th ERCIM Workshop "User Interfaces for All,"* Paris, 23–25.

Hammerton, L., and Luckin, R. (2001). How to help? Investigating children's opinions on help: To inform the design of Metacognitive Software Scaffolding. *AIED 2001*, San Antonio.

Hanna, E., Risden, K., Czerwinski, M., and Alexander, K. J. (1999). The role of usability research in designing children's computer products. In A. Druin (Ed.), *The design of children's technology* (pp. 4–26). San Francisco: Morgan Kaufmann.

Hanna, L., Risden, K., and Alexander, K. (1997). Guidelines for usability testing with children. *Interactions*, 4(5), 9–14.

Hartson, H., Rex, A., Terence, S., and Williges, R. C. (2003). Criteria for evaluating usability evaluation methods. *International Journal of Human-Computer Interaction*, 15(1), 145–181.

Hayes, N. (2000). *Doing psychological research*. Maidenhead, UK: Open University Press.

Hendersson, V., Lee, S.-W., Brashear, H., Hamilton, H., Starner, T., and Hamilton, S. (2005). Development of an American sign language game for deaf children. *Proceedings of Conference on Interaction Design and Children*, Boulder, CO.

Hertzum, M., and Jacobsen, N. E. (2001). The evaluator effect: A chilling fact about usability evaluation methods. *International Journal of Human-Computer Interaction*, 13(4), 421–443.

Hill, M. (2005). Ethical considerations in researching children's experiences. In S. Greene and D. Hogan (Eds.), *Researching children's experience* (pp. 61–86). London: Sage.

Houde, S., and Hill, C. (1997). What do prototypes prototype? In M. G. Helander, T. K. Landauer, and P. Prabhu (Eds.), *Handbook of human-computer interaction* (2nd ed.) (pp. 367–381). Amsterdam: Elsevier Science.

Höysniemi, J., and Read, J. C. (2005). Wizard of Oz with children—ethical dilemmas and experiences from the field. *Proceedings of Conference on Interaction Design and Children*, Boulder, CO.

Höysniemi, J., Hämäläinen, P., and Turkki, L. (2003). Using peer tutoring in evaluating the usability of a physically interactive computer game with children. *Interacting with Computers*, 15(2), 205–225.

Höysniemi, J., Hämäläinen, P., and Turkki, L. (2002). Using peer tutoring in evaluating the usability of a physically interactive computer game with children. *Proceedings of International Workshop on Interaction Design and Children*, Eindhoven, The Netherlands, 144–152.

Höysniemi, J., Hämäläinen, P., and Turkki, L. (2004). Wizard of Oz prototyping of computer vision based action games for children. *Proceedings of Conference on Interaction Design and Children*, Baltimore, 27–34.

Höysniemi, J., and Hämäläinen, P. (2004). Describing children's intuitive movements in a perceptive adventure game. *Proceedings of Workshop on Multimodal Corpora: Models of human behaviour for the specification and evaluation of multimodal input and output interface*, Lisbon, 21–24.

Höysniemi, J., Hämäläinen, P., Turkki, L., and Rouvi, T. (2005). Children's intuitive gestures in vision based action games. *Communications of the ACM*, 48(1), 44–50.

Ibrahim, Z., Dimitrova, V., and Boyle, R. D. (2004). Capturing human teachers' strategies for supporting schema-based cognitive tasks to inform the design of an intelligent pedagogical agent. *Proceedings of Intelligent Tutoring Systems*.

Ingram, D. E. (1984). *Report on the formal trialling of the Australian second language proficiency ratings (ASLPR)*. Studies in Adult Migrant Education, Department of Immigration and Ethnic Affairs. Canberra: Australian Government Publishing Service.

ISO. (1998). ISO 9241-11, Ergonomic requirements for office work with visual display terminals (VDTs)—Part 11: Guidance on usability.

Javal, E. (1879). Essai sur la Physiologie de la Lecture. *Annales d'Oculistique*, 81, 61–73.

Kahn, M. J., and Prail, A. (1994). Formal usability inpections. In J. Nielsen and R. L. Mack (Eds.), *Usability inspection methods* (pp. 141–171). New York: John Wiley.

Kail, R. V. (2002). *Children*. Englewood Cliffs, NJ: Prentice Hall.

Kano, A., Read, J. C., Dix, A., and MacKenzie, I. S. (2007). ExpECT: An expanded error categorisation method for text input. *Proceedings of BCS HCI*, Lancaster, UK.

Keats, D. M. (2000). Cross-cultural studies in child development in Asian contexts. *Cross-Cultural Research*, 34(4), 339–350.

Kelley, J. F. (1984). An iterative design methodology for user friendly natural language office information applications. *ACM Transactions on Office Information Systems*, 2(1), 26–41.

Kemp, J. A. M., and van Gelderen, T. (1996). Co-discovery exploration: An informal method for iterative design of consumer products. In P. W. Jordan, B. Thomas, B. A. Weerdmeester, and I. L. McClelland (Eds.), *Usability evaluation in industry* (pp. 139–146). London: Taylor and Francis.

Kipp, M. (2001). Anvil—A generic annotation tool for multimodal dialogue. *Proceedings of 7th European Conference on Speech Communication and Technology (Eurospeech)*, Aalborg, Denmark, 1367–1370.

Korhonen, H., and Koivisto, E. M. I. (2006). Playability heuristics for mobile games. *Proceedings of Mobile HCI*, 9–14.

Krosnick, J. A. (1991). Response strategies for coping with the cognitive demands of attitude measures in surveys. *Applied Cognitive Psychology*, 5, 213–236.

Kuniavsky, M. (2003). *Observing the user experience*. San Francisco: Morgan Kaufmann.

Kuper, J. (1997). International Law Concerning Child Civilians in Armed Conflict. Oxford: Clarendon Press.

Laban, R. (1975). *Laban's principles of dance and movement notation* (2nd ed.). London: Macdonald and Evans.

Lewis, V., Kellett, M., Robinson, C., Fraser, S., and Ding, S. (Eds.). (2004). *The reality of research with children and young people*. London: Sage.

Loke, L., Larssen, A. T., and Robertson, T. (2005). Laban notation for design of movement based interaction. *Proceedings of 2nd Australaian Conference on Interactive Entertainment*, 113–120.

Luckin, R. (2001). Designing children's software to ensure productive interactivity through collaboration in the Zone of Proximal Development (ZPD). *Information Technology in Childhood Annual*, 13, 57–85.

MacFarlane, S., and Pasiali, A. (2005). Adapting the heuristic evaluation method for use with children. *Proceedings of Interact Workshop on Child-Computer Interaction: Methodological Research*, Rome, 28–31.

MacFarlane, S., Sim, G., and Horton, M. (2005). Assessing usability and fun in educational software. *Proceedings of Conference on Interaction Design and Children*. Boulder, CO, 103–109.

Mackay, W. E. (1995). Ethics, lies, and videotape. *Proceedings of SIGCHI Conference on Human Factors in Computing Systems*, Denver, 138–145.

MacKenzie, I. S., and Soukoreff, R. W. (2002). Text entry for mobile computing: Models and methods, theory and practice. *Human–Computer Interaction*, 17(2), 147–198.

Malone, T. W. (1980). What makes things fun to learn? A study of intrinsically motivating computer games. PhD Thesis, Stanford University, Palo Alto, CA.

Malone, T. W., and Lepper, M. R. (1987). Making learning fun: A taxonomy of intrinsic motivation for learning. In R. E. Snow and M. J. Farr (Eds.), *Aptitude, learning and instruction. Cognitive and affective process analysis* (vol. 3). Hillsdale, NJ: Erlbaum.

Markopoulos, P., Barendregt, W., Brus, M., and Plakman, I. (2005). The parent evaluator method. *Proceedings of Interact Workshop on Child-Computer Interaction: Methodological Research*, Rome.

Martin, D. W. (2005). *Doing psychology experiments* (6th ed.). Belmont, CA: Wadsworth Publishing.

Mayhew, D. (1999). *The usability engineering lifecycle*. San Francisco: Morgan Kaufmann.

Measelle, J. R., Ablow, J. C., Cowan, P. A., and Cowan, C. P. (1998). Assessing young children's views of their academic, social, and emotional lives: An evaluation of the self-perception scales of the Berkeley puppet interview. *Child Development*, 69, 1556–1576.

Metaxas, G., Metin, B., Schneider, J., Shapiro, G., Zhou, W., and Markopoulos, P. (2005). *SCORPIODROME: An Exploration in Mixed Reality Social Gaming for Children. Proceedings of ACE*, Valencia, Spain, 229–232.

Miles, M. B., and Huberman, A. M. (1994). *Qualitative data analysis: An expanded sourcebook*. London: Sage.

Molich, R., Laurel, B., Snyder, C., Quesenbery, W., and Wilson, C. (2001). Panel—Ethics in HCI. *Proceedings of CHI*, Seattle, 217–218.

Montemayor, J., Druin, A., Farber, A., Sims, S., Churaman, W., and D'Amour, A. (2002). Physical programming: Designing tools for children to create physical interactive environments. *Proceedings of CHI*.

Mota, S., Picard, R. W. (2003). Automated posture analysis for detecting learner's interest level. *Workshop on Computer Vision and Pattern Recognition*, Madison, WI.

Murray, R. (2004). *Writing for academic journals*. Buckingham: Open University Press.

Newell, A., and Simon, H. A. (1993). *Human problem solving*. Englewood Cliffs, NJ: Prentice Hall.

Nielsen, J. (2007). *Eyetracking Research*. Retrieved January 2008 from *http://www.useit.com/eyetracking/*.

Nielsen, J. (1994a). Enhancing the explanatory power of usability heuristics. *Proceedings of CHI*, 153–158.

Nielsen, J. (1994b). Heuristic evaluation. In J. Nielsen and R. L. Mack (Eds.), *Usability inspection method* (pp. 25–62). New York: John Wiley.

Nielsen, J. (1993). *Usability engineering*. Boston: Academic Press.

Nielsen, J., and Mack, R. L. (Eds.) (1994). *Usability inspection methods*. New York: John Wiley.

Nielsen, J., and Molich, R. (1990). Heuristic evaluation of user interfaces. *Proceedings of CHI*, Seattle.

Nielsen, J., and Pernice, K. (2007). *Eyetracking Web usability*. Indianapolis: New Riders.

Norman, D. (2002). *The design of everyday things*. New York: Basic Books.

Ohnemus, K. R. & Biers, D. W. (1993). Retrospective versus concurrent thinking-out-loud in usability testing. *Proceedings of Human Factors and Ergonomics Society 37th Annual Meeting*, Santa Monica, 1127–1131.

O'Malley, C. E., Draper, S. W., and Riley, M. S. (1984). Constructive interaction: A method for studying human–computer interaction. *Proceedings of IFIP Interact*, 269–274.

Palen, L., and Salzman, M. (2002). Voice-mail diary studies for naturalistic data capture under mobile conditions. *Proceedings of CSCW*, 87–95.

Papert, S. (1980). *Mindstorms, children, computers and powerful ideas*. New York: Basic Books.

Peterson, C., and Bell, M. (1996). Children's memory for traumatic injury. *Child Development*, 67(6), 3045–3070.

Piaget, J. (1970). *Science of education and the psychology of the child*. New York: Orion Press.

Plowman, L. (2003). A benign addition? Research on ICT and pre-school children. *Journal of Computer Assisted Learning*, 19, 149.

Poole, A., and Ball, L. J. (2006). Eye tracking in human–computer interaction and usability research. In C. Ghaoui (Ed.), *Encyclopedia of human–computer interaction*. London: Ideas Group Inc.

Preece, J., Rogers, Y., and Sharp, H. (2002). *Interaction design: Beyond human–computer interaction*. New York: John Wiley.

Prensky, M. (2001). Digital natives, digital immigrants. *On the Horizon*, 9(5), 1–2. Available from *www.marcprensky.com/writing/Prensky%20-%20Digital%20Natives, %20Digital%20Immigrants%20-%20 Part1.pdf*.

Price, S., Rogers, S., Scaife, M., Stanton, D., and Neale, H. (2003). Using "tangibles" to promote novel forms of playful learning. *Interacting with Computers*, 15(2), 169–185.

Pruitt, J., and Adlin, T. (2005). *The persona lifecycle: Keeping users in mind throughout product design*. San Francisco: Morgan Kaufmann.

Read, J. C. (2004). Designing multimedia applications for children. *Comp@uclan 3*.

Read, J. C. (2005). The ABC of CCI. *Interfaces*, 62, 8–9.

Read, J. C., Kelly, S. R., and Birkett, S. (2006). How satisfying is gaze tracking for children? Paper presented at the *CHI Workshop—Getting a Measure of Satisfaction from Eyetracking in Practice*, Montreal.

Read, J. C., MacFarlane, S. J., and Casey, C. (2001). Measuring the usability of text input methods for children. *Proceedings of Conference on HCI*, Lille, France.

Read, J. C., Gregory, P., MacFarlane, S. J., McManus, B., Gray, P., and Patel, R. (2002). An investigation of participatory design with children—informant, balanced and facilitated design. *Proceedings of Conference on Interaction Design and Children* (pp. 53–64). Eindhoven: Maastricht Shaker Publishing.

Read, J. C., MacFarlane, S. J., and Casey, C. (2002). Endurability, engagement and expectations: Measuring children's fun. *Proceedings of Conference on Interaction Design and Children* (pp. 189–198). Eindhoven: Shaker Publishing.

Read, J. C., MacFarlane, S. J., and Casey, C. (2003). What's going on? Discovering what children understand about handwriting recognition interfaces. *Proceedings of Conference on Interaction Design and Children*, Preston, UK, 135–140.

Read, J. C., MacFarlane, S. J., and Gregory, A. G. (2004). Requirements for the design of a handwriting recognition based writing interface for children. *Proceedings of Conference on Interaction Design and Children*, Baltimore, 81–87.

Read, J. C., MacFarlane, S. J., and Horton, M. (2004). The usability of handwriting recognition for writing in the primary classroom. *Proceedings of Conference on HCI*, Leeds, UK, 135–150.

Read, J. C., MacFarlane, S. J., and Casey, C. (2003). Good enough for what? Acceptance of handwriting recognition errors by child users. *Proceedings of Conference on Interaction Design and Children*, Preston, UK, 155.

Read, J. C., Mazzone, E., and Höysniemi, J. (2005). Wizard of Oz evaluations with children—deception and discovery. *Proceedings of Conference on Interaction Design and Children*, Boulder, CO.

Renshaw, T., and Dickenson, S. (2007). The integration of images and text by children learning how to read: An eye tracking study (submitted to *Early Childhood Research Quarterly*).

Richardson, D. C., and Spivey, M. J. (2004). Eye tracking: Characteristics and methods. In G. E. Wnek and G. L. Bowlin (Eds.), *Encyclopedia of biomaterials and biomedical engineering*. New York: Marcel Dekker.

Risden, K., Hanna, E., and Kanerva, A. (1997). Dimensions of intrinsic motivation in children's favorite computer activities. *Poster presented at the Meeting of the Society for Research in Child Development*, Washington, DC.

Robertson, J., and Wiemer-Hastings, P. (2002). Feedback on children's stories via multiple interface agents. *Proceedings of 6th Annual Conference on Intelligent Tutoring Systems*, Biarritz, San Sebastian.

Robins, B., Dautenhahn, K., and Dubowski, J. (2004). Investigating autistic children's attitudes towards strangers with the theatrical robot—a new experimental paradigm in human-robot interaction studies. *Proceedings of 13th IEEE International Workshop on Robot and Human Interactive Communication*. Karashiki, Japan.

Rode, J. A., Stringer, M., Toye, E. F., Simpson, A., and Blackwell, A. F. (2003). Curriculum-Focused design. *Proceedings of Conference on Interaction Design and Children*, Preston, UK, 119–126.

Rogoff, B. (1990). *Apprenticeship in thinking: Cognitive development in social context*. Oxford: Oxford University Press.

Rubin, J. (1994). Handbook *of usability testing: How to plan, design and conduct effective tests*. New York: John Wiley.

Santamaria, M. (2003). Web navigation recorder—eye tracking software application demo. *Proceedings of Interaction Design and Children*, Preston, UK, 166.

Scaife, M., and Rogers, Y. (1999). Kids as informants: Telling us what we didn't know, or confirming what we knew already. In A. Druin (Ed.), *The design of children's technology*. San Francisco: Morgan Kaufmann.

Scullin, M. H., and Ceci, S. J. (2001). A suggestibility scale for children. *Personality and Individual Differences*, 30, 843–856.

Sears, A. (1997). Heuristic walkthrough: Finding the problems without the noise. *International Journal of Human-Computer Studies*, 9(3), 213–234.

Seely, J. (2002). *Writing reports*. Oxford: Oxford University Press.

Seely, J. (2005). *Oxford guide to effective writing and speaking* (2nd ed.). Oxford: Oxford University Press.

Shields, B. J., Palermo, T. M., Powers, J. D., Grewe, S. D., and Smith, G. A. (2003). Predictors of a child's ability to use a visual analogue scale. *Child: Care, Health and Development*, 29(4), 281–290.

Shneiderman, B., and Plaisant, C. (2004). *Designing the user interface* (4th ed.). Boston: Pearson.

Siegel, S., and Castellan, N. J. (1988). *Nonparametric statistics for the behavioural sciences*. New York: McGraw-Hill.

Smith, P. K., Cowie, H., and Blades, M. (2003). *Understanding children's development* (4th ed.). Oxford: Blackwell.

Stone, D., Jarrett, C., Woodroffe, M., and Minocha, S. (2005). *User interface design and evaluation*. San Francisco: Morgan Kaufmann.

Strunk, W. I., and White, E. B. (1999). *The elements of style* (4th ed.). New York: Longman.

Thomas, J. C. (1976). *A method for studying natural language dialog* IBM, Thomas J. Watson Research Center.

Tobey, A., and Goodman, G. (1992). Children's eyewitness memory: Effects of participation and forensic context. *Child Abuse and Neglect*, 16, 807–821.

Tufte, E. R. (2006). *Beautiful evidence*. Cheshire, CT: Graphics Press.

Vaillancourt, P. M. (1973). Stability of children's survey responses. *Public Opinion Quarterly*, 37, 373–387.

van Kesteren, I. E., Bekker, M. M., Vermeeren, A. P., and Lloyd, P. A. (2003). Assessing usability evaluation methods on their effectiveness to elicit verbal comments from children subjects. *Proceeding of Conference on Interaction Design and Children*, Preston, UK, 41–49.

Verhaegh, J., Soute, I., Kessels, A., and Markopoulos, P. (2006). On the design of Camelot, an outdoor game for children. *Proceedings of Conference on Interaction Design and Children*, Tampere, Finland, 9–16.

Vermeeren, A. P. O. S., van Kesteren, I. E. H., and Bekker, M. M. (2003). Managing the evaluator effect in user testing. *Proceedings of IFIP 9th International Conference on Human–Computer Interaction—INTERACT*, Zürich, 647–654.

Verschoor, Y. (2007). Using a social robot as facilitator in usability-tests with children. Master thesis. University of Technology, Eindhoven, The Netherlands.

Ward, T. (2003). I watched in dumb horror. *The Guardian*, May 20.

Wartella, E. A., Lee, J. H., and Caplovitz, A. G. (2002). *Children and interactive media*: Research compendium update. Markle Foundation. Retrieved January 2008 from *http://www.markle.org/downloadable_assets/cimcomp_update.pdf.*

Woodhead, M., and Faulkner, D. (2000). Subjects, objects or participants? Dilemmas of psychological research with children. In P. Christensen and A. James (Eds.), *Research with children* (pp. 9–35). London: Falmer Press.

Woodward, E. H., and Gridina, N. (2000). *Media in the home 2000: The fifth annual survey of parents and children*. Philadelphia: University of Pennsylvania.

Zinsser, W. (2006). *On writing well* (30th anniversary ed.). New York: HarperCollins.

INDEX

A

Y